Terry Pratchett's Ethical Worlds

Terry Pratchett's Ethical Worlds

Essays on Identity and Narrative in Discworld and Beyond

Edited by KRISTIN NOONE and EMILY LAVIN LEVERETT

McFarland & Company, Inc., Publishers
Jefferson, North Carolina

ALSO OF INTEREST AND FROM MCFARLAND

Welsh Mythology and Folklore in Popular Culture: Essays on Adaptations in Literature, Film, Television and Digital Media (edited by Audrey L. Becker and Kristin Noone, 2011)

LIBRARY OF CONGRESS CATALOGUING-IN-PUBLICATION DATA

Names: Noone, Kristin, editor. | Leverett, Emily Lavin, editor.
Title: Terry Pratchett's ethical worlds : essays on identity and narrative in Discworld and beyond / edited by Kristin Noone and Emily Lavin Leverett.
Description: Jefferson, North Carolina : McFarland & Company, Inc., Publishers, 2020 | Includes bibliographical references and index.
Identifiers: LCCN 2020018832 | ISBN 9781476674490 (paperback ; acid-free paper ∞)
ISBN 9781476638034 (ebook)
Subjects: LCSH: Pratchett, Terry—Criticism and interpretation. | Pratchett, Terry. Discworld series. | Ethics in literature. | Identity (Philosophical concept) in literature. | Discworld (Imaginary place)
Classification: LCC PR6066.R34 Z88 2020 | DDC 823/.914—dc23
LC record available at https://lccn.loc.gov/2020018832

BRITISH LIBRARY CATALOGUING DATA ARE AVAILABLE

ISBN (print) 978-1-4766-7449-0
ISBN (ebook) 978-1-4766-3803-4

© 2020 Kristin Noone and Emily Lavin Leverett. All rights reserved

No part of this book may be reproduced or transmitted in any form or by any means, electronic or mechanical, including photocopying or recording, or by any information storage and retrieval system, without permission in writing from the publisher.

Front cover images © 2020 Shutterstock

Printed in the United States of America

McFarland & Company, Inc., Publishers
  Box 611, Jefferson, North Carolina 28640
  www.mcfarlandpub.com

Table of Contents

Introduction: Terry Pratchett's Ethical Worlds
    KRISTIN NOONE *and* EMILY LAVIN LEVERETT   1

Something That Gods Are: Acts of Creation
in Terry Pratchett's Early Science Fiction
    KRISTIN NOONE   5

Conan the Nonagenarian: Beyond Hyborian Hypermasculinity
with Terry Pratchett's Cohen the Barbarian
    MIKE PERSCHON   19

Carrot Ironfoundersson: Medieval Romance, Narrative
Causality and the Ethics of Choice in Terry Pratchett's
Guards! Guards!
    EMILY LAVIN LEVERETT   34

Self-Discovery, Free Will and Change: The Ethics of Growing
Up in the Fantasy Novels of Terry Pratchett
    KATHLEEN BURT   45

The Anglo-Saxon Ælf: Old English Influences
in Terry Pratchett's *The Wee Free Men*
and *The Shepherd's Crown*
    LIVIA BONGIOVANNI   61

Constructing Identity Through Language in Discworld
    ELISE A. BELL   77

Rhetoricity of Discworld: Magic and the Ethics of Footnotes
    AMY LEA CLEMONS   91

The Golempunk Manifesto: Ownership of the Means
of Production in Pratchett's Discworld
  JANET BRENNAN CROFT   110

Neomedievalism and the Ethics of Colonization in Pratchett
and Baxter's *The Long Earth* and *The Long War*
  SADIE E. HASH   124

Appendix: Works and Adaptations   141

About the Contributors   145

Index   147

Introduction

Terry Pratchett's Ethical Worlds

KRISTIN NOONE and EMILY LAVIN LEVERETT

Terry Pratchett's novels and stories have sold more than 85 million copies worldwide, and have been translated into multiple languages and multiple media: films, board games, cookbooks, pop-scholarly folklore and science texts, and more, including the recent Amazon series based on *Good Omens*. During his lifetime, he was appointed Officer of the Order of the British Empire (OBE) in 1998 and was knighted for services to literature in the 2009 New Year Honours, and his numerous literary awards include the World Fantasy Award for Life Achievement and the Carnegie Medal, among others. This vast influence and appeal have led to a growing body of Pratchett studies and scholarly discussions, in particular with regard to his use of comedic fantasy to explore larger social and moral questions: truth, justice, identity, community, relationships (or lack thereof) with the past, the purpose of creativity, and the importance of compassion. Focusing specifically on Pratchett's Discworld novels, Gray Kochhar-Lindgren observes that Pratchett's fantasy "disrupts the cosmos of putatively given 'good order' for the sake of a more just order. Justice depends finally not on law but on inventiveness" (Alton and Spruiell); Pratchett's work interrogates themes of inventiveness and justice—and the meaning of and interdependence of—these ideas via intertexuality (allusions, references, pop culture and folklore), identity (British and global, located in time and partaking of the heterotemporal), adaptation (novels, films, plays, board games), and genre-crossing (young adult, fantasy, satire, science fiction). This complexity invites further study of the impact of Pratchett's contributions to fantasy, literacy, and theories such as narrative causality, and in this project, our aim has been to make a gesture toward unifying some of these disparate areas of Pratchett studies and bringing them productively into conversation with each other. Terry Pratchett's works celebrate the possibilities opened up by inventiveness and creation; taking this as our thematic core, the essays collected here examine the ways in which Pratchett constructs an ethical stance that values and valorizes informed self-aware choice, knowledge of the world in which one makes those choices, the value of play and humor in crafting a compassionate worldview, and acts of continuous self-examination and creation.

Previous Pratchett scholarship has followed three main threads: (1) examination of Pratchett within specific genres, for instance fantasy (e.g., Farah Mendlesohn and Edward James' *A Short History of Fantasy*); (2) commentary on Pratchett as a young adult author (the category in which he has achieved most critical attention and awards) and his contributions toward children's literacy (as noted, for example, in famed science fiction critic John Clute's essay "Coming of Age"); and (3) focus on Pratchett's Discworld universe in particular, the best-developed, longest-running, and most mature sequence of the author's work (an example of this focus is Anne Hiebert Alton and William Spruiell's *Discworld and the Disciplines*, referenced earlier). Here, we hope to weave together some of these threads of questioning: what impact, for instance, does Pratchett's early science fiction writing have on his later turn toward fantasy, in terms of genre shifts? How might an investigation of Pratchett's fondness for mythology and British folklore deepen our understanding of contemporary British identity and its complex relationship to colonialism? In what ways do themes of identity formation and exploration resonate in both the young adult novels and the novels for older readers, and to what extent do we see Pratchett's *non*–Discworld stories reflect or extend or even critique the predominant themes *within* Discworld, which must be understood not as a singular phenomenon but in dialogue with the rest of his work?

To this end, the essays gathered here combine elements such as science fiction studies, the effects of collaborative writing (e.g., Pratchett's work with Neil Gaiman and Stephen Baxter), steampunk aesthetics, productive modes of "ownership," intertextuality and textual references, neomedievalism and colonialism, adaptations into other media, linguistics and rhetorics, and coming of age as an act of free will. Fundamentally, we suggest that throughout Pratchett's works, moments of deliberate transformative choice—in particular those which create or transform or play with the expectations of narrative, genre, and storytelling—are central to his construction of ethical identity around moral self-examination, internal awareness, and often difficult yet worthwhile acts of compassion.

Opening the collection, Kristin Noone's "Something That Gods Are: Acts of Creation in Terry Pratchett's Early Science Fiction" considers the author's early and more sf-influenced work, reading the novel *Strata* and the short story "#ifdefDEBUG + 'world/enough' + 'time'" to argue that Pratchett's early science fiction presents moments of creation as an ethical act necessary for a self-aware, responsible, and pleasurable life, and that these early texts might offer insight not only into prototype versions of the later Discworld but into the evolution of Pratchett's moral stance. Following on from this, Mike Perschon's "Conan the Nonagenarian: Beyond Hyborian Hypermasculinity with Terry Pratchett's Cohen the Barbarian" returns to the 1930s pulp-fiction hero Conan the Barbarian to explore the ways in which Pratchett's Cohen the Barbarian moves from simple parody to sophisticated post-postmodern exploration of intertextuality and adaptation of the heroic ethos. Similarly, Emily Lavin Leverett interrogates the linkage of past and present in "Carrot Ironfoundersson: Medieval Romance, Narrative Causality and the Ethics of Choice in Terry Pratchett's *Guards! Guards!*," which takes the character of Carrot Ironfoundersson as a focal point for an examination of multiple medievalisms, satire, and multi-temporality in the romance motifs of Carrot's character development over multiple novels.

Kathleen Burt's "Self-Discovery, Free Will and Change: The Ethics of Growing Up in the Fantasy Novels of Terry Pratchett" also addresses the topic of maturation and moral agency in response to social and narrative convention, arguing that Pratchett allows his protagonists to explore ethical practice and construction of self-identity by adding a social component in which characters must determine how to fit in with or break with social expectations. This linkage of specific sociocultural, spatial, and temporal influences with self-construction is further examined in Livia Bongiovanni's "The Anglo-Saxon Ælf: Old English Influences in Terry Pratchett's *The Wee Free Men* and *The Shepherd's Crown*," which focuses on Pratchett's medievalism and in particular the Anglo-Saxon origins of Pratchett's version of elves, suggesting that the development of Pratchett's elves demonstrates both the continuing relevance of a specifically localized—and physically significant in England's geography—medieval past, and also the importance of speaking for the voiceless and putting others before oneself. Elise A. Bell, in "Constructing Identity Through Language in Discworld," expands the discussion of Pratchett's non-human characters into the field of linguistics, arguing that the linguistic characteristics of his trolls, Igors, dwarfs, and goblins serve to evoke stereotypes about real-world language use and the ways in which particular aspects of language use reflect both positively and negatively on speakers, while also demonstrating ways in which individuals might take advantage of linguistic creativity to forge their own personal identities with regard to a larger community group.

Continuing this connection between language, narrative construction, and ethics, Amy Lea Clemons' "Rhetoricity of Discworld: Magic and the Ethics of Footnotes" explores the relationship between magic and rhetoric, noting how both terms carry with them questions of identity and authority with implications for ethics—both in terms of Pratchett's characters who use these rhetorical strategies, and Pratchett himself, who uses that rhetoric to "take care of" his audiences through the literary techniques of carefully selected style and his infamous footnotes. Pratchett's deliberate choices of style and genre for rhetorical investigations of care are also central to "The Golempunk Manifesto: Ownership of the Means of Production in Pratchett's Discworld," in which Janet Brennan Croft asserts the importance of the steampunk sensibility for Pratchett's ethics—emphasizing the social effects of technology, the value of hackability, technology made beautiful, and the Victorian-influenced setting, but also a growing awareness of racial inclusivity and concern for sexual and social equality, as seen in both the later Discworld novels and their film adaptations, in particular the treatment of the golems. Finally, in "Neomedievalism and the Ethics of Colonization in Pratchett and Baxter's *The Long Earth* and *The Long War*," Sadie E. Hash examines the *Long Earth* series (which Pratchett co-authored with Stephen Baxter) as an interrogation of the ethics of colonialism, with attention to the intimate connections of the Long Earth universe with medievalist texts and figures (elves, trolls, and others), which the narrative characterizes as early British folklore and intertwines with British and American history, thus disrupting expected genre conventions of science fiction. Ultimately, Hash claims, Pratchett and Baxter's neomedievalism complicates and critiques our perception of colonialism and reflects an ongoing concern with humanity's ethical progress.

In all these essays, the focus remains on Pratchett's constructed worlds and narratives—from Discworld to the Long Earth, from the comedically apocalyptic near-present setting of *Good Omens* to the science-fictional flat planet of *Strata*, from Anglo-Saxon England to a parody of Conan the Barbarian's Cimmeria—as spaces in which questions of identity, community, and relations between self and other may be productively discussed, debated, and reshaped. Pratchett's worlds thus become *ethical* worlds: fantasies in which language always matters, stories resonate with the past and the future, and the choices characters make reflect the importance of self-aware and ongoing acts of compassion and creation.

Works Cited

Alton, Anne Hiebert, and William C. Spruiell, eds. *Discworld and the Disciplines: Critical Approaches to the Terry Pratchett Works*. McFarland, 2014.
Clute, John. "Coming of Age." In *Terry Pratchett: Guilty of Literature*, 2d ed. Edited by Andrew M. Butler, Edward James, and Farah Mendlesohn, 15–30. Old Earth Books.
Mendlesohn, Farah, and Edward James. *A Short History of Fantasy*. Oxfordshire Libri, 2012.

Something That Gods Are

Acts of Creation in Terry Pratchett's Early Science Fiction

Kristin Noone

"Creation is not something that gods do," the heroine of Terry Pratchett's science fiction novel *Strata* is told by the Computers, those ancient relics of the mysterious Builders of distant worlds; rather, creation is "something they are" (201). Examining Pratchett's heroes and heroines, Farah Mendlesohn has observed that "the Pratchett comedic hero ... incline[s] more toward accommodation, forgiveness, compassion, and mercy" (240), a form of redemptive heroism which rests on a sense of identity based on the ability to make choices and decisions for oneself (244). Tellingly, Mendlesohn's own academic metaphor when reading Pratchett revolves around the verb "construct": "the more truthful (or integral) one's sense of identity," she notes, "the more one can construct a sense of honor which is grounded in reality" (249) "without the assumption that it will make us comfortable" (260). These themes—the linking of construction, self-aware and self-determined choice, and compassion for self and others—appear early on in Pratchett's science fiction narratives, notably present in both the novel *Strata* and the short story "#ifdef DEBUG + 'world/enough' + 'time.'"[1]

Much Pratchett scholarship has focused on Discworld, as the largest and most fully developed expression of Pratchett's increasingly complex stance on ethics, individuality, narrative causality, and identification. However, bringing Pratchett's early—and more science-fiction aligned—works into this discussion not only provides context for the author's later works, but constructs a more complex narrative of Pratchett-as-author, one who explores and tests out acts of creation which build thematic connections across genre and form, science fiction travelogue and fantasy, short novel and short story. Investigation of these forays into literal world-building and self-creation, as seen in the short novel *Strata* and the short story "world/enough," can offer insight not only into prototype versions of the later Discworld, but into the evolution of Pratchett's moral stance regarding creation, pleasure, and ethical choice. In other words, Pratchett's early science fiction work presents moments of creation as an ethical act necessary for a self-aware, responsible, and pleasurable life.

Farah Mendlesohn, exploring faith and ethics in Pratchett's fantasy novels, argues that for Pratchett's characters, moral weight rests on their identity and sense of self, which in turn creates a coherent ethical system that relies on free choice and inclines toward accommodation, compassion, forgiveness, and mercy (239–240). Similarly emphasizing both choice and the inclination toward compassion, John Clute claims that Pratchett's vast popularity among general readers and academics alike suggests a desire for stories that leave the world "transformed for the better" yet offer this ameliorative comedic effect "without piety" (16). These elements of choice, identity, and responsibility can be traced not only in Pratchett's fantasy novels, but also in his early science fiction. In narratives like *Strata* and "world/enough," these recurrent themes, intertwined with the literal science-fictional building of worlds, demonstrate the author's working-through of the connections between this sense of individual responsibility, acts of creation, and transformation for the better. Both *Strata* and "world/enough," while early in Pratchett's career and less ambitious in scope than the Discworld sequence, serve as valuable case studies in an exploration of this question. Both works portray the choice to create, and the importance of creation, as an ethically valuable and even redemptive act, building new worlds and new selves in acts of willing kindness that rescue both oneself and others.

Fantasy, Science Fiction and Genre: Mapping Pratchett's Worlds

Science fiction and fantasy rely equally upon conventions of creation and world-construction, and Pratchett's work has always both emphasized, and playfully teased the inadequacies of, mapping imagined spaces. Pratchett's own famous comment, "There are no maps. You can't map a sense of humor," has been often quoted; however, paratexts such as *The Discworld Mapp*, *The Compleat Discworld Atlas*, *The Tourist Guide to Lancre*, *The Streets of Ankh-Morpork*, or even the detailed map of a certain section of Ankh-Morpork streets found in the Discworld novel *Night Watch* all suggest that to a certain extent, in fact, you *can*—and the maps will increase both the pleasures of experiencing the fantasy and the awareness of the social concerns of constructed spaces. Matthew Hills, discussing fantasy mapping in general and the mapping—or non-mapping—of Discworld specifically, draws attention to the groundedness and social problems reflected in Discworld's constructed space: sites of revolution, of waste-processing, of crime, of memorial. For Hills, fantasy mapping—the active imagination and creation of spaces— "need[s] to be viewed as moral" (236), and Pratchett's work "both observes the coordinates of the fantasy genre and re-places those coordinates through a postmodern emphasis on waste and marginality rather than heroic centrality" (236). According to this reading, Pratchett's created worlds are always deliberate acts with purposeful ethical implications: a choice to emphasize not the clean-cut and shining heroes of prophecy but the people on the margins, the sites of revolution or protest, the gritty streets, the civilians and Watchmen and candle-makers and street-cleaners and waste-processors. This moral stance in terms of imagined worlds—worlds which center around the everyday, even the menial—is reflected not only in the fantasy novels of Discworld, as in Hills' discussion, but can be traced into the more science-fictional early texts and inspirations for Discworld, such as *Strata* and "world/enough," a point which will be returned to in discussions of both narratives.

If Pratchett's acts of world-building are never politically neutral, always taking an ethical stance in their emphasis, what ethical concerns do these narrative creations raise? Gray Kochhar-Lindgren claims that Discworld overall and *Hogfather* in particular "addresses questions of origins, identity, symbolic representation, and ethics: how shall we then live?" and goes on to propose that Pratchett's fiction in general "questions the status of that dull division between the real and the unreal, for these are not opposites but co-sanguinates" (85). In other words, Pratchett's stance destabilizes the separation of the "real" and the "imagined," by presenting the imagined world(s) as necessary and vital for existence, spaces for working out very pertinent and practical questions of community, relations to self and others, and how one constructs a life. As Pratchett himself writes in "Imaginary Worlds, Real Stories," the text of his 1999 lecture to the British Folklore Society, "the collaborative aspect is prominent; those sitting in the circle of firelight while the story is told are not passive listeners" ("Imaginary Worlds," 240): the audience is affected by stories in very real ways, and is not passive but active in response, becoming more thoughtful and inquisitive. A few years prior, in 1993, speaking to the Booksellers Association Conference, Pratchett advocates fantasy and science fiction as "the proper diet for the growing soul. All human life is there: a moral code, a sense of order, and sometimes great big green things with teeth" ("Let There Be Dragons," 109); fantasy is a genre that not only engages with morality and ethics but does so in terms of the past and the future and multiple temporalities, traditionally the province of science fiction. As Pratchett himself says, fantasy "speculates about the future, rewrites the past, and reconsiders the present. It plays games with the universe" ("Dragons," 105). Kochhar-Lindgren agrees, analyzing the ways in which Pratchett's fiction addresses questions of social order and philosophical truth through "the concoction of an alternative world" (85) and arguing that if the "alternative world" is always an invention, his readers clearly revel in the unreality of it, in particular the self-aware quality of Pratchett's fantasy. This assertion consequently invites the question: what happens when Pratchett, early in his career, explores science fiction rather than fantasy?

Pratchett seems to nearly conflate the genres in his "Let There Be Dragons" speech, moving easily from defenses of one to defenses of the other. He refers to science fiction as "a twentieth-century subset of fantasy," in which "it is a small mental step from time travel to paleontology, from swords 'n' sorcery fantasy to mythology and ancient history," because both genres are concerned with "look[ing] at the universe" ("Dragons," 107). In *The Seven Beauties of Science Fiction*, Istvan Cicsery-Ronay, Jr., describes science fiction as "the first to devote its imagination to the future and to the ceaseless revolutions of knowledge and desire that attend the application of scientific and technical knowledge to social life" (2), language that invokes simultaneously the possibilities of science, the consideration of social impact that is essential to the genre, and the importance of imagined worlds. Carl Kears and James Paz propose in their editorial introduction to their volume *Medieval Science Fiction* that an interdisciplinary triangular relationship might prove more useful that strictly defined genre boundaries, offering the formulation "medieval/science/fiction," which, in their terms, might rotate and combine and recombine (26) to permit new views of the linkages between science, medievalism, and fiction; in the same collection, Andy Sawyer applies this formulation to his reading of Discworld as science fiction, noting that while at the outset Discworld begins as a realm of magic, "in later Discworld novels we see developments which, despite their fantasy trappings, make them much more akin to the science fiction novels in which a conceptual breakthrough or a new technology ensures that the world is never the same again," citing the in-universe invention of the "clacks" (Discworld's semaphore system), the printing press, and the locomotive as examples (170–172). For Sawyer, Discworld can be read as medievalist science fiction because it "involves the development of technological and political systems (often intertwined) as increasingly complex technology opens up new challenges for the political players" (170–171). If the Discworld itself can be read as science fiction, exploring the challenges and social ramifications of technology, then a reexamination of Pratchett's works as science fiction is necessary; while Sawyer does not discuss non–Discworld narratives—an omission that once again highlights the need for more expansive Pratchett scholarship—this reading provides an obvious opening for connection across Pratchett's larger corpus.

John Rieder, in *Colonialism and the Emergence of Science Fiction*, draws attention to the ways in which the persistent presence of colonialism becomes part of the science fiction genre's texture, its relation to otherness and the "exotic other" as alternately sites of discovery, projection, datum, or fantasy, and consequently its construction of the potentially imaginable: science fiction is a genre in which "this play of antithetical possibilities is an important measure of science fiction's engagement with colonial history, ideology, and discourse" (15). Science fiction functions as a means of ideological investigation and discourse, using created worlds to explore tensions inherent in encounters with Otherness. Therefore, the genre becomes fertile ground for exploration of uneven cultural and economic distribution (Rieder 32–33). It is not a coincidence, then, that Pratchett's early work engages with precisely these science-fictional themes; while, as Hills and Kochhar-Lindgren have observed, this engagement with morality and marginality is carried out in complex ways in Pratchett's fantasy, the science fiction of "world/enough" and *Strata* asks these questions as well.

Time to Explore "world/enough"

Pratchett's short story "world/enough" has received very little critical attention—mainly brief mentions, collected into discussions of his shorter fiction—but bears examining as an early venture into constructed worlds and the science-fictional *novum*.[2] The science-fictional novum, the new thing, allows for extrapolation from the known, that single point of cognitive estrangement, as per foundational science fiction scholar Darko Suvin's definition, rather than the fantastic un-real or never-real; according to Istvan Cicsery-Ronay, Jr., the science-fictional novum is "usually a rationally explicable material phenomenon, the result of an invention or discovery, whose unexpected appearance elicits a wholesale change in the perception of reality" (6). This invention or discovery is grounded in the rational, material, predictable world; the rules are not arbitrary, but extrapolated from available science, though perhaps not physically achievable. Importantly, however, Cicsery-Ronay's definition emphasizes the shift in *perception* caused by the science fiction novum: science fiction, he suggests, is a genre built upon "two forms of hesitation: a historical-logical one (how plausible is the conceivable novum?) and an ethical one (how good/bad/altogether alien are the transformations that would issue from the novum?)" (3). Pratchett's "world/enough" explores the proposed second hesitation, that of the social and ethical transformation, in depth, and arguably addresses the first as well, as can be seen in his own introductory comments about the ways in which the story's subject feels very close to home.

"world/enough" deploys the science fiction novum of artificial virtual reality to examine the ways in which the "real world" itself may be a construct, an agreed-upon narrative that consists of a series of choices made by people in response to ethical dilemmas. In this short story, which dates from 1990 and was originally written for Dave Barrett's *Digital Dreams* anthology, Pratchett examines virtual reality, afterlives, and the ability to literally build a personalized "better world." His own retrospective perspective shifts are reflected in his introduction to the reprinted story in 2012's *A Blink of the Screen*: "I was tempted to update this—after all, it's about Virtual Reality, haha, remember that, everybody? I'm so old I can remember Virtual Reality!—but after all, what's the point? Besides, it would be cheating…" (119). In this sense, "cheating" would mean removing the story from its context and the impetus for its production, but would also involve a form of cheating in terms of world-creation: rewriting and re-marketing "world/enough" with an updated plot and technology would arguably replace, and therefore no longer be, the narrative as originally created by the author. Pratchett continues, "I just liked the idea of an amiable repairman, not very bright but good with machines, padding the streets of a dull quiet sleeping world. Things are breaking down, knowledge is draining away, and he's driving his van around the sleeping streets, helping people dream. Now, many years later, it appears rather chilly and maybe very close to home" (119). If it is close to home, it is so in that science-fictional question of plausibility in an era when, as Cicsery-Ronay notes, "sf is ingrained within the quotidian consciousness of people living in the postindustrial world; each day they witness the transformations of their values and material conditions in the wake of technical acceleration beyond their conceptual threshold" (5); virtual reality technology is, if not perfected, present in headsets and simulated environments, and the topic of a plethora of news articles and studies both academic and popular.[3] Pratchett's story may therefore indeed lie very close to home, as he himself says, though it is not necessarily chilly; "world/enough" is a fundamentally ambiguous story, in which Pratchett works through the difficulties and the desires of the choice to go on living in a knowingly purely constructed virtual world.

The story's narrator, Darren Thompson, introduces himself in the middle, or rather the aftermath, of the action, as he is sent to tidy up the scene after two bodies are found physically dead but linked into an artificial reality device. Darren works as a repairman of the devices in question: "they always call me in. Reliable, see. Dependable. You can't trust the big boys, they're all dealers and agents for the afer [artificial reality] companies, they're locked in. Me, I could go back to repairing microswatch players tomorrow. Darren Thompson, Artificial Realities repaired, washing-machine motors rewound"

(122). Darren is very good at his job, but also clings to an older practical reality and a sense of history, as when he muses about the etymology of the word *copper*,[4] or comments in an aside to his audience, "me, I prefer to settle down with a good book. People don't read books these days. Don't seem to do anything much. You go down any street, it's all dead, all these people living in their own realities" (133). Pratchett's dark humor aside—the bodies at the scene are "all dead," indeed, as Darren arrives to tidy up—this moment encapsulates Kochhar-Lindgren's claim that Pratchett's work destabilizes binaries. Darren would prefer to settle down with a book, but is impressively good at his high-tech job, the person they "always" call in; he complains about the way people don't seem to do "anything much" and makes a point of noting his own other skills, washing-machine motor rewinding included, but nevertheless his current job and his reputation rely on the artificial reality industry, and ultimately his knowledge of the technology will permit his central act of compassion in the story.

As "world/enough" opens, Darren has been called to the crime scene because the police suspect that the Artificial Realities device—which, if functioning properly, is supposed to remind people to wake up—has gone wrong and led to not one but two deaths. The deaths in question are not unknown citizens, but famous persons: Michael Dever—the inventor of the most popular technological form of access to the artificial reality world—and his wife Suzannah, who had been pregnant; he had been plugged into the artificial reality machine at the time of her physical death, apparently from a miscarriage. The "coppers" want to investigate the possibilities of deliberate foul play, or equipment malfunction that could make Dever's company liable, or accidental negligence; this is why Darren has been called to investigate the machine. According to one copper's somewhat dismissive suggestion as Darren arrives, maybe it's as simple as the fact that "something went wrong. She bled to death. And her just lying there, and him in the next room in his little porno world..." (127). "world/enough" presents this as a horrible possibility, and does not shy away from it; however, this theory turns out not to be the case, as our expert repairman finds: "Thing is, there wasn't anything wrong. It wasn't that I couldn't find a fault, it was there was nothing to say a fault existed. It was as if it'd just been told to shut down everything. Including him" (130). He gets out his own helmet to log into the last memory, and after viewing it—initially, without disclosing to the audience what he did in fact see—he agrees casually with the officers' theories: "you're saying, hey, I know what you saw ... maybe there was a kid's voice in the next room, the kid they never had, because, right, he'd sat there five years ago while she was still alive and done the reality creation job of a lifetime. And he was living in it, just sane enough to make sure he kept living in it" (130). The police believe this explanation because it provides a tidy answer, tragic but with no party left to prosecute, human or corporation, and thus becomes the constructed truth of the official report. However, Pratchett's story hints at a different, and perhaps more hopeful, possible construction.

As Darren—described in that introductory text by Pratchett as "amiable," a repairman simply doing his job, one of the marginal atypically heroic figures that, as Hills claims, Pratchett's work centralizes—continues telling the unofficial story to his audience, a more complex and more compassionate narrative emerges. "He owes me, anyway," Darren confides. "I got the machine going again and I never told them what she said to me, when I saw her in his reality. She said, tell him to hurry" (132). Both the master programmer Michael and his wife Suzannah are in fact *alive* in the reality they have constructed, the narrative in which they can rebuild their lives and their family, Suzannah has been existing in this new world for the past five years, while Michael's upload has been trapped by the glitch in the machine. They speak to Darren, and they are not mere memories or copies, but creative forces; Suzannah Dever is writing children's books, as Darren tells us, three of them published in the last five years, one of which even received an award, and they have been "seen" vacationing in Oslo, or at least their digital presences have. Darren, who simply reboots the machine, fixes Michael's upload problem, and deliberately chooses to allow the couple their privacy, without drawing disruptive attention to their new plane of existence: "People in machines," Darren muses, "I can live with that, and I wonder what compiler he used, and when I rebooted the machine I sort of initialized him and made sure he got sent out. Sort of like a godfather, me" (132). Darren's choice is one of kindness, allowing the Devers the privacy of their new life, and even wondering whether he himself might choose this radical (and potentially desirable) form of constructed existence someday: "Every time I switch a visor on I wonder if I'll spot them. Wouldn't mind knowing how they did it, might like to be a virus myself one day, could be an expert at it" (132).

"world/enough" ends with Darren's musings on the artificial reality world and the future:

> when I was a kid we thought the future would be all crowded and cool and rainy with big glowing Japanese adverts everywhere and people eating noodles in the street. At least you'd be communicating, if only to ask the other guy to pass the soy sauce. My joke. But what we got, we got this Information Revolution, what it means is no bugger knows anything and doesn't know they don't know…. You shouldn't turn in on yourself. It's not what being human means. You got to reach out [132].

Pratchett, via Darren, expresses concern about people turning inward and a loss of history, of word-origins, of communication, not denying potential losses in the construction of new realities; however, through their constructed virtual selves, Michael and Suzannah Dever have followed precisely this advice: not turning inward with their grief but engaging with the world, writing children's stories, going on vacation, loving each other. They exemplify the deconstruction of binaries, as discussed by Kochhar-Lindgren, and the ideological questions of science fiction regarding the moral and ethical implications of the science fiction novum. When Darren himself thinks about potentially choosing this virtual-reality afterlife, and when Pratchett presents it to us, "world/enough" offers a constructed space that provides room for recovery, love, compassion, and reaching out to others in an act of kindness, giving them a world of their own.

The Layers of Strata

Strata, in contrast to "world/enough"'s virtual and personal constructed realm, presents an *external* invented world—a flat world, a disc-world—which is nevertheless revealed to be a joyful act of play by the Creators, as depicted in the novel. Here, the science-fictional novum involves world-building technology, which is more or less commonplace and has both practical implications (population expansion) and social implications, as becoming planetary designer is an open-to-anyone profession, though a celebrated and high-status one, and even within the profession some architects are far more distinguished than others. John Clute, reading *Strata*, comments that "the flat world itself and its tiny surrounding cosmos—all built as a perfect replica of the Ptolomaic universe—is a kind of flaw in the carpet, a joke, a fingerprint" (30)—in other words, primarily playful, though this is not necessarily a negative assessment. Clute calls this early Pratchett novel, first published in 1981, "more determinedly and less successfully a gambol, set in what only seems to be an alternate universe markedly similar to our own: the final surprises of the story concern the exceedingly complex but satisfying manner in which it turns out that the universe is indeed ours, a long time ago" (23); *Strata*, then, is a story about human identity, about discovery, about the value of play, and about the importance of invention in the worlds we construct, both literal and metaphorical.

Strata's narrative centers around the Company official and planetary designer Kin Arad, and the ways in which she embodies the connection between creation and delight. Kin, according to Clute, is "too much of an adult, too sexually mature, for Pratchett to cope with (at this stage in his career) successfully," (30) making her a difficult character to analyze; in support of this claim, Clute references Pratchett's disinclination toward sexually mature themes in early Discworld novels as well. Importantly, however, though Kin is 210 years old, she has been rejuvenated and refreshed, and is capable of desires. Her primary desire, in fact, is one of curiosity and inquisitiveness, paralleling Pratchett's argument in "Let There Be Dragons" regarding the paramount importance of fantasy and science fiction in encouraging questions and exploration. Kin is intrigued by the rumors of a world that defies Company guidelines and regulations, a supposed completely flat or discworld, which challenges the in-universe conceptions of what a built world must resemble; she has previously written a book and given talks celebrating the theory of "continuous creation":

> races arose, and changed the universe to suit themselves, and then died. And the other races arose, changed the universe to suit themselves, and then died.... Kin had once heard a speaker refer disparagingly to the Spindles because they had manipulated worlds. She had stood up and said, "So what? If they hadn't earth would still be a mess of hot rocks and heavy clouds. They changed all this and they brought in a big moon but do you know the best of all? They gave us a past. They jiggered their strata machines to give us fossils of things that had never existed. Icthyosaurs and crinoids and chalk and ancient seas. Maybe they didn't feel at home unless they had a few hundred meters of fossil strata underneath them ... but I think they did it because it was their art. They didn't know anyone would see it, but they went ahead and did it" [59].

Kin Arad is herself an expert on world-construction and creation and play, a notion which appears mildly controversial in the text: the novel opens with her gentle scolding of much younger Company employees for inserting, during construction, a fossil plesiosaur holding an "End Nuclear Testing Now" sign (10). Kin comments to herself that "sooner or later everyone did it. Because every novice planetary designer with an ounce of talent felt like a king atop the dream-device that was a strata machine, and sooner or later yielded to the temptation to pop the skulls of future paleontologists. Sometimes the Company fired them, sometimes it promoted them" (10). Even Kin herself once upon a time built a mountain range in the shape of her initials (12), demonstrating the irresistibility of playfulness; from the beginning, then, *Strata* makes a claim in favor of the integral and innate nature of fantasy and fantastic creation: the desire for the deliberately unreal, the out of place, the purposely and visibly ridiculous and theatrical which might be dangerous—a firing, a loss of position, emotional trauma for those future paleontologists—but might also be rewarded with a promotion. The plot of the novel proper begins with the arrival of a mysterious message: "A flat world. Be there or forever wonder," and Pratchett italicizes the sense of wonder when he repeats the message as Kin reads it. The flat world—the deliberately strange, evocative, uncanny world—is a place of wonder.

Strata embraces, and indeed defends and rescues, this sense of wonder, in Kin's choice to not merely discover but to protect this created space. Once Kin and her crew find the fabled flat world, they also discover the Computers left to run it by the mysterious (never fully explained) vanished Builders; Kin makes a bargain with these Computers. They require her skills—which she believes means her skills as a planetary designer—because the flat world's machinery is at last wearing out; she asks to be told what amounts to the secret of the universe, insofar as the Computers know the Builders' intent. This bargain proves satisfactory, and Kin puts on the helmet of the Builders, at which point the novel contains a scene break, in much the same way that "world/enough" draws attention to the discrepancy between Darren's constructed story for the "coppers" and the true story about narrative construction he confesses to his audience: both texts depict moments in which the artificial narrative of narrative itself is foregrounded, and the choices of what to tell or not tell are made overt.

When Kin removes the helmet and awakens, she has been given a story of her own to share. "We're a colony universe," she tells her companions, "the Builders just moved in and built it, and because everyone needs a history, they gave us a history. Just as we do with the new worlds. Ancient bones. Fabulous monsters. Great Spindle kings, Wheelers. And we never realized it. We did it ourselves and we never tumbled to it" (199). Creation here provides a history, an identity, and even a sense of purpose, as the novel's "we"— humanity—create in unknowing imitation of our creators. But Pratchett complicates and humanizes this cosmology, in a move that Clute describes as a conclusion that "ends in shifts, delights, even a touch of awe," and "an open hinge which never swings shut" (24). Specifically, Pratchett's novel suggests that we ourselves are the gods of our own universe:

> Silver [a fellow crewmate] unfastened her couch straps, and looked across at Kin. "We built the universe, didn't we," she said. "Not us precisely, these lumps of bone and brain, but the thing inside us that makes us what we are. The thing that dreams while the rest of us are asleep."
> Kin smiled. "The computers wouldn't tell," she said. "But yes, you're right. I think the Computers had a certain extra function, they could suppress all the mental static so the—oh, hell, why avoid the word?—the god inside could surface for just a while and perform. That's why practically anyone could be the Disc master" [202].

In *Strata*'s cosmology and history, the Builders of the universe could be, indeed, practically anyone—any of us. *Strata*, then, leads us to Discworld's uses of fantasy and science fiction not only morphologically, in the literal world-building, but thematically: the identity of the universe depends on the choices we all have made and what we have chosen to build, or in Kochhar-Lindgren's terms, "'good order' ... depends finally not on law but on inventiveness" (88). This inventiveness is celebrated not by Kin being special, or destined, or a kind of particular Chosen One, but by the truth that it could have been, to paraphrase Pratchett's words, practically any human wearing the helmet of the Builders, rescuing the flat disc-shaped world. Once again, this returns us to Pratchett's emphasis on the centrality of the everyday; the simple facts of Kin's humanity and her ability to invent and design worlds are the precise qualities celebrated in *Strata*'s science-fictional "good order."

When Kin asks the Computers *why* the Builders built, they tell her, in capital letters reminiscent of Discworld's Death,[5] "Humans are inquisitive. That is a function of their humanity. The beings that built this universe did so because it was unthinkable that they should not. Creation is not something that gods do. It is something that they are" (201). Once the "beings that built this universe" and "humans" are revealed to be the same, *Strata* asks us to read this sentence differently: creation is not something *humans* do, but something *humans* are. Acts of invention are ethical acts, as Kin's choice to repair the flat world helps rescue and preserve it, a choice that protects; and she is rewarded with an explanation (a story) of existence that reframes creation as not simply a day job—being a "planetary designer" by trade—but as work that is integral to humanity. And, as in "world/enough," this is a narrative in which the central choice of the story, the moment which leads to the satisfying conclusion, involves an act of repair, recovery, and connection with others. In "world/enough," that moment consists of Darren's compassion for the Devers and their desire to begin a wholly new life without the pain of the old; in *Strata*, that moment comes when Kin Arad agrees to help the Computers rescue their failing flat world, and puts on the helmet of the Builders.

Conclusion: Something Humans Are

If, as Farah Mendlesohn and John Clute have argued, heroism in Pratchett's worlds is fundamentally presented as redemptive, with an emphasis on active engaged choice and compassion for others, any examination of those moments of choice must also include the earlier and less-studied narratives in which those choices are explored and worked out in myriad experimental ways. If science fiction, medievalism, and fantasy are intertwined, as Carl Kears and James Paz—and Pratchett himself—argue, then Pratchett's later fantastic works must also be read in dialogue with his earlier exploratory works, which play with length (short story versus novel) and genre (science fiction versus fantasy) as well as ethics and philosophy. Placing these works into dialogue with other Pratchett texts can better inform our readings of Pratchett overall; the narratives I've discussed here, *Strata* and "world/enough," open up only two of many possible avenues for further investigation, a Pratchett scholarship which may itself become more connected (as in the medieval/science/fiction triangulation, potentially inviting collaboration with other genres?), more inventive (exploring paratexts and fan texts and transformative works, perhaps?), and more intrinsically playful.

In keeping with this first suggestion, that of cross-disciplinary connection, I have argued elsewhere that Pratchett's work employs the fantastic, in particular the fantastic of a Shakespearean England, in order to explore very human desires; in the Witches sequence of the Discworld novels, supernatural abilities provide power and impact on a larger scale, but it is human action and choice that is ultimately required for happy endings ("Shakespeare in Discworld," 30). *Strata* and "world/enough" make use of more science-fictional, less purely fantastical, settings, but Pratchett's emphasis on choice—and especially *compassionate* choice, reaching out to others—can be seen developing in both texts. These early acts of creation thereby invite us to begin to ask the ethical questions that Pratchett will later develop in more extended sequences: when and how and why do we make active choices to create worlds and narratives, who is affected by those narratives, and what responsibility might we have to craft compassionate constructed worlds? In what ways might these worlds and narrative serve to metaphorically rescue others, as Kin Arad's capability to invent literally rescues the inhabitants of the disc-world in *Strata*, and in what ways might they provide solace or a more bearable future for ourselves, as Michael and Suzannah Dever—and possibly Darren, the narrator, as well—explore in "world/enough"? In what ways might we continue to ask these questions in our own relationships with past and present, with fantasy and identity, and the ways in which we create and construct the narratives of our lives?

Notes

1. For ease of reading, this story will be referenced as "world/enough" from here on.
2. To this end, further investigation might explore Pratchett's science-fictional desires and his later work in the context of science fiction, with the steampunk of *Raising Steam* or the worlds of the Long Earth novels.
3. To provide just one example of the pop-culture reach of VR discussions, the popular tech magazine and news site *Wired* has an entire dedicated Virtual Reality section: https://www.wired.com/tag/virtual-reality/.
4. As certain members of the City Watch will also, later, over in Discworld.
5. For readability, I have standardized the capitalization here.

Works Cited

Clute, John. "Coming of Age." *Terry Pratchett: Guilty of Literature*, 2d ed. Edited by Andrew M. Butler, Edward James, and Farah Mendlesohn, Old Earth Books, 2004. 15–30.
Csicsery-Ronay, Istvan, Jr. *The Seven Beauties of Science Fiction*. Wesleyan UP, 2008.
Hills, Matthew. "Mapping Narrative Spaces." *Terry Pratchett: Guilty of Literature*, 2d ed. Edited by Andrew M. Butler, Edward James, and Farah Mendlesohn, Old Earth Books, 2004. 217–238.
Kears, Carl, and James Paz, eds. *Medieval Science Fiction*. Boydell & Brewer, 2016.
Kochhar-Lindgren, Gray. "Tell It Slant: Of Gods, Philosophy, and Politics in Terry Pratchett's

Discworld." *Discworld and the Disciplines: Critical Approaches to the Terry Pratchett Works*, edited by Anne Hiebert Alton and William C. Spruiell. McFarland, 2014. 81–91.

Mendlesohn, Farah. "Faith and Ethics." *Terry Pratchett: Guilty of Literature*, 2d ed. Edited by Andrew M. Butler, Edward James, and Farah Mendlesohn, Old Earth Books, 2004. 239–260.

Noone, Kristin. "Shakespeare in Discworld: Witches, Fantasy, and Desire." *Journal of the Fantastic in the Arts,* Vol. 21, issue 1, 2010. 26–40.

Pratchett, Terry. "#ifdefDEBUG + 'world/enough' + 'time.'" *A Blink of the Screen: Collected Shorter Fiction.* Anchor Books, 2012.119–133.

_____. "Imaginary Worlds, Real Stories." *Once More* *with Footnotes*, NESFA Press, 2005. 239–251.

_____. "Let There Be Dragons." *A Slip of the Keyboard: Collected Nonfiction.* Doubleday, 2014. 103–109.

_____. *Strata.* Corgi Books, 1981.

Rieder, John. *Colonialism and the Emergence of Science Fiction.* Wesleyan UP, 2008.

Sawyer, Andy. "The Riddle of Medieval Technology." *Medieval Science Fiction.* Edited by Carl Kears and James Paz, Boydell & Brewer, 2016. 153–176.

Suvin, Darko. *Metamorphoses of Science Fiction: On the Poetics and History of a Literary Genre.*: Yale UP, 1979.

Conan the Nonagenarian: Beyond Hyborian Hypermasculinity with Terry Pratchett's Cohen the Barbarian

MIKE PERSCHON

Some heroes just can't die. And in the case of Conan the Barbarian, it isn't for a lack of trying. This is true within the story world of the Hyborian Age where despite Conan's life of ever-present danger, neither his creator Robert E. Howard nor Howard's imitators could bring themselves to kill the seminal fantasy barbarian. This is also true in the real world, where Conan's popularity has waxed and waned, but never withered entirely. One need only differentiate between the original Conan of Cimmeria, 1930s pulp hero, and the popular designation "Conan the Barbarian" as *the* iconic barbarian of fantasy, in prose pastiches, comics, cartoons, television series, films, and games tabletop and desktop to understand the breadth of that popularity. Recent examples include *Conan Exiles*, a multiplatform video game set in the Hyborian Age which proved to be "the best and fastest-selling game in developer Funcom's history" (*Variety*), as well as *Robert E Howard's Conan: Adventures in an Age Undreamed Of*, a critically and financially successful tabletop roleplaying game (the third Conan roleplaying game since the 1980s). After more than a decade of Conan comics from Dark Horse comics, Marvel comics announced that it had reclaimed Conan to their roster with a new series launching in January 2019, while French publisher Glénat is releasing its own ongoing line of Conan books based on Howard's original stories. Conan lives on! But isn't it the hero's lot to die in battle?

According to *Cohen the Barbarian*, Terry Pratchett's parody of Conan, it is. In Pratchett's *Interesting Times*, Cohen muses on the wisdom of his father, who "had taken him to a mountain top, when he was no more than a lad, and explained to him the hero's creed and told him that there was no greater joy than to die in battle" (114). Pratchett, as is his style, takes the opportunity for a joke: "Cohen had seen the flaw in this straight away, and a lifetime's experience had reinforced his belief that in fact a greater joy was to kill the other bugger in battle and end up sitting on a heap of gold higher than your horse" (114). But in *The Last Hero*, the next Discworld book Cohen appeared in, this avoidance of death has been utterly abandoned in favor of running *towards* death, not away from it; Cohen and his equally decrepit, equally aged companions intend to blow up Cori Celesti, the mountain of the gods of the Discworld, because those gods "let us grow old" (47). While *The Last Hero* involves a few of Pratchett's signature of parallel plotlines, this apocalyptic suicide-heist is at the heart of the book. In those parallel plotlines, factions attempting to stop Cohen know that he's attempting the destruction of Cori Celesti, but are puzzled as to his motivation. And while Cohen voices anger at not being allowed to die in battle, Pratchett's explorations of age and heroism are more nuanced than reification of the idea that true heroes must die in battle. An investigation of those nuances offers the opportunity for a closer look at both Conan (the object of parody) and Cohen the parody.

As stated in the preface to *Terry Pratchett: Guilty of Literature*—the seminal academic anthology on Pratchett's work—a chapter devoted to Cohen (as well as a number of other recurring Discworld characters) seemed a glaring omission, and one which remained unaddressed in the book's second expanded edition (Butler, et al. x, xii). The passing references to Cohen in that anthology's submissions provide little illumination of Pratchett's intent when he parodied Conan, parodied heroic fantasy in general, and reinvented the iconic fantasy barbarian for the 21st century, at a time when Robert E. Howard's pulp hero in all his manifestations, both faithful and derivative, seem to lack cultural currency, save among devoted fans. While this absence was not the impetus for the writing of this essay, it is certainly an affirmation, especially given how little attention[1] Conan the Barbarian, Cohen's literary and cultural antecedent, receives in academic circles.

Admittedly, I wanted to write about Cohen because I'm a Conan fan who has grown up, and like so many critics of Conan, can see that the original barbarian hero is a bit like James Bond—he's an artifact, a relic of another time, be it historical time or a period in many (mostly male) fantasy fans' lives when they want their stories simple, direct, and to the swordpoint. And while some recent iterations of Conan in comics, such as the Dark Horse/Dynamite team up of *Conan and Red Sonja* by Jim Zub and Gail Simone, have attempted to take some of the potential barbarism out of the barbarian—his misogyny, his unthinking penchant for violence—it's difficult to see, even with Jason Aaron's socially aware 2019 reboot of the Marvel comics Conan series, how that hero will speak to a complex global village striving to find softer, gentler solutions to conflict amidst diversity.

Which brings me to why I am a fan of Cohen, and knew I wanted to write about him: I think, especially in *The Last Hero*, that Pratchett *has already rewritten Conan for the post-postmodern world*. What began as simple parody grew into a thoughtful exploration of where barbarians go when they can't die—not into the grave, nor even into the halls of Valhalla, but beyond the worlds which birthed them, adapting to survive in new times and new worlds. In this case, it's an exploration of where Terry Pratchett takes said immortal barbarian: to a space of questioning hypermasculine heroism and zero-sum violent solutions.

On the surface, a study of Cohen also charts how Pratchett grew as a writer in the fifteen years between *The Light Fantastic* (1986) and *The Last Hero* (2001), demonstrating how the Discworld began as mere parody of other people's fantasy characters, franchises, and worlds, but became a fantasy world in its own right, with its own characters: in the case of Cohen, a character who evolved from an elderly version of Conan the Barbarian into a more complex exploration of the ethos underlying heroic fantasy.

Cohen was not Pratchett's first attempt to lampoon the brawny barbarian. In *The Colour of Magic*, the wizard Rincewind and the hapless tourist Twoflower accompany "Hrun the Barbarian" into a temple of evil. The fact that Hrun is from "Chimeria" is an obvious reference to Conan's home of Cimmeria. He is described as spectacularly stupid, relying instead on his prodigious muscles and prowess in combat: the typical barbarian with more brawn than brains, a clear reference to Conan as pop culture in the 1980s understood him. Consequently, Hrun is not a parody of Howard's Conan. Howard's Conan is clever and articulate. He is not the monosyllabic grunter of Pratchett's Hrun. If Hrun is considered as parody of Conan at all—and it is just as likely that he is more a parody of all barbarians and heroic fantasy heroes, from Conan to Moorcock's emo–Conan, Elric of Melnibone (Hrun carries a sentient magical sword which is "the sort of black that is less a colour than a graveyard of colours" with a "highly-ornate runic inscription on the blade" [*The Colour of Magic*, 131])—he is a parody of Schwarzenegger's Conan, given how original 1980s audiences and critics derided the Austrian bodybuilder's thick accent as evidence of a lack of intelligence.

But even Cohen, when he appeared in *The Light Fantastic*, the sequel to *The Colour of Magic*, was not a direct parody of Howard's Conan alone. The presence of Herenna the Henna-Haired Harridan is an obvious reference to Red Sonja, whose connection to Howard's Conan is tenuous at best: while Howard wrote a female hero named Red Sonya of Rogatino in the short story

"Shadow of the Vulture," the Red Sonja parodied by Herenna is the Sonja of Marvel and now Dynamite comics. She is to the idea of the warrior-woman-in-a-chainmail-bikini what Conan is to the typical barbarian. This is one of many indications in *The Light Fantastic* that Pratchett is not parodying any one particular instance of heroic fantasy, but the idea of heroic fantasy as mediated through a synthesis of multiple media: of Howard's original prose re-released in paperback alongside other authors' Conan pastiches; of Frank Frazetta and Boris Vallejo's colorful and compelling cover art for most of those paperbacks, the image of John Buscema's iconic comic version in the Marvel comics series, bare-chested and brooding in his bearskin-loincloth and boots, and of course, Arnold Schwarzenegger as the cinematic Cimmerian in John Milius's 1982 film version.

In "'Barbarian Heroing' and Its Parody," the only extensive academic exploration of Cohen I have come across, Imola Bulgozdi identifies Cohen as a reaction solely to the popularity of Conan onscreen, which might admittedly be the most famous iteration of the character. Bulgozdi then argues that Cohen "becomes a far more complex figure, often displaying links with the original Conan of the short stories," by which she means the original Conan stories written in the 1930s by pulp writer Robert E. Howard. The bulk of Bulgozdi's comparative study of Cohen is taken up with references to Howard's fiction, perhaps because Howard's prose has gained a marginal amount of academic acceptance, while Milius' film remains a B-movie unworthy of scholarly attention.[2]

It seems unlikely that Pratchett was referencing Howard's version of the barbarian so much as the concept of Conan as the sum of many parts. I appreciate how Andrew M. Butler obliquely describes Cohen as a parody of what Conan "might get up to in later life if his career was as long as his creator's successors made it" (10), since it is arguably Howard's successors, not so much Howard himself, who Cohen is a reaction to. If someone says, "I'm a fan of Conan," the response needs to be, "which one?" Do you mean the original pulp hero created by Howard? Or do you mean the paperback hero of pastiche and rewrites under L. Sprague de Camp's watchful eye (or by his own hand)? What about the Conan of Frank Frazetta's celebrated oil paintings which graced the covers of the Ace paperbacks? Or perhaps you preferred the smoother airbrushed approach of Boris Vallejo or other artists in the 1980s. You might be a fan of the comics, but then we'd want to ask Marvel or Dark Horse? And of course, you might be a fan of the films (and again, I'd have to ask, "Schwarzenegger or Momoa?"), or even the lesser known and much maligned television series.

Consequently, in investigating Cohen, the inquiry begins with the question, "which Conan was Pratchett responding to?" While I won't completely discount the possibility of Pratchett having read Howard's Conan, I think it unlikely that Cohen is meant to directly reference the original stories alone. Even if Pratchett meant to reference Howard's work, it's not in only the areas Bulgozdi identifies. For example, Howard's Conan is comfortable in the clothing of many cultures, while Cohen and his silver Horde chafe at being dressed in anything but their utterly chafe-prone leather loincloths; consequently, Conan is more flexible and versatile than Cohen and company (Bulgozdi 196). However, the "civilized" garb Cohen and the Horde are forced to wear in *Interesting Times* is that of eunuchs. Pratchett's reference is less about Howard clothing Conan in "the garb of various countries with natural elegance" (196) than it is making an off-color joke about old men who exemplify traditional Western masculinity unknowingly masquerading as emasculated palace servants. Furthermore, it's not far off from a direct parody of Schwarzenegger's Conan and his companions dressing in temple garb in *Conan the Barbarian* to infiltrate the Temple of the Serpent, or Conan mugging a priest for his robes to assassinate the film's villain, Thulsa Doom. Pratchett plays on the ridiculousness of making heroes who are used to rushing in recklessly sneaking around *incognito* again in *The Last Hero*, in which Cohen and the Silver Horde masquerade as ridiculous deities like "the God of bloody Swearing" or "God of Bein' Sick" (140). This is less a reference to Howard's Conan than it is a series of quick and easy gags. In general, the connection to Howard's Conan is tenuous at best, though Bulgozdi makes much of these perceived connections throughout her article.

Bulgozdi argues that Howard's Conan has largely been "overwritten in popular fiction by the 1982 hit, *Conan the Barbarian*." As stated earlier, she then links the film to the "1986 debut of the Discworld character, Cohen the Barbarian in Terry Pratchett's *The Light Fantastic*" (193). If we pursue this line of inquiry further, she'd have discovered stronger connections between Cohen and the cinematic or popular Conan.

Once again using Bulgozdi's example of the Horde and their dislike of any clothing other than the "tiny leather loincloths and bit and pieces of fur and chainmail," (46, *The Last Hero*), the reference is obviously made, not only to both 1980s Conan films, but the deluge of cheap, direct-to-video imitations that followed in the wake of their sandaled and codpieced hero. Although *Conan the Barbarian* featured a somewhat more diverse and convincing use of fur and leather in the costume designs, in *Conan the Destroyer*, Schwarzenegger is constantly one prodigious codpiece away from being naked but for his footwear, headband, and scabbard. I couldn't help but think of the promotional photographs of Conan in that leather codpiece when I read the description of Cohen's first appearance in the Discworld in *The Light Fantastic*:

> By the light of the torches he saw that it was a very old man, the skinny variety that general gets called "spry," with a totally bald head, a beard almost down to his knees, and a pair of matchstick legs on which varicose veins had traced the street map of

quite a large city. Despite the snow he wore nothing more than a studded leather holdall and a pair of boots that could have easily accommodated a second pair of feet [99].

Leather holdall aside, the obvious contrast between Schwarzenegger's Conan as massively muscular in his youthful prime and Cohen as skinny, bald, and very old should indicate that Pratchett's parody is focused on the more popular, less precise idea of Conan as quintessential fantasy barbarian, as Patrice Louinet describes him in his introduction to *The Coming of Conan the Cimmerian*: "Howard's creation has been diluted to the point that it is often nearly impossible to recognize Howard's character in the iconic image of the fur-clad, hyper-muscled super-hero he has become in the public's mind" (xix).

This is further supported by how many of the cheap imitations of Milius's film utilized the same approach to costuming. Independent filmmakers saw opportunity in those strips of leather and fur: you could make a pretty cheap film if you could find enough bodies that looked all right in next-to-nothing. And in the 1980s, with the craze of fitness videos and the rise of steroids, you didn't have to look far to find aspiring actors and actresses willing to show off the fruits of their physical labors onscreen. Initially, a few of these cheap imitations made it to the silver screen: only months before *Conan the Barbarian* was released, Albert Pyun's *The Sword and the Sorcerer* fulfilled fan anticipation for gratuitous gore and scantily clothed heroes and heroines. In many ways, that film's hero, Talon, bears greater resemblance to Howard's Conan than Schwarzenegger's performance did, save that, as Alec Worley notes, television star Lee Horsely is a "rather puny barbarian swordsman padded out with furs and a mane of over-styled hair" when contrasted with Schwarzenegger. However, he's clever and charismatic—and while he carries a sense of royal destiny, he never fulfills it. By contrast, Milius' Conan is nearly being a Chosen One, an idea utterly antithetical to Howard's Conan. The film sets him up with a powerful sense of destiny, a concept Charles Hoffman argues is alien to Howard's Conan:

> Other fantasy heroes' exploits take place within the context of their "noble destiny," their special mission.... Howard never resorts to this distressingly familiar motif ... most of [Howard's successors'] series are chronicles of the hero fulfilling his "noble destiny." In each of Howard's stories, Conan creates and carries out his own destiny. When Conan becomes king, he is not acting out a role already preordained by fate; rather, he seizes the opportunity to make himself a king ["Conan the Existential"].

This is parodied in Pratchett via Cohen's usurpation of the Agatean Emperor's throne in *Interesting Times*, which mirrors Conan's overthrow of Aquilonia's throne. And it's King Cohen who potentially demonstrates that Pratchett was parodying Conan as cultural phenomenon, not just as Howard's hero or Schwarzenegger's breakout role.

While I can't discount the possibility that Pratchett read Howard's work before creating Cohen, it would have been mixed in with the pastiches and rewrites it sat alongside in the paperback editions released between the 1960s and 80s with various covers and marketing strategies. It's well known in Conan/Howard studies that those paperbacks are filled as much with the work of L. Sprague De Camp as Robert E. Howard. De Camp enlisted a few other writers to assist him with the Ace paperbacks: Bjorn Nyberg and Lin Carter. Either by original pastiches or reworkings of Howard's finished works or half-finished drafts, de Camp filled the demand for more Conan, albeit with some of the worst prose in the history of the genre. This, in addition to a series of pastiches by writers like Poul Anderson, Robert Jordan, Andrew J. Offutt, Harry Turtledove, and sword and sorcery author Karl Edward Wagner, rendered Conan less the sole providence of Robert E. Howard and more a quintessential archetype of "Barabarian Hero" by 1986.

But even those Ace paperbacks are unlikely literary culprits of Cohen's provenance. It's as likely that Pratchett was exposed to Conan the Barbarian through Marvel Comics, without necessarily even having to ever read an issue. In the 1980s, Conan appeared frequently in Marvel advertising, in a form iconified by John Buscema, who had rendered the Cimmerian once and for all shirtless in a bearskin loincloth with a hairstyle sharing strong affinity with members of metal bands like Iron Maiden. It would take years for comic artists to break with that image; the proof of this was the run legendary comic artist Gil Kane did on Conan in the 1980s, collected in *The Creation Quest and Other Stories*: despite the superiority of Kane's line art and sequential storytelling, it was a short-lived run on the book. Kane's work on the series had been the result of Buscema quitting because writer J.M. DeMatteis had introduced child-companions for Conan, and Buscema was opposed to this vision of Conan. In addition to introducing child-companions for Conan, DeMatteis had also deviated from the terribly episodic nature of most Conan comic stories, crafting a quest narrative, which, as stated earlier, would be antithetical to Howard's Conan. Once again, Howard's Conan (and apparently Buscema's) is not a Chosen One. Howard hardly ever sent Conan on a quest—the closest he came to it was Conan's return to the throne in *Hour of the Dragon*, wherein Conan seeks to regain his throne. As Farah Mendlesohn notes in her *Rhetorics of Fantasy*, Howard's Conan stories belong under her categorization of immersive fantasy, not portal/quest fantasies: "For Howard, the action itself is the point; the finding of the object sought after, or the completion of a task is almost irrelevant" (37). In this regard, Pratchett's Cohen shares a strong affinity.

Both Conan and Cohen randomly enter other, bigger stories than their own, and bash about a bit before exiting to go back on their way. Again, Mendlesohn, along with Edward James, says that Howard created a different sort of fantasy hero in Conan, one who frequently "breaks up other people's narrative" (37). This is most clearly evident in one of Howard's greatest short stories, "The Tower of the Elephant," where Conan breaks into a supposedly impregnable tower to steal a precious gem. Along the way, he intrudes upon the work of a famous and accomplished thief (my students and I have joked that Conan wouldn't have made it all the way into the tower if he hadn't had this serendipitous meeting), consequently blundering into a conflict between an ancient alien being and his sorcerer-jailer. Conan acts out his part in this conflict, but he has largely stumbled into a story greater than his own.

Likewise, Pratchett's Cohen stumbles into the tale of Rincewind the Wizard and Twoflower the Tourist in *The Light Fantastic*, journeys with them for a time, and then wanders back out of the story. In *Interesting Times*, a former schoolteacher turned barbarian companion succinctly summarizes his propensity for such picaresque appearances: "Cohen came into people's lives like a rogue planet into a peaceful solar system, and you felt yourself being dragged along simply because nothing like that would ever happen to you again" (202). Pratchett's inclusion of Cohen as a force of chaos, as a seemingly random wrecking ball parallels how Conan is not a chosen one, not a Quest-driven hero.

There's another parallel between the literary Conan and Cohen, and it is indicative of how Pratchett constructs his intertextual webs. On the surface, Cohen is a simple parody of Conan the Barbarian: hard bodied hypermasculinity rendered gaunt geriatric. There's no arguing with that; as Bulgozdi artfully argues, Cohen is not only a parody of Conan, but of traditional masculinity typified by representations of Conan. But Pratchett also seems to have known enough about the theme of barbarism vs. civilization in Howard's writing to weave it into *Interesting Times*, having Cohen decry "civilized" behavior in a way very familiar to Conan fans. After learning of the civilized customs of the HungHung's nobility such as foot binding and the emasculation of eunuchs, Cohen declares, "I'm learning a lot about civilization, I am.... Long fingernails, crippled feet, and servants running around without their family jewels. Huh" (230). Robert E. Howard's Conan stories are filled with the idea of barbarism as superior to civilization In "Iron Shadows in the Moon," Conan inadvertently rescues the "daughter of the king of Ophir" who had been sold "to a Shemite chief, because [she] would not marry a prince of Koth." When Conan grunts in surprise at this revelation, Olivia admits that "Aye civilized men sell their children as slaves to savages, sometimes," and then reminds Conan that "[t]hey call your race barbaric." Conan's reply establishes the shared code of barbarians, be they pulp or parody: "'We do not sell our children,' he growled, his chin jutting truculently" (*Coming*, 190).

This barbarian manifesto is most clearly manifest in Conan's statement from "Beyond the Black River": "Barbarism is the natural state of mankind. Civilization is unnatural. It is a whim of circumstance. And barbarism must always ultimately triumph" (*Conquering Sword*, 100). Cohen's speech on barbarism and civilization later in *Interesting Times* echoes Howard.

> Barbarism! Haha! When we kills people we do it there and then, lookin' 'em in the eye, and we'd be happy to buy 'em a drink in the next world, no harm done. I never knew a barbarian who cut up people slowly in little rooms, or tortured women to make 'em look pretty, or put poison in people's grub. Civilization? If that's civilization, you can shove it where the sun don't shine! [253].

The correspondences become richer and more nuanced as we move on to *The Last Hero*.

Bulgozdi notes that by the writing of *Interesting Times* and *The Last Hero*, Cohen "becomes a far more complex figure;" in fact, The Last Hero contains arguably the most interesting of all Pratchett's intertextual weavings between the quintessential barbarian and his aged lampoon. In *The Last Hero*, Cohen and the Horde *do* go on a quest, but it's one we can imagine Conan going on as well. It's a quest to blow up Cori Celesti, the home of the gods. The reason for this journey? Payback for the gods having let these heroes live so long. After all, as stated in both *Interesting Times* and *The Last Hero*, a hero is supposed to die in battle, not waste away in the ignominy of decrepitude. It's one last hurrah for Cohen and the Horde, who encounter old friends and enemies along the way to the home of the Gods: Evil Harry, a minor dark lord whose minions seem more parodies of James Bond villains and the Stormtroopers of *Star Wars* than many fantasy villains, and Vena, the Ravenhaired, an obvious reference to Xena, Warrior Princess. And it's that last hurrah which reveals just how Cohen becomes Bulgozdi's "far more complex figure."

Stories about aging heroes feeling like they've overstayed their welcome are fairly common, as evidenced in cinematic instances like *Space Cowboys* and the screen adaption and sequel of the comic book *Red*. But *The Last Hero* has several intertextual references which indicate that Pratchett is referencing a far more literary intertext than these aging-action-hero films. Even more interesting in terms of Cohen's relationship to Conan, it's a literary intertext *Last Hero* seems to share with one of the despised Conan pastiches.

Alfred Lord Tennyson's poem "Ulysses" is a Romantic poem, wherein Homer's wandering hero Odysseus is mashed up with the Ulysses of Dante's *Inferno* as an aged king, dissatisfied with ruling the home he had worked so hard to return to in *The Odyssey*. Legendary Tennyson scholar Christopher Ricks, while noting *The Odyssey* as inspiration, calls Dante "the more important source" (614), and this is noteworthy for our discussion, since Dante's treatment of Odysseus (as Ulysses) is a transformation of Homer's hero, and Tennyson's treatment is a further transformation. We might see a parallel to Conan in Odysseus, a hero who cannot die, but keeps being reborn repeatedly throughout world literature: both Dante and Tennyson reinvent Odysseus to suit a different age, a different literary intention than Homer's or Virgil's. In both Dante and Tennyson, Ithaca holds no joy for the wandering hero, which is a departure from Homer's version: in Tennyson, he admits that his son Telemachus would do a better job of ruling the kingdom, and leaves him to the task. He calls upon his old companions (who had all died in Homer's version) to go on one last adventure with him. As in Dante's own revision of Odysseus' story, Ulysses sets out with these friends to the edge of the known world, seeking out places no one else has seen, and deeds no one else has accomplished. However, in Dante such striving is vice, deserving hell as punishment; for Tennyson it is virtue, and the poem reinvents Dante's Ulysses to be as silver-tongued in defending this virtue as Homer ever did. Ulysses' call to adventure is an irresistible siren song in Tennyson's hands. Small wonder that L. Sprague de Camp, Lin Carter, and Pratchett all succumbed to it.

In de Camp and Carter's *Conan of the Isles*, an aged King Conan leaves the ruling of his kingdom to his son, Conn, to go on an adventure, which would prove to be his last. By the end of the book, Conan has sailed into the West, beyond the edges of the map of the Hyborian world found in many of the paperback editions of Conan's adventures. Likewise, Cohen leaves behind an empire, giving up the soft life of a sovereign ruler to go on one last adventure with his Horde, wherein they will strive against the Gods, and by the end of the book, has ridden off into the stars, to arguably explore "all those other worlds out there" that "one lifetime" wouldn't afford the time to explore (157, 169–70).

Some might resist the idea that a Conan novel, let alone one of the dreaded pastiches, would make so elevated a literary allusion as Tennyson's "Ulysses." But it's tough to argue that "Ulysses" played no part in de Camp and Carter's inspiration, given how the introduction to *Conan of the Isles* ends a summary of Conan's life up to his rule as the King of Aquilonia by saying that "[a] growing restlessness perturbed and irritated him" (18). The italicized epigraphs which de Camp constructed to link Howard's short stories with the pastiches and rewrites states in *Isles* that after the death of his queen, "Conan finds the routine of a peaceful reign increasingly irksome" (20). The first chapter describes his restlessness in greater detail:

> On the throne, Conan glowered down upon the quivering litigant. From the depths of his soul he loathed these tiresome, wordy, labyrinthine tax cases, with their plausible lies and their mathematical calculations of skull-cracking complexity. How he would have liked to hurl his crown at the fat face of the greedy fool before him, stride from the hall, clamp his legs about a stallion's barrel, and ride off for a day's hunting in the forests of the North!

A pox upon this business of kinging it! he thought. It drained every last drop of juice from a man's tissues, leaving him a querulous old hairsplitter without enough red blood in his veins to swing a broadsword. Surely, after twenty weary years of wearing the crown, a man was entitled to throw over honors and titles and *set out toward dim horizons* for one last, gore-spattered adventure before Time's all-felling, implacable scythe cut him down... [23, emphasis mine].

The prose is, as Michael Moorcock argued in "The Heroes of Heroic Fantasy," "mindless, silly, heartless stuff which would disgrace even a schoolboy imitator of Conan, let alone one of the most careful writers in the sf world. The work is almost certainly Carter's ... but de Camp surely owes it to the Howard he admires to ensure better editing, for Conan was never more dead than he is in these travesties of the original stories" (qtd. in Herron, "The Dark Barbarian" 168–69). As a Howard scholar and devotee, Herron has made much of de Camp's inferior prose. But the quality of de Camp's Conan pastiches never prevented their popularity, and it is the popular concept of Conan that Pratchett is most often parodying. Furthermore, de Camp and Carter's *King Conan* shares a strong kinship with Tennyson's Ulysses, who is described as "an idle king" who "cannot rest from travel" (Tennyson in Ricks, 615). Unlike Homer's hero whose only goal was to get home and stay home, Tennyson's hero ponders how "dull it is to pause, to make an end/To rust unburnish'd, not to shine in use!" (617). Like Conan, he dislikes the work of statecraft, which Tennyson describes as meting and doling "Unequal laws unto a savage race/That hoard, and sleep, and feed, and know not me" (615).

Both Conan and Ulysses turn over the work of governing the kingdom to their sons: Conan to Conn, and Ulysses to "mine own Telemachus/To whom I leave the sceptre and the isle." There are differences here: Conn is much like his father, and Conan muses that his son shares his own dislike of royal duties: "Doubtless the lad was also dreaming of flinging off these stifling robes of state and riding off for a day's hunting, or perhaps a night of wenching in waterfront dives" (de Camp and Carter 23). Tennyson's Telemachus is described as being well-suited to the work Ulysses leaves him to, but in both cases, the father leaves home "to seek a newer world," to go on one final adventure.[3]

Just as I cannot discern with confidence whether Pratchett ever read the Conan stories or simply absorbed their core themes through an osmosis of popular culture, I cannot prove that he ever read *Conan of the Isles*. It seems unlikely to me that he'd have gotten much farther than I did as an adult, had I not needed to read it as part of this chapter. But it's impossible to deny the correspondences between "Ulysses," *Conan of the Isles*, and *The Last Hero* when considering references to old age and last adventures.

Howard's Conan often adventures alone. If he has companions, they are temporary: they either die in the current story, or in the case of many of Conan's female companions, are discarded by the next tale. The cultural Conan sometimes differs: Schwarzenegger's Conan had companions in both films. Tennyson's Ulysses, unlike Homer's Odysseus who lost all his companions along the journey home, still has comrades to accompany him on this last adventure:

> My mariners,
> Souls that have toil'd, and wrought, and thought with me—
> That ever with a frolic welcome took
> The thunder and the sunshine, and opposed
> Free hearts, free foreheads—you and I are old;
> Old age hath yet his honour and his toil;
> Death closes all: but something ere the end,
> Some work of noble note, may yet be done,
> Not unbecoming men that strove with Gods [618–19].

Cohen and his Silver Horde are certainly men who have toiled and wrought together, though Pratchett's parody of Barbarian heroism rarely includes thought. They are long-time companions, with many prior adventures which Pratchett alludes to throughout *The Last Hero*. When the Horde meet up with Evil Harry and Vena the Raven-haired, the reader immediately understands that these characters have a history together. And like Ulysses and his companions, despite admitting old age, they recognize they might yet achieve some great work worthy of an immortalizing saga. At one point, Pratchett seems to make a direct reference to Tennyson's poem, echoing the line "Made weak by time and fate, but strong in will," in the estimation of Cohen and the Horde whereby "Age hadn't weakened here—well, except in one or two places. Mostly, it had hardened" (43).

Yet they would likely contest that "old age hath yet his honour and his toil." For them, old age has stolen their dignity. Once again returning to the leather, fur, and chainmail of their uniforms which the Horde wear "in deference to their profession," Pratchett also describes the changes needed for them to keep wearing that uniform: "In deference to their advancing years, and entirely without comment among themselves, these had been underpinned now with long wooly combinations various strange elasticated things" (46). Cohen wears false teeth. One of the Horde named Mad Hamish is in a sledge/wheelchair, and is nearly deaf. One of the book's running jokes involves the Horde's indignation over the death of another aged hero, Old Vincent the Ripper, who choked to death on a cucumber: "That's no way for a hero to die," declares Cohen, "all soft and fat and eating big dinners. A hero should die in battle" (55).

And so, as "men who strove with Gods," Cohen and the Horde go boldly into the Citadel of the Gods, carrying with them "a fifty-pound keg of Agatean Thunder Clay," to exact their revenge for being denied a hero's death. But along the way, Cohen's interactions with a bard, kidnapped to write the saga of this last hurrah (this bard is yet another reason to consider the intertextual relationship between *The Last Hero* and Tennyson's "Ulysses"), opens a new vista of possibility for these heroes who have outlived their due date. As Cohen, his companions, and the bard stare into the night sky, Evil Harry muses, "They say every one of 'em's a world." Cohen asks the bard how many of these worlds there might be. "I don't know," the bard replies. "Thousands. Millions." Cohen laments that humans are only given one hundred years, when millions of worlds are out there, waiting to be explored (119). Cohen and his Horde have experienced much on the Discworld: "Their eyes said that wherever it was, they had been there. Whatever it was, they had done it, sometimes more than once. But they would never, ever, *buy* the T-shirt" (25). From the slopes of the mountain of the Gods, Cohen notes "I bin to everywhere I can see." Like the Emperor Carelinus, a Discworld analogue of Alexander the Great, Cohen laments that "there were no more worlds to conquer" (92).

Consequently, when they are convinced to give up their scheme to destroy the home of the Gods, which will also destroy the Discworld, Cohen and the Horde sacrifice themselves before the Agatean Thunderclay can explode, taking it ten miles down the slopes of Cori Celesti in a spectacular fall. When the Valkyries of the Discworld arrive to deliver them to Valhalla, the Horde refuse and with the help of Vena disguised as a Valkyrie, steal the Valkyries' winged horses to fly off towards the stars, towards other worlds, once again evoking shades of Tennyson:

> Come, my friends,
> 'Tis not too late to seek a newer world.
> Push off, and sitting well in order smite
> The sounding furrows; for my purpose holds
> To sail beyond the sunset, and the baths
> Of all the western stars, until I die [619].

Unlike Tennyson's Ulysses who seeks only death, Cohen genuinely seeks another world. While Pratchett's characters suggest that they can deny death and do something else, Tennyson's Ulysses can only die doing something he loves. One might even say that Pratchett's Cohen surpasses Tennyson's Ulysses, and by extension, Howard's Conan. Arguably, Cohen *has* died, but then cheats death, effectively discovering that death was just another obstacle in his adventure. And so Cohen passes from the Discworld, and from the imagination of Terry Pratchett. But in his passing, we cannot ignore the admiration Pratchett accords his parody of Conan. While he began as a simple mockery of the easiest of targets, the hypermasculine barbarian, it's clear by *Interesting Times* that Pratchett admires the Heroic Code he has constructed for Cohen and his Horde. There's a grudging admiration from the characters who encounter them, and a clear admiration from Pratchett, making this final parody of Conan the most successful of all. I read somewhere, a long time ago in a time before meticulous citation, that the best of all parodies contained an admiration for the object of ridicule. Repeatedly, one senses this admiration in Pratchett's ridicule of the fantasy genre. He's not making fun of it because he hates it; he's making fun of it because he loves it. And insofar as his love of Cohen and by extension Conan, it is made most clearly near the conclusion of *The Last Hero*, as the minstrel ponders his lost companions: "He'd never been keen on heroes. But he realised he needed them to be there, like forests and mountains ... he might never see them, but they filled some sort of hole in his mind. Some sort of hole in everyone's mind" (168).

My guess, moreover my hope, is that we cannot expect to do away with Conan or his fellow barbarians any time soon. I will not resort to speaking of archetypes or the need for any essential heroism, for I subscribe to neither as ways of understanding literary fiction. Pratchett was certainly no fan of essentialism. Instead, he regularly transformed tired old types into new and vital variations. But if Conan can be salvaged in the form of a very old man, then what other forms might Howard's barbarian adapt to? To date, he's proven to be remarkably resilient, but perhaps it's time for a more drastic change, one that buries the hypermasculine lone wolf, and allows for a rebirth: for example, there's an air of Conan about the Iconic Barbarian[4] Amiri, a female tribal warrior clad in fur and leather who wields a giant's sword in the popular *Pathfinder* roleplaying game; the warrior of the video game *Gauntlet Legends* is clearly modeled on Conan (named Thor for avoidance of copyright infringement), but travels in the company of an elven archer, an aged wizard, and a virtuous Valkyrie, a step beyond the rugged individualism of Howard's Conan—this is Conan as part of the fantasy roleplaying world's balanced party, an echo of Tolkien's *Fellowship of the Ring*. It's never too late to seek a newer world, and perhaps it is time for fans of heroic fantasy to do so with newer versions of Howard's seminal hero. Transformation, not termination, is the direction Pratchett's Cohen points—the barbarian is arguably adept at adaptation in order to secure their survival, living on beyond the Hyborian Age, beyond hypermasculinity, beyond limiting ideas of heroism: "To strive, to seek, to find, and not to yield" (Tennyson 620).

Notes

1. Of course, by "little attention," I do not mean "no attention whatsoever." I am well aware of Don Herron's *The Dark Barbarian: The Writings of Robert E. Howard: A Critical Anthology*, the first academic work on Howard's writing, which contains a number of excellent essays on Conan; yet even in *The Dark Barbarian*, Conan is only the focus of two out eight of those essays. More recently, Jonas Prida's *Conan Meets the Academy: Multidisciplinary Essays on the Enduring Barbarian* collected ten essays focused entirely on Conan, dividing the book into the two Conans I talk about in this chapter: the "Literary Conan" and the "Cultural Conan." In addition to these anthologies, there have been several articles published in academic journals on the literary Conan, but none to discount my contention that academic attention for Conan is rare.

2. Again, this is not to say there is no work on the Conan films, but simply that the bulk of Conan studies takes Howard's work very seriously, while the films receive less attention: when given the option between pulp-era prose and steroidal Sword and Sorcery cinema, even a Conan scholar chooses dusty tomes. The exceptions to this avoidance of studying the cinematic Conan often lie outside Howard studies: Both Alex Worley's *Empires of the Imagination* and Kevin M. Flanagan's "'Civilization ... ancient and wicked": Historicizing the Ideological Field of 1980s Sword and Sandal Films" in Michael G. Cornelius's *Of Muscles and Men* closely examine the Schwarzenegger Conan films and cinematic heroic fantasy of the 1980s. In the aforementioned anthology, *Conan Meets the Academy*, it's noteworthy to observe that the majority of the articles are about the literary Conan, while only one of the four chapters on the "Cultural Conan" is concerned with the Schwarzenegger film: "Arnold at the Gates: Subverting Star Persona in *Conan the Barbarian*" by Nicky Falkof.

3. de Camp and Carter conclude *Conan of the Isles* with Conan sailing "into the unknown West" to a "new world," uncertain of what may come. While the uncertainty is rendered in what some consider a typical reaction for Conan ("Crom knows!"), and the references to "new world" may simply be the Hyperborean World's equivalent of the undiscovered Americas, the mood certainly mirrors Tennyson's poem in less artful diction (188–89).

4. This means that in all official Pathfinder content from rulebooks, adventure modules, and tie-in comics, Amiri is the representation of the Barbarian character class: not the giant hypermasculine male the word "barbarian" would usually conjure, but a fit and fierce female.

WORKS CITED

Bulgozdi, Imola. "'Barbarian Heroing' and Its Parody: New Perspectives on Masculinity." *Conan Meets the Academy: Multidisciplinary Essays on the Enduring Barbarian*, edited by Jonas Prida, McFarland, 2013.
Butler, Andrew M. *Terry Pratchett*. Pocket Essentials, 2001.
De Camp, L. Sprague and Lin Carter. *Conan of the Isles*. 1968. Ace Fantasy Books, 1984.
DeMatteis, J.M., et al. *The Creation Quest and Other Stories*. Dark Horse Books, 2009. The Chronicles of Conan, Volume 17.
Flanagan, Kevin M. "'Civilization ... Ancient and Wicked": Historicizing the Ideological Field of 1980s Sword and Sandal Films." *Of Muscles and Men: Essays on the Sword & Sandal Film*, edited by Michael G. Cornelius, McFarland, 2011, pp. 87–103.
Herron, Don. "The Dark Barbarian." *The Dark Barbarian: The Writings of Robert E. Howard: A Critical Anthology*, edited by Don Herron, Wildside Press, 1984, pp. 149–181.
Hoffman, Charles. "Conan the Existential." *The Dark Barbarian That Towers Over All: The Robert E. Howard LitCrit Megapack*, edited by Don Herron, The Cimmerian Press, 2014. Kindle.
Howard, Robert. E. *The Coming of Conan the Cimmerian*. Del Rey, 2003.
_____. *The Conquering Sword of Conan*, Del Rey, 2005.
Louinet, Patrice. "Introduction." *The Coming of Conan the Cimmerian*. Robert E. Howard, Ballantine Books, 2003, pp. xix–xxv.
Mendlesohn, Farah. *Rhetorics of Fantasy*. Weslyan UP, 2008.
Mendlesohn, Farah, and Edward James. *A Short History of Fantasy*. Libri Publishing, 2012.
Pratchett, Terry. *The Colour of Magic*. 1983. Corgi Books, 1985.
_____. *Interesting Times*. Corgi Books, 1995.
_____. *The Last Hero: A Discworld Fable*. 2001. Gollancz, 2002.
_____. *The Light Fantastic*. Corgi Books, 1986.
Tennyson, Alfred Lord. "Ulysses." *The Poems of Tennyson in Three Volumes*, 2d ed, edited by Christopher Ricks, Longman. 1987, pp. 613–620.
Vincent, Brittany. "'Conan Exiles' Becomes Developer Funcom's Biggest, Fastest-Selling Game Ever." *Variety*. Variety Media, 5 Jul. 2018. Web. 11 Jul. 2018.
Worley, Alec. *Empires of the Imagination: A Critical Survey of Fantasy Cinema from George Méliès to* The Lord of the Rings. McFarland, 2005.

Carrot Ironfoundersson

Medieval Romance, Narrative Causality and the Ethics of Choice in Terry Pratchett's Guards! Guards!

Emily Lavin Leverett

Terry Pratchett's Discworld covers 41 novels and a myriad of other texts including short stories, maps, children's books, and cookbooks, among other things. Given its dozens of settings and hundreds of characters, Discworld is a place rife with possibilities and interpretations. As Anne Hiebert Alton and William C. Spruiell note,

> Pratchett's Discworld books are inherently interdisciplinary. He merrily deploys innumerable genres and literary conventions (often within the same book), only to overturn them and transform them into self-critiques as well as often highly targeted social satire. [...] By his appropriation and reconstruction of discourse types, he provides readers with models for gaining a measure of conscious and playful control over what can otherwise be an impenetrable hegemonic maze [Introduction, 2014, pp. 4–5].

In this essay, I look at the way in which Pratchett "deploys" and then "transforms" one particular genre: the medieval English Romance. Specifically, this essay argues that Carrot Ironfoundersson of the Night Watch novels is a reworking of what Helen Cooper calls the trope of "Restoring the Rightful Heir" (*The English Romance in Time*, 324–360). Finally, I examine how Pratchett, like many medieval English Romance authors, is using this genre to explore national identity and critique what he calls "narrative causality."

One of Pratchett's many locations of satire is the medieval fantasy genre, specifically those texts which are primarily derivative: "I started writing the *Discworld* books in the eighties as an antidote to all the bad Fantasy that was around—third or fourth hand copies of Tolkien that weren't really adding anything new, and they were just an endless rehash of the same Fantasy elements" (Freiburg and Schnitker, 180). Pratchett is engaging in a medievalism that is particularly interesting for its temporal ripples. If medievalism is (re)working the Middle Ages into the present in some way, then Pratchett is doing that, and more. He's engaging in satirizing multiple medievalisms through the one he himself produces. The multi-temporality found in Pratchett's world—including the medieval alongside the Victorian, pre- and post-industrial revolution, and so on—is increasingly common in popular medievalism: "In the realm of popular medievalism, this notion of asynchronous collocations applies, [...] in many cases, to the way the Middle Ages themselves are represented in many pop cultural forms" (D'Arcens and Lynch, xxiii). This blending, and the results that Pratchett achieves, are visible in his treatment of Carrot.

Of all the many characters on the Disc, Carrot Ironfoundersson is one of the most explicitly connected to traditional fantasy and medieval romance. His story arc—a foundling child raised outside the kingdom who returns to save it from a horrific evil—fits a pattern established by medieval romance: restoring the rightful heir. Helen Cooper identifies each of these patterns as "a romance motif": a unit within literature that proves so useful, so infectious, that it begins to take on a life of its own. She refers to them as "a 'meme,' an idea that behaves like a gene in its ability to replicate faithfully and abundantly, but also on occasion to adapt, mutate, and therefore survive in different forms and cultures" (3). Carrot's character arc reflects this shift in general terms, and also specific ones.

Carrot hits several markers of this medieval romance hero (who is almost universally male): he is handsome and attractive; he is superiorly strong and/or skilled with weapons; he has an unknown parentage; he has a physical evidence of kingship or lineage, such as possession of a token or weapon, and/or a physical mark on his body; and he is concerned with restoring and/or enforcing the law for the common good (Cooper, *The English Romance in Time*). While these are general guidelines, not all of these appear in every example of an heir restored. However, Carrot's story is strikingly similar to that of a particular medieval English romance: *Havelok the Dane*.[1] While *Havelok* might be unfamiliar to contemporary audiences as such, its footprint is not. Indeed, it fits all of the romance motifs of the restored heir, as well as other elements common in medieval English romance:

> [*Havelok the Dane*] contains exile-and-return, a popular hero (in both senses of the word), evidence of oral and local cultural connexions [sic] and probably origins, a positive, even good-humored view of the past as a locus of creative fantasy for the present, a view of a cohesive society, of physical strength used in support of legal rule, of personal relationships contributing to social stability. It could be argued that

the "Havelok-type" even if it is only a group of one, has had a disproportionate effect on the modern awareness of the English medieval narrative [Field, p. 39].

There are several moments in Carrot's arc in *Guards! Guards!* that parallel or rework moments from *Havelok the Dane*.[2] A comparison between both Pratchett's text and the medieval poem reveals some of the ways that Pratchett adapts medieval English Romance for his own uses.

To begin, Carrot Ironfoundersson is certainly strong. As he has been raised by dwarves, but is human, he is of course comparatively tall already. That said, at six feet tall, he's taller than the rather average tradesman Mr. Varneshi, who is five-foot (Pratchett, *Guards! Guards!*, 24). Havelock, too, has the benefit of height: "Than was Havelok bi the shuldren more/Than the meste that ther kam" ("Havelok the Dane," 983–984).[3] [The tallest man came up only to Havelok's shoulder.][4] While Carrot is tall, like Havelok, Carrot's build is especially impressive:

> The young man is called Carrot. [...] It is because of his shape. It is the kind of tapering shape a boy gets through clean living, healthy eating, and good mountain air in huge lungfuls. When he flexes his shoulder muscles, other muscles have to move out of the way first [p. 21].

This passage clearly invokes the image of classic heroes like Conan the Barbarian, in terms of body shape, but also of the youthful goodness that suggests a kind of naiveté, and Carrot does prove to be naive when he first comes to Ankh-Morpork. However, Carrot also is charismatic—he speaks and people listen. Though the degree to which his charisma is connected to his role as a lost king grows throughout the Discworld series, it starts in *Guards! Guards!* with a comment by Sergeant Fred Colon: "'Something odd about that boy,' said Colon, as they limped after [Carrot]. 'He always manages to persuade us to follow him, have you noticed?'" Something about him is stately and evokes the power of command.[5] Havelok is similar:

> It was nevere man that yemeded
> In kinneriche that so wel semede
> King or cayser for to be,
> Than he was shird, so semede he [pp. 976–979].
> [There was never a man that ruled in the kingdom that looked so much like a king or like Ceasar, than Havelok when he was appropriately clothed.]

In all, then, Pratchett uses the romantic motif of the strong, powerful young man, who has all the markings of royalty (or at least leadership).

The restoration of the heir motif also generally includes a loss of identity. Usually the heir is lost or, more often, deliberately driven away by some evil force, whether human beings or nature. In Havelok's case, his father leaves control of the kingdom to Havelok's uncle, a man his father believes will be a good steward. The uncle slaughters Havelok's sisters in front of him, and then, because the uncle fears becoming a king-slayer, he hires a fisherman to kill Havelok. Instead of killing the boy, the fisherman recognizes him as the rightful heir and flees England, raising Havelok as his own and with his own family. Carrot has a similar origin story. Thought he has been raised by dwarves, his "father" must finally tell him that he is not a dwarf, but a human. Carrot, like Havelok, survived a treacherous encounter.

> The thing is, [...] we found you in the woods one day. Toddling about near one of the tracks [...] Thing is, you see ... there were these carts. On fire, as you might say. And dead people. Um, yes. Extremely dead people. Because of bandits. [...] So we took you in, of course, and then, well, it was a long winter, like I said, and your mam got used to you, and, well, we never got around to asking Varneshi to make enquiries. That's the long and short of it [pp. 24–25].

Like Havelok, the events leading to Carrot's loss of his family and, presumably, his kingdom are tragic and violent. It is hard to say whether bandits simply missed him in the attack, leaving him to wander, or if someone hid him in the woods. Either way, he was subject to violence, barely escaped the violence, and then was saved by good people who knew, at least to some extent, who he was and that he would need to return to the world someday. Although Pratchett gives Carrot no memory of his human parents, unlike Havelok, the similarities in their stories remain. Pratchett uses the classic framework of the restored heir to set up Carrot's story, to drive him to Ankh-Morpork, setting him out on a quest, another very typical romance and fantasy fiction motif.

Carrot's path, a childhood living in exile followed by a quest, allows him to reach another milestone in the restoring the heir trope: the assertion of strength for the sake of justice. When the dragon is defeated, lying prone and vulnerable on the ground, a mass of locals, all armed, surround it with the intent to execute it. Carrot does not allow it because, Vimes told him, "prisoners weren't to be molested" (319), and Carrot has arrested the dragon, thereby making her a prisoner.[6] The medieval romance can be used to

> promote the well-being of the realm, the common weal. [... T]he rightful king is also the good king. Prowess in battle, faithfulness in marriage (a consistent element of English romance, for men as much as for women[7]), due reward of his followers, firm rule in accordance with the law, and keeping his word, all mark a kingship that carries the approval of God and the goodwill of the people [Cooper, *The English Romance in Time*, p. 340].

Carrot fought off a large group of people, and he is doing so not to defend a particular person (or animal), but to defend the rights of prisoners according the law. Even though the mob surrounding the dragon are not happy with Carrot at the time, his devotion to the law, even in the face of civic rebellion, make him a clear example of this meme.

Carrot's protection of the dragon also demonstrates his prowess:

> It was quite a large and heavy roof timber and it scythes quite slowly through the air, but when it hit people, they rolled backwards and stayed hit. [...] Carrot turned slowly, the roof beam held like a staff. His gaze was like a lighthouse beam. Where it fell, the crowd lowered their weapons and looked merely sullen and uncomfortable. "I must warn you," Carrot went on. "that interfering with an officer in the execution of his duty is a serious offense. And I shall come down like a ton of bricks on the very next person who throws a stone." [p. 391].

Visually, Carrot is standing on a pile of rubble, which has come down on and more or less pinned down a dragon, so his choice of language here is backed up by a compelling visual. His ability to freeze the crowd with his stare, too, speaks to the charisma that Sergeant Colon noted earlier. They are also immobilized by the threat of action. However, he is not particularly violent. He would rather not hurt anyone and insists on a warning. In terms of medieval English romance, once again Carrot is very similar to Havelok. Havelok is housed in the home of Bernard, a merchant. In the night, enemies of Bernard attack. They begin by launching a stone through the door. Havelok fights seven in turn, and ultimately ends up killing twenty of them. The whole episode is well over one hundred exciting, brutal lines. One section in particular, though, is relevant to Carrot:

> [The stone broke through the door.]
> [H]avelok it saw, and thider drof
> And the barre sone ut drow,
> That was unride and gret ynow,
> And caste the dore open wide
> And seide, "Here shal I now abide!
> Comes swithe unto me—
> Datheyt hwo you henne fle!"
> "No," quodh on, "that shaltou coupe";
> And bigan til him to loupe,
> In his hond his swerd ut drawe,
> Havelok he wend thore have slawe,
> And with him comen other two
> That him wolde of live have do.
> Havelok lifte up the dore tre
> And at a dint he slow hem thre.
> Was non of hem that hise hernes
> Ne lay ther ute ageyn the sternes [pp. 1794–1809].

[Havelok saw it happen and ran to the door and grabbed the door bar and drew it out of the rubble. It was huge, big enough. He opened the door wide and said, "Here I am, come quickly to me—curses on anyone who runs away!" In return, one said "no, you shall pay," and ran at Havelok. He drew his sword and would have slain Havelok. He came with two others that would have robbed Havelok of life. Havelok lifted up the door-bar, and in one stroke killed all three of them. All of them lay there with their brains bashed out, visible to the stars.]

While there is more violence here than in Pratchett's scene, they are strikingly similar. Both men are defending the law, both men are using huge wooden beams from building rubble, and both declare their prowess and intent. Carrot and Havelok are also both in the middle of the journeys home—both these take place in their original and future homes. While Carrot never claims the Ankh-Morpork throne, it becomes increasingly obvious that he belongs to the city, and the city to him. Havelok will go on to overthrow his corrupt uncle and become king of both England and Denmark.[8]

The final clear parallel between Pratchett's Carrot and Havelok in the restored heir motif is the king mark—the indisputable evidence that a person is indeed the heir. This can happen in multiple ways, including magic, miracles, physical objects, and/or natural evidence (Cooper, *The English Romance in Time*, 324). In *Guards! Guards!*, Pratchett engages two: a sword and a birthmark. Probably the most well known of identifying objects, thanks to T.S. White, is the sword pulled from the stone by Arthur, son of Uther Pendragon. Carrot, too, comes with a sword, which has been presented to him in "mysterious circumstances" (21). Furthermore, it is well used: "The blade was dull and short, and notched like a saw. It was well-made, and there might have been an inscription on it once, but it had long ago been worn into indecipherability by sheer use" (353). That Carrot uses it well, too, adds to the power of the sword as a meme for kingship. The other king mark present in the novel is a literal mark—a birthmark that Carrot has, which he himself describes as shaped, "like a crown thing" (353). Havelok, too, has a king mark: "On hise rith shuldre a kynmerk,/A swithe birth a swithe fair" (605–6) [On his shoulder was a king mark, so bright and so fair]. Both men have the marks on their upper body. While Carrot's is explicitly a crown, Havelok's is only identified as a king's birthmark, perhaps suggesting that at the time *Havelok the Dane* was written, the trope was already so well established as to be recognizable by that audience.[9]

Up to this point, I've laid out the ways in which Pratchett uses romance motifs, or memes, to invoke the persistent elements of medieval romance stories that have since been translated into fantasy fiction. Now, I want to turn to how Pratchett manipulates and reworks these memes for his own purpose: in particular, Pratchett disrupts the memes in order to challenge what he calls "narrative causality": "the idea that there are 'story shapes' into which human history, both large scale and at the personal level, attempts to fit" ("Imaginary Worlds, Real Stories," 166). Pratchett's own manipulation of tropes demonstrates the necessity of *not* allowing tropes to govern behavior, instead empowering characters to make their own choices. Ultimately,

Pratchett uses these motifs and memes to present characters who refuse to be governed by them, and, as a result, end up becoming responsible, ethical beings.

The first major upset in the use of the romance memes is Pratchett's creation of a universe in which they are fully visible. In other words, the characters already know how stories work and expect life to follow patterned stories. Guards know that a single fighter, particularly an old man, will always defeat a group of guards (Pratchett, *Guards! Guards!*). Colon and Nobby believe that million-to-one chances *always* come in (Pratchett, *Guards! Guards!,*). And the average Joe on the street—or in the secret cabal summoning dragons—knows how a hero always turns up at the right moment:

> Yeah. They do that you know. [...] Happens all the time. You read about it. Skions, they're called. They go lurking around in the distant wildernesses for ages, handing down the secret sword and birthmark and so forth from generation to generation. Then just when the old kingdom needs them, they turn up and turf out any usurpers that happen to be around. And then there's general rejoicing [p. 11].

Rather than being worried about such an event, the villain—the Supreme Grand Master—is counting on it. He even has a ready-made "skion" to bring out when they conjure the dragon. Here, Pratchett turns the hero narrative on its head, allowing the villain to use it to manipulate the people into the behavior that he wants.

Other characters, though, including Carrot, have a different perspective on heroes. Even though he has a sword, and a birthmark in the shape of a crown, and even though he and his friends in the Watch have defeated the dragon, saved the damsel, and been publicly rewarded by the Patrician, he insists he doesn't fit the narrative:

> "Kings' swords are big and shiny and magical and have jewels on them and when you hold them up they catch the light, *ting*. [...] I'm just saying you can't go round giving people thrones just because of stuff like that. [...] It's not the kind of thing for the likes of Us—" he looked proudly—"guards" [p. 354].

Carrot, Vimes, Sybil, Colon, and Nobby have actually been the heroes that the city needs. Carrot may well be the long-lost king. But to Carrot's mind, those things—the actual heroic actions—are not the definition of a king. Shiny swords and sparkling smiles are as important, if not more so, than action. Carrot is better, though, for the *choice*. Pratchett's emphasis here is on doing the right thing, not because it is what the story says, but because it is character's choice.

Interestingly enough, it is Colon, who is often considered the least intelligent, or at least the slowest, of the members of the Watch in *Guards! Guards!,* he who actually connects Carrot's attributes to what a real, useful king might be:

Colon had been momentarily lost in a little world of speculation. Real kings had shiny swords, obviously. Except, except, except maybe your *real* real king of, like, days of yore, he would have a sword that didn't sparkle one bit but was bloody efficient at cutting things. Just a thought [p. 354].

Indeed when looked at from this point of view, Carrot seems uniquely qualified for the position. This is also a case where one of the best qualifications for being a king (or hero) is to not think you should be king. Carrot's desire to continue being a guard, to protect and serve the law, and to treat people well are in fact good qualities. Though in this case, the choices worked out well in the end, Pratchett does not make that guarantee. As Farah Mendlesohn notes: "Pratchett is *not* trying to assert that morality leads to success, nor that moral actions provide morals outcomes, rather to make it clear that it is morality which makes us who we are" (259). The final image of the book reinforces this point. Errol the swamp dragon and the Noble Dragon he defeated are let go—free to leave Ankh-Morpork and, eventually, Discworld itself. The justification for this is not pragmatic (how would one put a dragon in prison, even to await execution for murder?), but rooted in the possibilities of choice. The dragons are given the choice to try to live, despite the fact that they may not survive:

> On the dark crescent, where the old light of sunset had barely drained from the deepest valleys, two specks, one big, one small, flew out of the shadow, skimmed low across the swells of the Rim ocean, and struct out determinedly over the totally unfathomable, star-dotted depths of space. Perhaps the magic would last. Perhaps it wouldn't. But then, what does? [p. 355].

Pratchett himself, along with many authors of medieval English romance, might argue that the answer to that question is *the story*. In the end, Pratchett is successfully reworking the memes because they remain in the service of story. Carrot, in particular, invokes not only classical fantasy heroes, but the restored heir trope of medieval romance, and his connection to *Havelok the Dane*, whether deliberate or not, demonstrates the power of narrative causality.

As a coda to this, I want to turn to one of the many purposes of medieval English romance: identity. In the genre in general, "there is a turning of history into romance, or romance into history" (Cooper, "When Romance Comes True," 14). Given that all of the medieval period is to contemporary readers the (at least somewhat) distant past, it can be hard to decipher the ways in which medieval literature itself is often representing its own past. However, like contemporary authors using medievalism today, medieval authors reflected their own historical moments as well:

> romance as we know it is the product of identifiable and specific changes in social practices, and therefore much more closely modelled on the immediate conditions of

contemporary life than our association of the form with dragons allows [Cooper, "When Romance Comes True," p. 16].

The same could be said of fantasy fiction today—despite the knights and dragons and other tropes, each text is written in a particular moment and under the influence of particular texts.

Here, once again, Carrot and Havelock share a connection. Both the anonymous *Havelok* author and Terry Pratchett use their stories to explore the idea of being English (or British for Pratchett). So, not only was *Havelok the Dane* a quintessential example of many of the tropes of medieval romance, it was also a text that sought to create and establish England's identity through the construction of a heroic past *and* it specifically used the tropes for romance for this project: "the Middle English *Havelok* employs narrative strategies endemic to romance to forge a sense of emergent national identity" (Faletra, 348). While he might not explicitly be discussing the state of the UK as a whole, Pratchett does acknowledge that current events have an effect on his writing: "the last ten books maybe, have been subtly influenced by moderately current affairs" ("Discworld & Beyond," p. 73) and "topicality is certainly woven into Discworld books" ("21 Years of Discworld," 58). Furthermore, Pratchett considers writing to be something other than his telling a story to people who take it in: "remember above all that writing is a collaborative process to which the reader also brings something" ("Imaginary Worlds, Real Stories," 159). Finally, he offers the possibility that the reader may take more than he is deliberately or knowingly giving: "I know what I put in; what you get out is between you and your God. You might get out more than I put in" ("A Conversation with Terry Pratchett—Part 2"). In both cases, though the fictional works are telling stories of other times and/or places, both connect to the current situations of the authors.

So, how does Pratchett use Carrot to comment on the world? One way is the fact that he deliberately refuses to allow Carrot to fulfill the trope of restored heir. As Gideon Haberkorn notes,

> Carrot, who is the heir apparent, is constantly involved in narratives which negotiate questions of kingship, and he constantly subverts the tradition, simply by remaining hidden. Instead of assuming his rightful position above the law, he is happy and content being a servant of the law [p. 331].

This also suggests that the law, and the keepers of it, have the responsibility in the modern day that a mythic king figure would in the Middle Ages. For Pratchett, justice comes in the form of law. While Pratchett subverts the *idea* of kings through his most fantasy-trope-king-character, he reinforces the *purpose* of kings as worthwhile and important. As Edward James notes, "[Pratchett] deconstructs the traditional views of kings and kingship. But at the same time he shows Carrot to be almost everything that the monarchists expect of a king" ("The City Watch," 203–204).¹⁰ Practhett reworks the memes of medieval English romance and fantasy fiction at the same time, ultimately using Carrot as a foil for ideas of the past and complications of the present day. While writing in his made-up world of Ankh-Morpork, he wrote about his own Britain, too.

The memes of medieval romance have become so ubiquitous as to almost be unnoticeable, a testament to the success of medievalism not only now, but for centuries. Terry Pratchett not only adopts those memes, but also demonstrates their flexibility in the ways he manipulates and reworks them to his own ends. Ultimately, what I hope I have shown here is the through line that we see from the romances of the Middle Ages to the Discworld novels. In seeing this continuity, we can begin to appreciate how deftly Pratchett weaves his stories together. Yet, for all the tropes he gives us, his best, most complex characters are those who reject narrative causality, the narrative that the world has planned out for them, in favor of choosing their own roles. As for Pratchett's advice for his readers and their own stories? *"Fabricati [tua] Diem [tuum], Pvnk"* (51).

Notes

1. While Carrot resembles Havelok in story, Pratchett uses the name "Havelok" elsewhere: the patrician of Ankh-Morpork is named Havelok Vetinari. Pratchett's choice, while intriguing, is not a part of my discussion here.
2. While Pratchett's uses of Medieval Romance span far beyond both Carrot and *Guards! Guards!*, for the sake of time and space, I am limiting my discussion here to those alone. For a discussion of how Samuel Vimes also fits into romance tropes, see Emily Lavin Leverett, "'At Times Like This it's Traditional that a Hero Comes Forth': Romance and Identity in Terry Pratchett's *Guards! Guards!*" Ed. Marion Rana. *Terry Pratchett's Narrative Worlds: From Giant Turtles to Small Gods* (Palgrave Macmillan, 2018) 159–175.
3. All citations from this edition. Line numbers, not page numbers, are listed here.
4. All translations are my own.
5. For a discussion of Carrot's charisma and its connection to Havelock in the Night Watch novels after *Guards! Guards!* see Field, 41–42.
6. The dragon is explicitly female.
7. Later in the Night Watch books, Carrot fulfills this trope through his development of a faithful love match with Sergeant Angua, a werewolf in the Watch.
8. Another interesting similarity is the dual-kingdom. Havelock marries Goldeboro, the heir to Denmark, which is the land where he was raised while in exile. Though Carrot never marries Angua, her family does partly rule Uberwald, where Carrot was raised in exile.
9. See Field, 40–42.
10. For a discussion of how Carrot specifically, and the Watch in general, are used by Pratchett to discuss racism and prejudice, see James 203–216.

Works Cited

Cooper, H. *The English Romance in Time: Transforming Motifs from Geoffrey of Monmouth to the Death of Shakespeare.* Oxford UP, 2004.
Cooper, H. "When Romance Comes True." In N. Cartlidge (Ed.), *Boundaries in Medieval Romance* (pp. 13–27). D.S. Brewer, 2008.
D'Arcens, L., and Lynch, A. "Introduction: The Medieval, the International, the Popular." In

L. D'Arcens and A. Lynch (Eds.), *International Medievalism and Popular Culture* (pp. xi–xxx). Cambria Press, 2014.

Faletra, M. "The Ends of Romance: Dreaming the Nation in the Middle English Havelok." *Exemplaria*, 17 (2) (2005): 347–380.

Field, R. "The Curious History of the Matter of England." In N. Cartlidge (Ed.), *Boundaries in Medieval Romance* (pp. 29–42). D.S. Brewer, 2008.

Freiburg, R., and Schnitker, J. "'Fantasy Is the Whole Cake': An Interview with Terry Pratchett." In R. Freiburg, J. Schnitker, R. Freiburg and J. Schnitker (Eds.), *"Do You Consider Yourself a Postmodern Author?" Interviews with Contemporary English Writers* (pp. 175–199). Transaction Publishers, 1999.

Haberkorn, G. "Cultural Palimpsests: Terry Pratchett's New Fantasy Heroes." *Journal of the Fantastic in the Arts*, 18 (3) (2007), 119–339.

Havelok the Dane. In R. Herzman, G. Drake and E. Salisbury (Eds.), *Four Romances of England* (pp. 73–186). K: Medieval Institute Publications, Western Michigan University, 1999.

Hiebert Alton, A., and W. Spruiell, "Introduction." In A. Hiebert Alton, W.C. Spruiell, A. Hiebert Alton, & W.C. Spruiell (Eds.), *Discworld and the Disciplines: Critical Approaches to the Terry Pratchett Works* (pp. 4–5). McFarland, 2014.

James, E. "The City Watch." In A. Butler, E. James and F. Mendlesohn (Eds.), *Terry Pratchett: Guilty of Literature* (pp. 193–216). Old Earth Books, 2004.

Leverett, E.L. "'At Times Like This It's Traditional That a Hero Comes Forth': Romance and Identity in Terry Pratchett's *Guards! Guards!*" In M. Rana (Ed.), *Terry Pratchett's Narrative Worlds: From Giant Turtles to Small Gods* (pp. 159–175). Palgrave Macmillan, 2018.

Mendlesohn, F. "Faith and Ethics." In A. Butler, E. James, and F. Mendlesohn (Eds.), *Terry Pratchett: Guilty of Literature* (pp. 239–260). Old Earth Books, 2004.

Pratchett, T. "A Conversation with Terry Pratchett—Part 2." (S. Silver, Interviewer) SF Site, March 2000.

_____. "Disworld & Beyond." *LOCUS*, 4 (December 1999): 73–76.

_____. *Guards! Guards!* HarperCollins, 1989.

_____. "Imaginary Worlds, Real Stories." *Folklore*, 111 (2) (2000): 159–168.

_____. "21 Years of Discworld." *LOCUS*, 8–9 (May 2004): 58–59.

Self-Discovery, Free Will and Change

The Ethics of Growing Up in the Fantasy Novels of Terry Pratchett

KATHLEEN BURT

A key theme in Terry Pratchett's writing is discovery of self. Many of Pratchett's novels revolve around the protagonist embarking on a journey of self-discovery, upon realization of which the protagonist and those around them then go about beginning to set themselves up in the position in which they can do the most good for themselves and others. In the process, not only does the main character achieve greater consciousness of themself, but so do side characters who align themselves with the protagonist. The consistent presentation of individual self-discovery aligns closely with elements of John Locke's conceptualization of "identity." Locke's emphasis on time and consciousness as key elements of "personal identity," and his theory that a person's "identity" consists of layered components that remain largely stable over time, factor heavily into many of the Discworld narratives. Pratchett adds to Locke's concepts by focusing consistently on the maturation process in his characters, and their realizations of how to best place themselves to do good and promote change in the world once they have grown up.[1]

John Locke's theory of identity considers elements of substance, identity, identity of man, and personal identity. Substance has both physical and immaterial levels, with the immaterial referring to thought process.[2] "Identity" consists of observed attributes of a subject at a given location and time, with same attributes in the current moment of observation as when compared to the subject in the past (Locke 1). The general concept of identity then is tied to time and place, and includes a component that distinguishes between individuals which is "consciousness" (*ibid.* 9–10). Locke also attributes an ethical dimension to his definition of person, saying, "It is a forensic term, appropriating actions and their merit; and so belongs only to intelligent agents, capable of a law, and happiness, and misery" (26). As Shoemaker points out, Locke's conception of personal identity includes the condition of moral agency, or ownership of and responsibility for one's actions and decisions.[3] Pratchett explores themes of realizing ethical practice and use of self-identity by adding a social component in which many of his characters must determine how to fit in with or break with social expectations.

The general concepts of conscious awareness and time and place appear with particular clarity in *Pyramids*. In *Pyramids*, time and place are also important to identity. As long as the pyramids are used to stop the movement of time within the kingdom's borders, Dios' and Dejelibeybi's shared identity remains in place. Dios is the First Minister and high priest of the kingdom, and the power behind the throne that ensures all proper rituals are observed and traditions remain unbroken; for much of the novel, he thwarts Teppic's efforts to update the kingdom. Early in the final confrontation between Dios' traditionalist position and Teppic's more practical modern worldview, Teppic finds out that the kingdom has been frozen in time and that he must destroy the pyramids which are the cause. Once time starts moving at the end of the novel, Teppic points out, "I've inhumed a pyramid, a pantheon, and the entire old kingdom" (*Pyramids* 283). Dios gets thrown back to what is likely the beginning of his time and place, and forgets who he was, but Pratchett hints that Dios has *only* forgotten, and as Locke points out, forgetting or sleep are only temporary suspensions, and not actual loss of identity.[4] Dios appears poised to begin his same life all over again, stuck in some sort of time loop, as suggested by the new feature on his staff: "Each snake had its tail in its mouth" (*Pyramids* 284).

Locke creates a distinction for what makes human identity a unique entity. In determining what the identity of a (hu)man consists of, Locke claims that it is "participation of the same continued life, by constantly fleeting particles of matter by succession vitally untied to the same organized body" (6–7). He disagrees with the idea that the soul alone defines the identity of a person (Locke 7), and argues that person, substance, and man are in fact three separate things (*ibid.*). Myria LeJean, an Auditor of Reality who spends *Thief of Time* experiencing and grappling with nature of corporeal existence, helps illustrate how identity does have a physical component, as acquiring a physical body separate from the other Auditors is what allows her to begin developing an individual identity. Because of the way in which Death functions in the Discworld, her identity as Unity survives in the continued existence of her "shade" after the destruction of her physical body (*Thief of Time*

427).⁵ Although the body allows Unity to gain her identity, her body is not the only thing that defines it. While physical substance is a part of identity, it is only one component; as Locke notes, "identity depends on not a mass of the same particles, but on something else" (5). That something else is awareness, or in Locke's term "consciousness." This is how Borrowing works for the witches; as Nanny Ogg notes, "It was all very well entering the minds of animals and such, but too many witches had never come back" (*Lords and Ladies* 49). Tiffany similarly observes, "It was dangerous witchery, for an inexperienced witch risked losing herself in the mind of the other and never coming back" (*Shepherd's Crown* 41). In order to Borrow successfully, the witch needs a strong sense of personal identity to maintain her awareness of herself while also cooperating with the consciousness of the animal.

According to Locke, "the same consciousness that makes a man be himself to himself, personal identity depends on that only" (10). It is the discovery of this awareness that drives many of Terry Pratchett's Discworld novels. *Pyramids*, the seventh novel in the series, follows Pteppic from his departure from home to Ankh-Morpork for education, and then his return as a young adult. Place and its relationship to time and change in the formation of identity, personal and otherwise, are at the core of the story. Pteppic's father, the king of Dejlibeybi, remembers promising his late wife to send their son to school outside of the kingdom, because "'People never learn anything in this place,' she'd said. 'They only remember things'" (*Pyramids* 17). The idea of memory is related to Locke's concept of the importance of awareness of self as an element of identity, or in the case of Teppic's homeland, awareness of the past is the only thing giving them an identity as the kingdom cannot progress and evolve for reasons that are gradually revealed through the story.⁶ While at home, Teppic believes that he "hadn't been educated. Education had just settled on him, like dandruff" (*ibid.* 21). Teppic is sent to the Assassin's Guild in Ankh-Morpork for education, and he learns as much about modern life (including plumbing) as he does about the craft of inhumation.

Teppic's struggle to reintegrate into his new role of ruler of Djelibeybi illustrates the importance of change and self-awareness that Locke includes. As long as one's consciousness remains intact, then changes or pauses that come from life progress such as sleeping or growing up and finding a place in the world don't necessarily change identity. Teppic's initial struggles to synthesize his knowledge and experience from his years in Ankh-Morpork fail until the pyramids stop working properly. These malfunctions are critical to the story and the Lockean concepts invoked because "Pyramids are dams in the stream of time. Correctly shaped and orientated, with the proper paracosmic measurements correctly plumbed in, the temporal potential of the great mass of stone can be diverted to accelerate or reverse time over a very small area" (*Pyramids* 139). The problem is that people forget how the process is supposed to work (140), meaning no one in the kingdom can change without the passage of time, with the exception of a few stray ideas, such as the pyramid builder's son's interest "in this newfangled cosmic engineering" (*ibid.* 91). The loss of awareness of the function of time causes conscious creative self-identity to become impossible.

Teppic has been able to change throughout his adolescence, leaving home around age twelve and returning at about nineteen, because he has been able to experience the natural changes that come with the passage of time and growing up. While he may not have been aware of the changes directly, he was always aware of himself, and so Teppic maintains his personal identity. When the pyramids stop working correctly, Djelibeybi and the rest of the world end up in different temporal places of existence, and all the past monarchs wake up and emerge from their pyramids to get to Dios, who imprisoned them in the pyramids. Dios notes, "Memory is the first thing that goes. The pyramids don't seem to preserve it, strangely" (*Pyramids* 259). The problem of relying on memory for identity that Dios and Djelibeybi represent for much of the novel illustrates potential objections to Locke's ideas. Shoemaker considers the objections that memory presupposes personal identity and therefore cannot be a criterion for it, and that identity is transitive property while memory is not, so memory cannot be a criterion for identity.[7] He also notes the possible problem that "identity seems to persist through the loss of memory" (sec. 1). Pratchett works around these objections in his narrative by illustrating on the static nature of memory without time; Dios has his memories, but little awareness of his personal self. After Dios tells the resurrected past rulers of the kingdom that he can't remember having a family or his exact age, he says, "'Memory goes from the head. But it is all around me. Every scroll and book.' 'That's the history of the kingdom, man!' 'Yes. My memory'" (259). Dios has no personal memories or sense of self that are his alone; all he has are the seven thousand years' worth of the kingdom's existence. Memory alone does not define personal identity, but together with the passage of time, and awareness of both self and society, such as what Teppic gains while away from his homeland, memory functions as an element of personal identity.

The unification of Teppic's sense of time and place in his consciousness allows him to finally reconcile who and what he is, and determine the best course of action for himself and his kingdom. Once he learns about how the pyramids work from an Ephebean philosopher, Teppic realizes the intertwined nature of time and place: "His body had been away for seven years but his blood had been in the kingdom for a thousand times longer" (*Pyramids* 207). By forcing the great Pyramid to give off its stored time with a boost from his ancestors, Teppic restores his kingdom to reality, but in doing so he wipes out the gods and his ancestors, and leaves to seek his own fortune, while Ptraci takes over ruling the kingdom and bringing it more up to date with the rest of the world. When Ptraci asks him what he plans to do, Teppic decides, "I've inhumed a pyramid, a pantheon, and the entire old kingdom. It may be worth trying something else" (*ibid.* 283). When time changes, the kingdom and its inhabitants have to create a new identity for themselves, one that Teppic now realizes needs to be based on new ideas, not those that his family lineage represents. Ptraci, as his half-sister, is of the right family to rule, but she also represents a willingness to change, which the kingdom needs.

Thief of Time makes similar use of the concepts of time and consciousness as key components to self-identity. The clock at the center of the story can measure the smallest unit of time, the cosmic quantum tick, but since only part of the clock existed in the real world and part outside the universe: "It wouldn't go with the flow. It was trying to count the tick, not move with it" (*Thief of Time* 191). The Auditors have the idea that if they get the clock built, "All that will happen is that time will stop. Everything thereafter will be neat. Alive, but not moving. Tidy" (*ibid.* 196). During the ensuing struggles, Lobsang and Jeremy both develop new awareness of self and society; throughout much of the story both characters begin to learn to work with other people, Jeremy with Myria LeJean and Igor, and Lobsang with Lu-Tze and Susan Sto Helit. Of the main cast, Susan and Lu-Tze already have clearly established self-identities. Jeremy, Lobsang, and Myria LeJean all end up discovering their identities through interactions with the attempts to control time which ends up altering their consciousnesses.

Myria LeJean starts out as an Auditor in disguise, but through the disguise she gains personhood, then consciousness and personal identity. While giving a status report, Lady LeJean notes, "But it is essential for humans to use the personal pronoun. It divides the universe into two parts. The darkness behind the eyes, where the little voice is, and everything else. It is … a horrible feeling. It is like being … questioned, all the time" (*Thief of Time* 197). Another Auditor asks, "What is the little voice?" to which Lady LeJean responds, "Sometimes thinking is like talking to another person, but that person is also you" (198). While preparing another progress report, she thinks, "Oh, yes. We, not they. I must remember I'm a we" (242). She has at this point developed a more clearly defined consciousness, but still requires time to develop the awareness of herself to herself that Locke requires of personal identity. Once other Auditors decide to join her in physical bodies, she realizes, "It's in the darkness where your eyes can't see. The universe becomes two halves, and you live in the half behind the eyes. Once you have a body, you have a 'me'" (*ibid.* 260).

Locke might disagree with her assessment that the physical body equals identity, but Lady LeJean has yet to fully realize herself as a distinct individual, and as such is still a part of the Auditors' existence, not fully her own, as she is still working her way through the process of building a "self"; as Pratchett notes, "It has to be said that Lady LeJean was not herself at this point. She didn't quite have a self to be" (*Thief of Time* 261). First she shows that the body is an essential component, embodying Susan's observation that "[m]y grandfather says that if an intelligent creature takes a human shape, it starts to *think* human. Form defines function" (304). Lady LeJean has now achieved the physical substance and "participation in the same continued life" (Locke 6) that constitutes Locke's "man," but she still needs the awareness and recognition of it to have a "self-identity." Once Lady LeJean joins forces with Jeremy and Susan against the Auditors who have become unstable thanks to their inability to adapt to the demands of a physical body, she gains the awareness and consciousness required[8]: "I *was* one of them," said Lady LeJean. "Now I rather think I'm one of me" (*Thief of Time* 331).

Her next step is a new name, which Susan gives her, "You're not many, you're one. OK? Just be … yourself. Unity … that'd be a *good* name" (*Thief of Time* 354). Eventually Unity concludes that "I am insane. I know this." and "It is a terrible thing to be different" (407). Susan, who had been growing irritated with Unity, "felt a stab of guilt. It wasn't Unity's fault, after all. People learn things as they grow up, things that never get written down. And Unity had never grown up" (408). Susan's observation serves as a response to Pierce's assessment of Unity's evolution as impossible. Pierce wonders, "Myria LeJean, once one of indistinguishable Auditors, after not having an individual identity, becomes one. But, if it was originally not an individual, what was it?" (144). Unity does fully achieve a personal identity, which is confirmed by, after her suicide by chocolate, Death's retrieval of an individual life-timer and the return of her spirit. Pratchett's narrative reality and Pierce's question illustrate the importance of awareness as Locke emphasized; Auditors can have personal or individual identities, but most of them never become aware of this potential and progress towards gaining individual consciousness.

Susan's observation about learning as an important component of identity is illustrated more directly by the hero of *Thief of Time*, Lobsang Ludd. Lobsang is a young man trying to learn what his place in the world is through education and experience, and only achieves that goal when he discovers who and what he is. When the Abbot and Lu-Tze are discussing his apprenticeship, the Abbot observes, "The boy needs to *mmm brmmm* find himself" (*Thief of Time* 99). Lobsang, who had previously been apprentice thief Newgate Ludd until he was discovered by the Monks of History, wonders what the Sweeper Lu-Tze can teach him:

[Lu-Tze] "You wish to face me in the dojo? For it's a very old truth: when the pupil can beat the master, there is nothing the master cannot tell him, because the apprenticeship is ended. You want to learn?"
[Lobsang] "Ah! I knew there was something to learn!" [132].

Lobsang's new name gives him a new identity, but one that doesn't quite fit him until he meets his literal other half. Susan tries to explain to Lobsang:

"I had to lead up to it," said Susan. "It's one of those things you have to get hold of a bit at a time, I'm afraid. He's not your brother. He's you."
"Then who am I?"
Susan sighed. "You. Both of you ... are you" [337].

This exchange fits Locke's concept of personal identity because, while at the instant before they touch Jeremy and Lobsang are not the same man, having different physical existences, they share the same perceptions (as when the unconscious Jeremy speaks the same words as Lobsang at the same time, or Lobsang feeling Susan pinch Jeremy); once they touch, their physical and immaterial selves combine and their identities merge into a single complete entity. Locke's focus on awareness is key; once Jeremy and Lobsang are aware of themselves upon Lobsang's touch, their personal identity coalesces.[9]

The critical component of memory concerning identity is also addressed in *Thief of Time*. Ronnie Soak has to reconcile his past and present in order to help fight the Auditors. After Lu-Tze suggests he may have become too human, Ronnie realizes, "He could remember the time when there was only him. It was *hard* to remember, because ... there *was* nothing" (361). He considers that people in the past had recognized him: "They *feared* old Kaos. But now— He opened his eyes and looked down at his dark, smoking hands. To the world in general, he said, 'Who am I now?'" (362). He realizes that people hadn't forgotten him as Kaos, but they had "found Chaos, which is Kaos with his hair combed and a tie on, and had found in the epitome of disorder a new order undreamed of. [...] Not dark, ancient Kaos, left behind by the evolving universe, but new shiny Chaos, dancing in the heart of everything. The idea was strangely attractive. And it was a reason to go on living" (373–374). When Ronnie rejoins The Four Horsemen, "'Some old man told me you live and learn,' he said. 'Well. I have lived, and now I've learned that the edge of a sword is infinitely long. I've also learned how to make damn good yoghurt, although this is not a skill I intend to employ today. Shall we go get 'em, boys?" (382). Locke's principle of how a body can change but still be the same personal identity also applies to Ronnie's awareness; his understanding of himself and his place in the world can also change, but Ronnie remains Ronnie. While it may be argued that he is no longer Kaos, but Chaos, he retains "Ronnie" and as such, his personal identity remains intact.

The idea of continuity and awareness inherent in Locke's definition of personal identity combine in the importance of memory, which manifest in similar ways in *Thief of Time* as it does in *Pyramids*, namely through the maturation of the main protagonist. In Lobsang's case, his concept of self had to change. As he tells Susan, "*Before, I was not me*" (*Thief of Time* 373). This comment reflects the references to Lobsang needing to find himself made throughout the story by the abbot of the Monks of History, Lu-Tze, and Wen. When Susan asks him if he Lobsang and/or Jeremy, he responds, "I will always remember both of them. But I would prefer if you called me Lobsang. Lobsang has better memories. I never liked the name Jeremy even when I was Jeremy." and that he is "everything about them that was worth being, I hope" (388). Lobsang's first words when he begins to re-manifest his physical self are first to confirm his name, and second concerning Susan's query about his whereabouts, "*We are just a memory. And I am weak.* […] *But I will grow strong*" (346). Once he manages to regain a physical self to guide Susan towards the clock, he tells her:

"Don't talk to me! I've got to remember!"
"Remember what?"
"Everything!" [384].

In Teppic's case, his maturation depends on his being able to accept and merge the two parts of his experience and understanding, the historic Djelibeybi and the modern Ankh-Morpork. Lobsang's maturation involves a more literal merger, but they both have to face the human and the godlike characteristics they possess, and both make the same decision: they want to remain as human as possible. Teppic becomes annoyed with plants growing at his feet (*Pyramids* 255, 268, 272) and nearly forgets to make the sun rise (269), while Lobsang struggles to remain in human form once he becomes Time. After the destruction of the Great Pyramid Teppic notices with relief that he doesn't have the grass problem (*Pyramids* 272), and Lobsang makes the conscious decision to stay human. When Lobsang returns to the monastery to visit Lu-Tze, he tells his master, "But I'm partly human. I want to stay partly human. That means doing things the right way round. Please?" (*Thief of Time* 412). Once they know who and what they are, both young men make conscious decisions about what they going to do with that knowledge. Teppic decides to go back to the city, leaving Djelibeybi in his sister's hands, and Lobsang takes over his mother's job.

Tiffany Aching illustrates the growing up emphasis, as her story shows her begin to realize her personal identity as a child, and grow into it by the final novel. Teppic is about nineteen and Lobsang sixteen or seventeen when they grow into their personal identities and places in the world, and in Tiffany's final story *The Shepherd's Crown* she is at a similar age. At the beginning of her journey, in *The Wee Free Men*, Tiffany is "nine years old and felt that Tiffany was going to be a hard name to live up to. Besides, she'd decided only last week that she wanted to be a witch when she grew up, and she was certain Tiffany just wouldn't work" (11). In *The Wee Free Men*, Tiffany begins the process of gaining her personal identity. Near the end of the story, Granny Weatherwax tells her that the thing about witchcraft "'is that it's not like school at all. *First* you get the test, and then afterwards you spend years findin' out how you passed it. It's a bit like life in that respect.'" (*Wee Free Men* 306). Tiffany's test is to face the Elf Queen, who tries to manipulate through dreams and illusions. Tiffany manages to fight her way into one of her own dreams, where she reminds herself: "'I'm *me*! I am careful and logical and I look up things I don't understand! When I hear people use the wrong words I get edgy! I am good with cheese. I read books fast! I *think*! And I always have a piece of string! That's the kind of person I am!'" (263–4). She has an idea of her identity, but she has not matured quite enough to be fully aware of enough aspects of herself and her place in the world.

The beginning of Tiffany's narrative illustrates the key role that thought plays in developing personal identity, which is mentioned in *Thief of Time*, but is emphasized in *The Wee Free Men* as a first step. When the Queen follows Tiffany home, the Queen tells her, "You *think* too much, and now your precious thinking has let *you* down" (*Wee Free Men* 278). Tiffany wonders: "how can I stop thinking? And thinking about thinking? And even thinking about thinking about thinking? She saw the smile in the Queen's eyes, and thought: Which one of all those people doing all that thinking is *me*? Is there really any *me* at all?" (*ibid.*). Tiffany begins to struggle, and "She could feel her self disappearing" (279). What gives Tiffany the strength to fight back is the memories of the land she grew up on and of her Granny Aching.[10] The memories give her the idea she needs to defeat the Queen: "All witches are selfish, the Queen had said. But Tiffany's Third Thoughts said: Then turn selfishness into a weapon! Make all things yours! [...] How dare you try to take these things, because *they are mine*!" (282). As Tiffany faces the Queen, she proclaims, "I have woken up and I am real. I know where I come from and I know where I'm going. You cannot fool me anymore" (291). In order to beat a creature who uses illusions and doubt as weapons, Tiffany is forced to become aware of the difficulties and realities of identifying as a witch, which she is able to accept with the consciousness of her past and the meanings of her memories.

Consciously giving meaning to memories is a component of identity, and Tiffany's practice of self-reviewing through Second and Third Thoughts provides a response to the main objections to the memory part of Locke's theory.[11] Perry points to Butler's concern that Locke's focus on memory does not account for the futurity of the same self.[12] Towards the end of *I Shall Wear Midnight*, when Tiffany encounters her older self, she asks:

"Won't I be you one day? And then will I talk to me now, as it were?"

"Yes, but the you that you talk to won't exactly be you … throughout the rest of time, somewhere an old Tiffany will be talking to a young Tiffany, and the fascinating thing is that every time they do, they will be a little bit different" [340–1].

This explanation returns to Locke's concept of awareness. No Tiffany is aware of any of the other Tiffanys' exact memories, and therefore they are different identities. Yet with the current pair, older Tiffany retains her younger self's memories and awareness, which according to Locke means that they should share the same Tiffany self-identity, except that older Tiffany has memories beyond her younger self's, so she is in fact a unique identity as older Tiffany suggests. This scene illustrates that it is not only memory that is important to identity; awareness and thought are critical as well.

Tiffany reflects on two lessons which reveal how she's started to build a personal identity. Her first reaction is that she needs to remember that what happened was true and real. First, when she reunites with the Feegles, she thinks, "*But I must remember that it wasn't a dream*" (*Wee Free Men* 294), and she has a similar thought when she asks Ronald to take Wentworth home, "*No, it's all true*, she said to herself. *I must remember that, too*" (297). Her second realization is about becoming a witch: "You can't give lessons on witchcraft. Not properly. It's all about how you are … you, I suppose" (303). Tiffany needs to retain the memories and the lessons she learned while in Fairyland in order to become a witch, and her new butter stamp at the end of the novel hints that her observations were correct, "a gibbous moon and, sailing in from of the moon, a witch on a broomstick" (318).

The final novel in the Tiffany saga, *The Shepherd's Crown*, shows Tiffany realizing her full identity as a witch, and establishing her place in the world with it.[13] She is accompanied by Geoffrey in her journey to establish place in the world, and Lady Nightshade, who is trying to discover her personal identity. Nightshade is the former Elf Queen Tiffany encountered in *The Wee Free Men* and, much like Myria LeJean, Nightshade grapples with creative thinking, identity, and awareness of a personal self. Tiffany's challenge in the final Discworld novel is to help one companion find his place in the world, help the other figure out her personal identity, and to use her (Tiffany's) own identity to establish her place in the world.

At the beginning of *The Shepherd's Crown*, Tiffany is about sixteen, the same age as many other Discworld characters when they realize their identities and the direction they need to take in life. The event that begins her final stage of development is the death of Granny Weatherwax, who names Tiffany as her successor. Tiffany struggles to handle both Granny's territory and her own, and to live up to Granny's reputation as a witch. A fundamental part of being a witch in this world is a strong sense of self identity, which is emphasized throughout the story. Tiffany herself notices, when Nightshade first tries to influence her, "that her sense of self was being changed" (180). When Tiffany asks Nightshade to demonstrate her glamour, the more experienced witches brace themselves with reminders.[14] Magrat points out, "To be a witch is to be full of yourself—and in charge of yourself as well" (229), and after Tiffany is shocked that Mrs. Earwig isn't affected at all, Letice Earwig emphatically states the idea, "No one can stop me being me!" (230)

The element of memory is also emphasized after the battle against the elves. In a scene closely reminiscent of the end of her first encounter with Nightshade, Tiffany is determined to remember the events, repeating three times the importance of remembering (*Shepherd's Crown* 258). The old men who help save the day also know the importance of memory: "We happy few, we extremely elderly few, have scorned the horrible elves. They say old men forget, but we won't. Not by a long chalk" (260). For them, the reminder that their age does not limit them as much as most people (including themselves) had thought serves to illustrate how, as Locke argued, it is possible to retain self-identity in cases of temporary loss of awareness. Captain Makepeace and his friends realize, "We thought we were old—but today we found we were still young" (260). They have discovered that the men they were when they were younger are still a part of their self-identities. They had not lost or changed identities so much as they needed a reminder.

Geoffrey and Nightshade represent the need to find one's place and construct a self-identity respectively. Geoffrey has a sense of self-awareness when he is introduced; he knows he is different from his brothers and father, but he does not know where he fits in with the world. Thanks to Mr. Wiggall, his tutor as a child, "Geoffrey started to discover what he might make of himself" (*Shepherd's Crown* 13). After Geoffrey decides to leave his father's house, McTavish, a servant friendly with Geoffrey, decides to loan him some cash "till you finds out where you wants to be" (19). McTavish and Mr. Wiggall serve as guides to Geoffrey much as Lu-Tze does for Lobsang, and the parallel is reflected in the language of "needing to find oneself." In contrast, Nightshade has to determine who and what she is after she is kicked out of Fairyland. Like Unity, Nightshade is separated from a collective identity and must construct a personal one, and she needs to do it by gaining awareness of herself and her place in the world in which she now exists. Tiffany starts to teach her about concepts like empathy and friendship, and Nightshade's last words are, "There are … other ways. [...] I have learned this. And this girl"—she pointed at Tiffany—"is my *friend*" (253).[15] Because Nightshade has gained knowledge and thought processes that are exclusively her own, she starts to construct a personal identity. She does not get the chance to fully realize that identity or to figure out her place in the world because she is killed moments later, but because she never has this chance, she represents the concept of identity separate from place in the world.

Tiffany, Lobsang, and Teppic all share the features of ending up as young adults with firm ideas about their personal identities, and stable although not always specific ideas about how they fit into the world. The narrative in each case is driven by the protagonist developing their growing awareness of their self-identities in terms of the society which surrounds them in a way that benefits not only the individual, but also their society. This social component of self-identity is not from Locke, and as such represents more Pratchett's own ideas about ethical use of self-awareness and social responsibility. Particularly in Tiffany's case and her final choice to establish herself on the Chalk and allow Geoffrey to mind Granny's former steading, the necessity of benefit to both the community and the individual is clear. Tiffany's final realization encompasses the idea that in order to best serve her community, she can't do everything by herself, and she has to be herself, not Granny or anyone else.

This emphasis on using one's personal identity once established for the benefit of others is particularly notable in *Good Omens*, which shows a younger protagonist, Adam Young, discovering his identity as the Antichrist, and figuring out how he will use that power and to whose benefit. Once Adam's son of Satan abilities start to manifest: "Something was happening inside his head. It was aching. Thoughts were arriving there without him having to think them. Something was saying *You can do something, Adam Young. You can make it all better. You can do anything you want.* And what was saying this to him was… him. Part of him, deep down. Part of him that had been attached to him all these years and not really noticed, like a shadow" (215). Adam has the idea to better the world by remaking it and putting his friends in charge of various areas, but realizes that in doing so he would violate his friends' free will:

> "Oh, if that's all that's worryin' you, don't you worry," said Adam airily, "'cos I could make you all just do whatever I wanted—"
> He stopped, his ears listening in horror to the words his mouth was speaking. The Them were backing away.
> Dog put his paws over his head.
> Adam's face looked like an impersonation of the collapse of empire.
> [...]
> "No, I din't mean it—" he began. "You're my friends—" [302].

Adam's realization of the need to consciously think accords with Lock's definition of "person," and his realization of awareness presents his pending recognition of his personal identity and ethical responsibility.

Adam soon shows that he has gained the conscious awareness that Locke requires of personal identity, and needs to decide what he is going to do with it: "Whatever had been standing in the old quarry before, Adam Young was standing there now. [...] Possibly more of Adam Young than there had ever been before" (*Good Omens* 302). When the representatives of Heaven and Hell are trying to convince Adam to complete Armageddon, the Metatron tells him:

> "You can't run counter to the Great Plan. You must *think*. It's in your genes. *Think*."
> Adam hesitated. The dark undercurrent was always ready to flow back, it reedy whisper saying yes, that was it, that was what it was all about, you have to follow the Plan because you were a part of it— [351–2].

Adam's decision to act according to what he believes is right and keep the world as it is, Johnsonites and all, reflects Pratchett's emphasis on following one's values and acting for the benefit of those around the character as opposed to following a collective will or one imposed on him.[16] Adam shows the exercise of his own will when he reasons, "I don't see why it matters what is written. Not when it's about people. It can always be crossed out" (353).

Good Omens is co-authored with Neil Gaiman, and while both Terry Pratchett and Neil Gaiman enable their heroes to evolve through sharing new experiences with new people and places, Pratchett's heroes often discover their identities, while Gaiman's emphasis is on characters learning to see and face the darker realities of their worlds regardless of the age of the protagonist. For example, early in *Neverwhere*, the narrative observes, "Three years in London had not changed Richard, although it had changed the way he perceived the city" (9). This is doubly true at the end of the novel, as Richard Mayhew has changed in how he views London again, having gained knowledge of London Below. He faces his ex-fiancée Jessica and she asks if he's met someone else, he reflects on some of the women he met on his adventures in London Below, and tells her, "'No. No one else,' he said. And then, realizing it was true as he said it, 'I've just changed, that's all.'" (362). What has changed about Richard is that he is now more aware of the worlds around him, and he has gained courage in dealing with people and the world which he had previously lacked.

Even Gaiman's *Stardust*, which features a teenaged protagonist, focuses on Tristran's discovery of new environments and people and learning how to adapt in the face of challenges, not his personal identity. Tristran's critical realization throughout the course of the story is that "he could no longer reconcile his old idea of giving the star to Victoria Foster with his current notion that the star was not a thing to be passed from hand to hand, but a true person in all respects, and no kind of thing at all" (*Stardust* 198–199). Yvain's personhood is what Tristran realizes, not his own. Tristran does learn about his birth mother and his inheritance from her, but this information does not change his awareness of himself, nor does it change his perception of the world around him. At the beginning of the novel, Tristran dreams "strange guilty fantasies, muddled and odd, of journeys through forests…. He was a gangling creature of potential, a barrel of dynamite waiting for someone or something to light his fuse" (38). He has his adventures and gets to rescue the girl, yet the last words he speaks in the novel include, "But there are still so many places we have not seen. So many people still to meet" (232). While his situation certainly changes from misfit to partner to king and his worldview expands to include Faerie, how he identifies himself changes very little.

Neil Gaiman's heroes often already have their identities when their stories begin and instead must focus on adapting their perspectives to their world and choosing which world they prefer, in contrast to Terry Pratchett's typical hero beginning to change their world upon discovery of their identity. Teppic, Lobsang, and Tiffany all make substantial changes to the world around them. In *Good Omens*, upon realizing his identity as the Antichrist (Pratchett's contribution) and the true natures of Heaven and Hell, Adam chooses to keep the world as it is. What Gaiman adds is the emphasis on acknowledging and facing the darker realities of the world within the status quo, much like Richard Mayhew's recognition of London Below, or Tristran's identification with Faerie and its people. Many of Neil Gaiman's narrators choose to leave the mundane world for the new one they discover, but they do not change either their old or new worlds. Adam Young's decision to stay in the world he started in is another place where Pratchett's influence is visible.

The concerns with gaining both a sense of personal identity and using that knowledge and awareness for the betterment of society is unique to Terry Pratchett's fantasy. His focus on the ethical applications of realized self-identity is a consistent factor in his Discworld novels, as most protagonists have to grow up, realize their self-identities, reconcile their understandings with preconceived notions, and decide how to make the most socially responsible use of their awareness and skills. Supporting thematic elements that are consistent through Pratchett's corpus include free-will, and the nature of time and change. Pratchett's addition to Locke's descriptions of self-identity of social responsibility both enhances the Lockean tradition while at the same time illustrating some of the complexities in ways only possible in fantasy fiction.

Notes

1. Haberkorn and Reinhardt point out that young protagonists "finding his or her way in the world" are a feature of Pratchett's fantasy (43).
2. Santos and Sia explain the idea of the immaterial "thinking substance" (27–28).
3. Shoemaker, section 1. Santos and Sia also emphasize the ethical nature of Locke's definition by arguing that the theory can only be fully understood in ethical terms (15, 44–45).
4. Locke 23.
5. Neely emphasizes an alliance between Death and humanity against the Auditors, which represents the conflict between individuality and collective (228–229).

6. The second of McCrossin's four concerns, that if memory can be segmented, why not personhood, is relevant here. He raises the possibility that maybe individuals do change (including identity) but that the process is gradual enough that we don't notice (176–177). The answer, revealed throughout the story of *Pyramids*, is that memory alone does not sustain or constitute identity. Memory must work in combination with several other factors that result in a final personal identity that stabilizes when a young person is mostly grown up.

7. Shoemaker, Section 1: "Historical Highlights of the Relation."

8. The irony in this inability of most Auditors to adapt to a more creative individualized existence is pointed out by Neely, who notes that the Auditors get more creative in each appearance in the Discworld (236).

9. Again, Pierce's concerns about the possibility of separate physical but shared consciousness are answered here by the necessity of combining memory, awareness, and physical elements for a personal identity to exist (see Pierce 151–152).

10. This idea is similar to Webb who argues, "For Tiffany, this sense of responsibility for the land she inhabits grounds her selfhood. Once she understands this relationship, she can reject as unimportant the Queen's allegation of her heartlessness" (277).

11. Again, there is some similarity with Webb, who argues, "[Tiffany's story] also examines the ways in which alert individuals can consciously respond to and manipulate those beliefs in order not only to shape their own identities but to revise community expectations" (106).

12. Perry 145–147. Perry ultimately disagrees with Butler's reasoning, but considers the potential problem with the future relevant.

13. The Afterword of the book points out that this novel was finished and published after the author's death in 2015, but that "Terry had been thinking about the key elements in Tiffany Aching's and Granny Weatherwax's last story for a few years. […] *The Shepherd's Crown* has a beginning, a middle and an end, and all the bits in between. Terry wrote all of those. But even so, it was, still not quite as finished as he would have like when he died" (276).

14. Fellows details how the witches in the Discworld act on both individual and collective levels to maintain morality and justice (223).

15. This argument is an extension of Neely's point that "This emphasis on individuality is central to the ethics of care" (241).

16. Adam's situation and reasoning coincides with Haberkorn and Reinhardt's suggestion, "Adolescence is the time when we traditionally pick most of our mental furniture. Some of it we get used, some is prefabricated, some we have to assemble ourselves, some we get from scratch" (44).

Works Cited

Fellows, Jennifer Jill. "Categorically Not Cackling: The Will, Moral Fictions, and Witchcraft." *Philosophy and Terry Pratchett*. ed. Jacob M. Held and James B. South. Palgrave Macmillan, 2014. 204–227.
Gaiman, Neil. *Neverwhere*. Headline, 2013.
_____. *Stardust*. Spike Books, 1999.
Haberkorn, Gideon, and Verena Reinhardt. "Magic, Adolescence, and Education on Terry Pratchett's Discworld." *Supernatural Youth: The Rise of the Teen Hero in Literature and Popular Culture*. ed. Jess Battis. Lexington Books, 2011, 43–64.
Locke, John. "Of Identity and Diversity." *An Essay Concerning Human Understanding*. Vol. 1, bk. 2, chap. 27. 1690; Project Gutenberg, 2017. http://www.gutenberg.org/cache/epub/10615/pg10615.html
McCrossin, Trip. "Being One's Me: (Witchy) Personal Identity on the Discworld." *Discworld and Philosophy: Reality Is Not What It Seems*. ed. Nicolas Michaud. Open Court, 2016. 173–184.
Neely, Erica L. "The Care of the Reaper Man: Death, the Auditors, and the Importance of Individuality." *Philosophy and Terry Pratchett*. ed. Jacob M. Held and James B. South. Palgrave, 2014. 228–248.

Perry, John. *Identity, Personal Identity, and the Self.* Hackett Publishing Company, Inc., 2002.
Pierce, Jeremy. "Becoming Vetinari: Personal Identity on the Discworld." *Discworld and Philosophy: Reality Is Not What It Seems.* ed. Nicolas Michaud. Open Court, 2016. 143–156.
Pratchett, Terry. *I Shall Wear Midnight*, Harper, 2010.
_____. *Lords and Ladies.* Harper Torch, 1992.
_____. *Pyramids.* Corgi Books, 1992.
_____. *The Shepherd's Crown.* Harper, 2015.
_____. *Thief of Time.* Corgi Books, 2001.
_____. *The Wee Free Men.* Doubleday, 2003.
Pratchett, Terry, and Neil Gaiman. *Good Omens.* Corgi Books, 1991.
Santos, Ferdinand, and Santiago Sia. *Personal Identity, the Self, and Ethics.* Palgrave Macmillan, 2007.
Shoemaker, David. "Personal Identity and Ethics." *Stanford Encyclopedia of Philosophy.* Stanford University. Article published December 20, 2005; last modified December 21, 2016. https://plato.stanford.edu/entries/identity-ethics/
Webb, Caroline. *Fantasy and the Real World in British Children's Literature: The Power of Story.* Routledge, 2015.

The Anglo-Saxon Ælf
Old English Influences in Terry Pratchett's The Wee Free Men *and* The Shepherd's Crown

Livia Bongiovanni

Whether consciously borrowing or working from an internalized set of conventions, contemporary fantasy writers continue to take inspiration from some of the earliest English sources.[1] In her article, "On the Ambiguity of Elves," British folklorist Jacqueline Simpson affirms that modern fantasy derives many of its magical elements from pre-existing folklore. Regarding the origin of elves in the popular fantasy novels of British authors J.R.R. Tolkien and Terry Pratchett, Simpson writes, "The elves of Tolkien and Pratchett, different though they are, can both claim descent from the highly ambiguous concept of elves found in Germanic mythology, in so far as this can be reconstructed from the fragmentary evidence of Old English and Old Icelandic sources" (77–8). Pratchett's use of Old English source material in his writing is often understated, especially when compared to his more recognizable references to modern history, popular culture, and significant social movements. When Pratchett does engage in so-called "high" fantasy, he does so usually for the sake of parody. Two of his young adult novels, however, *The Wee Free Men* (2003) and *The Shepherd's Crown* (2015), rely heavily on Anglo-Saxon folklore for their depiction of elves as well as the overall message they impart to their young audience. The extent to which Pratchett's elves retain the key characteristics of their Anglo-Saxon ancestors can be measured against H. Stuart's criteria laid out in "The Anglo-Saxon Elf." Using evidence derived exclusively from Old English texts, primarily the *Lacnunga* and the leechbooks, Stuart identifies "five different and equally incompatible descriptions of the elf" (313). Elves are described as (1) the source of unexplained illness, (2) having the ability to possess humans, (3) related to human beings through a common lineage, (4) female nature spirits with specific habitats, and (5) overall benevolent creatures associated with wisdom and strength (Stuart 313–14). As this list shows, Anglo-Saxon elves possess both positive and negative aspects, depending on the source to which one refers. Since Pratchett only mentions these positive traits for the purpose of subverting them, the first three descriptions that Stuart provides are the most relevant. A comparison of Old English scholarship and Pratchett's *The Wee Free Men* and *The Shepherd's Crown* reveals three common characteristics: that elves are amoral creatures capable of doing great harm as well as good, that they are in some way related to human beings, and that they are the source of mental and physical disease. When read within the context of their Anglo-Saxon origins, Pratchett's elves emerge as morally ambiguous, humanoid creatures with a penchant for inducing nightmares as a means of possessing and controlling humans.

In *The Wee Free Men*,[2] Pratchett's thirtieth novel in the *Discworld* series and his second novel written for children, nine-year-old Tiffany Aching must venture into Fairyland to rescue her baby brother Wentworth from the queen of the elves (referred to in the first novel only as the Queen) with the help of the Nac Mac Feegle, "the most feared of all the fairy races" (*Wee Free Men* 6). Both *The Wee Free Men* and *The Shepherd's Crown* take place in the Chalk Hills of the Discworld, located somewhere between the kingdom of Lancre and the city of Ankh-Morpork. The physical landscape of the two novels, which is based on the geography of Southeast England, compliments Pratchett's use of Anglo-Saxon elves and allows for the incorporation of historical Anglo-Saxon beliefs surrounding the relationship between supernatural beings and the land. According to Simpson, *ælf* compounds such as water-elf, wood-elf, and mountain-elf, found primarily in the Latin glosses, "imply that for the English it seemed appropriate to locate elves in the landscape of earth, not in a remote mythological realm" (78). The extent to which Pratchett's elves dwell within the landscape varies, but neither the Nac Mac Feegle nor the Queen can be said to reside in some "remote mythological realm." In fact, both live in close proximity to humans. The Queen's land exists on the border of the physical realm, and can be entered through certain doors in the natural world. The kelda, the matriarch of the Nac Mac Feegle clan, cautions Tiffany as to the nature of these peripheral worlds as Tiffany prepares to venture into Fairyland:

> there are more worlds than stars in the sky.... They are everywhere, big and small, close as your skin.... Some ye can see an' some ye canna, but there are doors, Tiffan [*sic*]. They might be a hill or a tree or a stone or a turn in the road, or they might e'en be a thought in your heid, but they are there, all aroound ye. You'll have to learn to see 'em, because you walk among them and dinna know it. And some of them ... is poisonous [*Wee Free Men* 112].

The kelda's mention of geographical land markers in this passage echoes the close relationship between Anglo-Saxon elves and the natural world, a folkloric motif identified by Simpson. Tiffany must locate one such door in order to rescue her brother, and she eventually manages to gain entry through a circle of standing stones. Although there is no anthropological evidence, as Sarah Semple states, "of supernatural entities associated with stone circles or henge monuments" (Semple 115), Pratchett's elves are nevertheless firmly entrenched within "the landscape of the earth," (Simpson 78).

The Nac Mac Feegle, to whom the title of *The Wee Free Men* refers, embody this concept more literally, taking shelter in the burial mound of a long-forgotten king. According to Semple's article on the place of the prehistoric burial mound in Anglo-Saxon culture, "etymological evidence demonstrates that barrows were not just associated with dragons but also with goblins, elves and Woden himself" (111). Pratchett may have had this particular piece of folklore in mind when he chose to set his novel in a fictional version of England's downlands, which contain several such burial mounds according to Semple's study. In addition to the Nac Mac Feegle residence, Pratchett makes at least two other references to mound structures in *The Wee Free Men*, even alluding to *Beowulf* at one point in the text: "Tiffany knew there was a story that a hero had once fought a dragon up there and its blood had burned the ground where it fell. There was another story that said there was a heap of treasure under the hill, *defended* by the dragon,[3] and *another* story that said a king was buried there in armor of solid gold" (*Wee Free Men* 37). Although Tiffany isn't sure of the exact legend surrounding the burial mound, the mound itself clearly has supernatural significance for the people of the Chalk. These geographical details, along with their allusions to Anglo-Saxon mythology, establish Pratchett's text within the landscape of Anglo-Saxon belief, creating the expectation for a similar awareness of how supernatural creatures such as elves operate within this culture.

Based on their portrayal in the Old English medical texts as well as the Latin glosses, medieval scholarship tends to classify elves as amoral rather than immoral beings, arguing that the association between elves and malevolence accompanied the arrival of Christianity. Karen Jolly discusses the merging of these two belief systems in her book *Popular Religion in Late Saxon England: Elf Charms in Context*, arguing that "amoral creatures such as elves were gradually 'demonized' to fit into the Good-Evil paradigm of the Christian moral universe" (136). Likewise, Stuart writes, "It seems that until Christianity came along, and for some time afterwards, the elves and their relations were considered not so much immoral as amoral" (316). Although Simpson agrees that elves are naturally ambiguous both before and after the conversion of Anglo-Saxon England, she argues that "Pratchett draws on [elves'] negative traits ... to draw a wholly negative picture" (78). While

Pratchett does indeed portray elves in a decidedly negative light, classifying them as entirely evil is problematic. As Simpson and other scholars have stated, *ælf* was originally a blanket term referring to all manner of "minor supernatural beings" (Simpson 77). She reminds us that elf or *ælf* "was a standard word in English until it was gradually superseded, from the thirteenth century onwards, by the more elegant and aristocratic French loanwords 'fairy' and 'fay'" (77). Because the Nac Mac Feegle originate from the same realm as the Queen and her servants, they can, arguably, be classified as elves. These fairy folk are famous for drinking, fighting, and stealing anything they can lay their hands on, yet we come to learn that they do indeed possess a sense of right and wrong. As Pratchett writes, "The Nac Mac Feegle would fight and steal, certainly, but who wanted to fight the weak and steal from the poor?" (*Wee Free Men* 149). The Nac Mac Feegle's sense of morality becomes the key factor in their rebellion and subsequent banishment from Fairyland, and their expulsion from the supernatural realm places them in a unique position within the text. Having been cast out by their queen, they are no longer officially "elves," nor are they entirely human. This liminal status may explain why they appear to exhibit more of a conscience than their elven counterparts.

Unlike the Nac Mac Feegle, the Queen is incapable of discerning right from wrong, which associates her more closely with the Anglo-Saxon concept of *ælf*. Yet even the Queen may not be definitively evil. According to Stuart's interpretation of the presence of elves in *Beowulf*, "man, the moral animal, can appreciate the rights of his fellow beings to life, happiness, and material comfort: elves and monsters cannot" (316). The queen, keeping in line with Stuart's definition, cares only for her own happiness. By her very nature, she is *unable* to consider the needs of others. When Tiffany asks the kelda why the Queen would kidnap her brother, she replies, "The Quin likes children. She has none o' her own. She dotes on them. She'll give the wee boy everything he wants, too. *Only* what he wants" (*Wee Free Men* 112). The Queen steals children simply because she likes them (until she grows bored). She acts not out of spite, but out of solipsism. Even Rob Anybody, the Big Man and head warrior of the Feegle clan, seems to regard the Queen's self-centered worldview as an inseparable part of her being rather than a conscious choice, commenting, "The Quin'll try to be kind to him, but she disna know how. She's an elf. They're no' very good at thinking of other people" (*Wee Free Men* 150). Rob's remarks make it clear that this kind of egomania is a species trait shared by all elves, as the elf courtier Peaseblossom later demonstrates in *The Shepherd's Crown*: "[Tiffany] felt the tug of his glamour but rage was a useful tool, and she hated that grinning face. It was so self-centered. It loved itself beyond any other thing" (252). Whether or not the Queen's behavior is morally correct is something of an insoluble question because the Queen and her elves are only ever *capable* of thinking of themselves. During their eventual confrontation in *The Wee Free Men*, young Tiffany realizes that the Queen "[doesn't] know *anything* about people. [She's] just ... a child that's got old" (201). Put another way, the Queen lacks the necessary mental capacity to empathize with others. She has never developed the ability to understand the possibility that someone might experience thoughts and feelings that are contrary to her own.

The Queen's inability to imagine and therefore empathize with the needs of others may also have something to do with her inability to use her magic to create anything original. Pratchett's definition of Fairyland is, consequently, a kind of "robber world that [lives] off the real worlds" (*Wee Free Men* 188). It exists just on the periphery of the "real" world and can be found only by those who know where to look. Unable to create anything of her own, the Queen manipulates the fears and fantasies of mortals to shape her own universe, attempting to create a world that closely mimics the aesthetics of the human realm:

> Tiffany listened, at the end of the shadowy wood, to the story of a little world where nothing grew, where no sun shone, and where everything had to come from somewhere else. It was a world that took, and gave nothing back except fear. It raided—and people learned to stay in bed when they heard strange noises at night, because if anyone gave her trouble, the Queen could control their dreams [*Wee Free Men* 149].

Anything of substance (food, animals, people, etc.) must come from a different reality. As William the gonnagle, a nod to the famed poet William McGonagall and perhaps even a take on the Anglo-Saxon sceop, explains, "Fairies can't make music, ye ken. She'll steal a man awa' for the music he makes" (*Wee Free Men* 150). Unable to conceive of an original thought or idea, Pratchett's elves can only mirror human invention and creativity. Further examples of this mirroring occur when Tiffany is forced to navigate a series of dreams intended as traps to distract her from her mission to rescue Wentworth. Because the Queen and her subjects are not capable of original thought, each dream is based on the experiences of the dreamer, and Tiffany quickly concludes that each dream "must make use of what it finds in your head" (*Wee Free Men* 168). Roland, another of the Queen's stolen children and the long-lost son of the local Baron, confirms that the Queen "picks up dreams from everywhere. She collects them" (*Wee Free Men* 189). The Queen's power lies not in manufacturing her own illusions, but in manipulating the imaginations of those around her.

The link between elves and dreams, especially nightmares, is well documented in Old English texts. According to Jolly, "Elf-disease remedies appear in close proximity to or combined with remedies for demon possession, nightmares, madness, fevers, and other mind-altering afflictions of seemingly malevolent origin that aggressively attacked humans or cattle" (135). Bonser concurs, stating "the elves were regarded as the source of apparitions, especially at night, and therefore of nightmare. Thus, one finds charms against 'the elf-kind and nocturnal goblins,'" (360). According to Stuart, elves' ability to invade the mind of a sleeping person and control their dreams became associated with demonic forms of possession with the arrival of Christianity: "The ability to enter into a man and assume control of his mind and body can be viewed as an addition to the original elvish properties derived from the [New Testament] concept of penetrating demons" (314). However, this association may have pre-Christian origins. Stuart goes on to state that "from the [Old English] sources alone it can be deduced that earlier Germanic peoples believed that a certain type of disease was caused by the victim's being 'ridden' by a supernatural creature: originally a mare, sometimes a dwarf. By this concept they explained the occurrence of epileptic fits and other spasms" (314). The Queen's expertise at manipulating dreams may also be interpreted as a kind of possession. The Queen proclaims to young Tiffany, "'I can make you think whatever I please'" (*Wee Free Men* 235), suggesting that she has some power over the will of her victims. Although Tiffany can usually differentiate between dreams and reality, and at times may even exert some control over the dream, the Queen still governs the sensory perceptions of the dreamer. She repeatedly attempts to control Tiffany's thoughts by subjecting her to hallucinatory states of mind. Perhaps the most troubling and definitive evidence of this type of possession is that elves continue to influence and manipulate the minds of mortals long after they break free from their enchantment, as the witch Nanny Ogg observes in *The Shepherd's Crown*: "That's the trouble with elves, they will keep comin' back [...] People tell stories about 'em, Tiff [...] They make 'em sound fun—it's as if their glamour hangs around after they've gone and stays in people's heads, tellin' 'em that elves is no problem. Just a bit of mischief" (197). The king of the elves confirms Nanny's theory shortly thereafter, calling stories "a way into the minds of your peoples" (*Shepherd's Crown* 204) when Tiffany visits his barrow in Lancre to solicit his assistance during the elven invasion of her homeland.

Pratchett appears to be well aware of the relationship between the Anglo-Saxon *ælf* and these "mind-altering afflictions" (Jolly 135). His afterword to *The Wee Free Men* credits the 19th-century painter Richard Dadd, known for his illustrations of elves and fairies, for partially inspiring the novel. Dadd, who struggled with severe mental illness, was committed to Bethlehem Hospital after killing his father during a hallucinatory episode. He continued painting during his incarceration, creating one of his best-known works, *The Fairy Feller's Master Stroke*, during his time in Bethlehem Hospital. Pratchett directly references this painting in *The Wee Free Men* in Tiffany's illustrated book of fairy tales, where Tiffany comments that it "looked as if it had been done by an artist who painted what was in front of him," (47)[4] and again when Tiffany enters Fairyland. In *The Wee Free Men*, madness is defined as an inability to differentiate between what is real and what is not. As in the Old English texts, this type of madness is caused by dreams brought about by elves. The Queen is so adept at controlling these dreams that her victims are no longer able to tell the difference between the dream world and reality: "There's dreams inside dreams," Roland tells Tiffany, "There's ... other things that live inside dreams, horrible things. You never know if you've really woken up. And the Queen controls them all" (*Wee Free Men* 174). Likewise, Rob cautions, "Live in dreams for too long and ye go mad—ye can never wake up prop'ly, ye can never get the hang o' reality again" (*Wee Free Men* 151).

Rather than attributing this connection between elves and madness to medieval Christian influences, Alaric Hall argues that this association can be found within the word itself: *ælfisc* (122). Drawing on evidence from the Latin glosses, Hall translates *eluesce wehte* as "*ælfisc* beings," which he contextualizes as "delusions" or "delusory beings" (123). Hall argues that "although the phrase *eluesce wehte* remains somewhat problematic, the implication is that *ælfe* were sufficiently closely associated with causing delusion that a derived adjective could be used with a meaning along the lines of 'delusory' by a glossator seeking to elucidate a Latin term" (123). Hall also points to later linguistic evidence in the form of a Middle English sermon "where *elvich* seems most unlikely to mean 'to do with elves' or any such literal reading, but rather to mean 'delusory'" (123). Finally, Hall looks at the meaning of the word *ælfsīden*, roughly translated as "elf magic" which "occurs in three different remedies," noting that "*ælfsīden* was caused by *ælfe* and specifically was associated with fever; this association connects more generally to an association of *ælfe* with causing delusions" (119, 140). The linguistic evidence that Hall provides demonstrates that this association likely has pre–Christian origins and is an indigenous part of Anglo-Saxon folklore.

As previously mentioned, elf-illnesses often involve symptoms of fever. This is especially true in elf-remedies involving the word *ælfsīden*. While none of the characters ever experience fever explicitly, Tiffany does find herself momentarily trapped in a dream that could be described as feverish:

> The heat struck like a blowtorch, so sharp and sudden that she gasped. She'd had sunstroke once, up on the downs, when she'd gone without a bonnet. And this was like that; the world around here was in worrying shades of dull green, yellow, and purple, without shadows. The air was so full of heat that she felt she could squeeze smoke out of it [*Wee Free Men* 179].

The Queen and her subjects live in a land of eternal winter (perhaps a nod to C.S. Lewis), and Tiffany must travel through this frigid landscape as she encounters one dream after the next. The above passage occurs as Tiffany steps from winter into summer, finding herself in a dream inspired by *The Fairy-Feller's Master Stroke*. The heat is so overwhelming that Tiffany momentarily believes that she is actually in a world of summer. That is to say, the "fever" brought about by the dream, inflicted on her by the queen of the elves, causes her to experience delusions. These fevered hallucinations are so convincing that Tiffany has to rely on someone else's perceptions in order to identify reality:

> She ducked under a round leaf much bigger than she was and took out the toad again.
>
> "Whap? It's sti' cooold," said the toad, hunching down on her hand.
> "Cold? The air's baking!"
> "There's just snow," said the toad. "Put me back, I'm freezing!"
> Just a minute, thought Tiffany. "Do toads dream?" she said.
> "No!"
> "Oh ... so it's not really hot?"
> "No! You just think it is!" [*Wee Free Men* 182].

Because the toad, another of Tiffany's traveling companions, can't experience dreams, he is not subject to the same kind of delusions. Up until this moment, Tiffany remains convinced that she is experiencing the sensation of real heat. Perhaps most significantly, this dream is the *only* one in which Tiffany is unable to discern reality for herself. One could say that the rise in temperature, a metaphorical fever, has made her temporarily insane.

All these examples of possession, madness, and fever point to a well-established association between elves and illness in both the Anglo-Saxon world and Pratchett's universe. Hall even suggests that this association goes beyond those mentioned in the leechbooks, writing that "the medical texts themselves are not the only material with a bearing on *ælfe's* associations with illness. Some more tangential evidence derives also from glosses and a plant-name containing *ælf-*" (98). As Hall goes on to explain, "the associations of *ælfe* with illness seem to be part of a wider and presumably older tradition. Perhaps significantly, the evidence is mainly West Germanic" (98). What sets Pratchett apart from these Old English sources is that his work depicts elves not just as the bringers of disease, but as a kind of parasite in and of themselves. The extent to which the Queen steals from humanity borders on vampirism, and the elves literally feed on the human world in order to survive. Rob Anybody likens them to sheep ticks, a metaphor easily recognizable to the shepherds of the Chalk:

> "Ye ken them wee bitty bugs that clings on to the sheeps and suck theirsel' full o' blood and then drop off again? This whole world is like one o' them."
> "You mean like a, a tick? A parasite? A *vampire*?"
> "Oh, aye. It floats aroound until it finds a place that's weak on a world where no

one's paying attention, and opens a door. Then the Quin sends in her folk. For the stealin', ye ken" [*Wee Free Men* 148-9].

For Pratchett, the very existence of elves is harmful to one's health. Elves have the potential to destroy not just individuals, but entire worlds. They may even be able to *transform* said worlds into a reflection of their own empty reality, if the word "vampire" is any indication. The "other world" is a "parasite with its evil little hooks in the gateways of stone" (*Shepherd's Crown* 50). Put into terms of disease, Pratchett's elves are like a virus, feeding off the host world until it withers and dies.

Yet despite the casual cruelty and lack of empathy for which elves are known, Pratchett suggests that, under the right circumstances, elves and humans are not all that different. In "The Anglo-Saxon Elf," Stuart argues that "the *Beowulf* poet depicts the race of elves as basically human, but outlawed from human society" (314). The following passage, translated by R.M. Liuzza, groups elves into the same category as Grendel and the biblical Cain, which, according to Stuart, demonstrates that "the *Beowulf*-poet saw familial similarities" (316) between these three subjects:

> Wæs se grimma gæst Grendel hāten,
> mære mearcstapa, sē Þe mōras hēold,
> fen ond fæsten; fifelcynnes eard
> wonsǣlī wer weardode hwīle,
> siÞðan him Scyppend forscrifen hæfde
> in Cāines cynne—Þone cwealm gewræc
> ēce Drihten, Þæs Þe hē Ābel slog;
> ne gefeah hē Þǣre fǣhðe, ac hē hine feor forwræc,
> Metod for Þȳ mane mancynne fram.
> Þanon untȳdras ealle onwōcon,
> eotenas ond ylfe ond orcneas,
> swylce gīgantas, Þa wið Gode wunnon
> lange Þrāge; hē him ðæs lean forgeald

> This grim spirit was called Grendel,
> mighty stalker of the marches, who held
> the moors and fens; this miserable man
> lived there for a time in the land of giants,
> after the Creator had condemned him
> among Cain's race—when he killed Abel
> the eternal Lord avenged that death.
> No joy in that feud—the Maker forced him
> far from mankind for his foul crime.
> From thence arose all misbegotten things,
> trolls and elves and the living dead,
> and also the giants who strove against God
> for a long while—He gave them their reward for that [102–114].

Stuart stresses that "whether the link was derived from clerical lore or stemmed from the poet's own imagination is not as important as the fact that it *could* be made, that it was a connection both feasible and convincing to the poet's audience. Thus, man and all *untydras* or 'misbegotten creatures' were descended from two brothers, one of whom had forfeited his sense of morality" (316). Stuart suggests here that the Anglo-Saxons conceptualized elves as an offshoot of humanity originating from the same set of parents. If elves are descendants of Cain, then they must be related to humans in at least some capacity. Alaric Hall disagrees with Stuart's interpretation, arguing that classifying elves as descendants of Cain represents a conscious attempt to reframe the Anglo-Saxon world in Christian terms: "*Beowulf's* situation of *ælf* in alliterative and semantic collocation with *eotenas* can be read rather as a self-conscious (and perhaps ostentatious) realignment of the *ælf*, demonising [sic] them by association with monsters traditional (*eotenas*), Classical (*orcneas*) and biblical (*gigantas*)" (73). Although he disagrees as to the poet's motive for linking elves with Cain, Hall's research nevertheless supports a relationship between elves and humans: "Although it is not conclusive, the early Old English evidence suggests corporeal anthropomorphic beings mirroring the human in-groups which believed in them" (68).

Such mirroring occurs in Pratchett's text when Tiffany recalls how a member of her own "human in-group" once kidnapped a child. Prompted by the Queen's assertion of "all I wanted was a little bit of company" (*Wee Free Men* 193), Tiffany launches into a moment of external analepsis, one of many in the text, where she recounts the story of Miss Female Infant Robinson. Miss Robinson, who came to work in Tiffany's village as a young woman, is now "quite old" (*Wee Free Men* 193) and without any family. Having lost some measure of her mental faculties with age and loneliness, "Miss Robinson," we are told, "had stolen a baby" (*Wee Free Men* 194):

> [Tiffany] picked up bits of conversation, though sometimes they seemed to be in a kind of code, like: "Never really had anyone of her own, poor old soul. Wasn't her fault she was skinnier'n a rake," and "They say that when they found her, she was cuddling it and said it was hers," and "The house was full of baby clothes she'd knitted!" That last one had puzzled Tiffany at the time, because it was said in the same tone of voice that someone'd use to say, "And the house was full of human skulls!" [*Wee Free Men* 194].

Neither Miss Robinson nor the Queen understands that taking a child from its parents is inherently wrong. Miss Robinson even thinks that the child belongs to her. Pratchett continues, "Tiffany had overheard bits of arguments all over the village, but the same phrases cropped up over and over again. Poor thing never meant no harm. She was a hard worker, never complained. She's not right in the head. The law's the law. A crime's a crime" (*Wee Free Men* 194). That Miss Robinson is "not right in the head" speaks not only to her cognitive state, but her morality as well. Like the Queen, she is inherently unable to differentiate between right and wrong. Instead, she acts only on her own impulses. Pratchett purposely parallels these two scenarios to show the reader exactly how thin the line between right and wrong, and consequently human and non-human, can be. As Miss Robinson shows us, human beings are capable of experiencing terrible loneliness and occasional bouts of insanity. The fact that Tiffany makes the connection between Miss Robinson and the Queen suggests that elves are capable of experiencing the same, emulating the human world of which they are a part.

There is an inherent duality, even uncertainty, imbedded in the Anglo-Saxon elf. Even the Old English word *ælf* is simultaneously associated with beauty and disease. Simpson notes several Anglo-Saxon given names containing the word *ælf*, such as Ælfred and Ælfric, which "support the idea of [elves as] beautiful and/or benevolent beings" (78). This duality carries over to Pratchett's elves primarily in their physical appearance, as we see when Tiffany strips away the Queen's glamour to reveal a "small and gray" creature[5] (*Wee Free Men* 241). Such contradictory associations, according to Simpson, are not mutually exclusive. Rather, they are representative of the ambiguous nature of everyday life in Anglo-Saxon England. "Clear-cut moral divisions," she explains, "do not reflect the way we experience life, where good luck and misfortune bear no relation to virtue and vice" (Simpson 82). The same would seem to be true of Pratchett's work, which consistently reflects the ambiguities of the real world. In recognition of these circumstances, young Tiffany banishes the Queen back to Fairyland with the parting words, "I hope there's someone who'll cry for you" (*Wee Free Men* 241). Tiffany is only eleven years old during the events of *The Wee Free Men*, and she has already learned that morality is hardly ever black and white, especially when faced with the qualifiers of old age and mental illness or even just *being an elf*.

Tiffany's pity for the Queen comes full circle several years later in *The Shepherd's Crown*, when the Queen is beaten and exiled following a coup led by the vindictive elf Lord Peaseblossom. This is the first time in the series that an elf expresses something approaching human emotions. The Queen "[appears] to have been crying" (*Shepherd's Crown* 162) when the Feegles find her out on the Chalk, and we finally learn the Queen's given name: Nightshade. The plant with which the queen shares a name has a long history of inducing as well as *treating* many of the same symptoms associated with elf-attributed illnesses (fever, nightmares, delirium, convulsions, etc.) such that the significance can hardly be coincidental. If anything, the name Nightshade reinforces the duality of elven nature as equal parts harmful and benevolent. It may even be possible that the Queen herself holds a potential cure for the parasitic affliction that is her people. "She has encountered ideas unknown to her," the now adult Tiffany observes after taking Nightshade under her protection, "Perhaps she might then go back to Fairyland and persuade other elves to think like her? To leave us alone" (*Shepherd's Crown* 191). Tiffany's burgeoning faith in Nightshade's ability to change her nature is the result of several days of education during which Nightshade accompanies Tiffany on her daily rounds, which generally involve looking after the poor, ill, and elderly in Tiffany's community. Nightshade initially struggles with the concept of mercy, asking Tiffany,

> "You could have killed me yesterday.... *I'd* have killed me. Why didn't you? You know I am an elf, and *we* are merciless."
> "Yes," said Tiffany, "but we are human, and we do know mercy. I also know I'm a witch, and I'm doing my job" [*Shepherd's Crown* 182].

Nightshade gradually learns that being a witch, and by extension being human, involves taking care of one another, even strangers, simply because they are people. The philosophy to which Tiffany adheres stems from a refusal to treat any sentient being as an Other, regardless of whether or not they are human: "although they are strangers, I simply think of them as people. All of them" (*Shepherd's Crown* 186). Doing so is not always easy, as Tiffany admits when she is later overcome with fury at the kidnapping of a human infant. In the blink of an eye, Tiffany kills three elves and must reckon with the consequences of her actions:

> And she had to stop herself there, suddenly appalled at what she had done. *Only a witch gone to the dark would kill*, she screamed at herself inside her head.
> And another voice said, *But they were just elves. And they were hurting the baby.*
> The first voice came sneakily back with, *But Nightshade is also just an elf....*
> And Tiffany knew that if a witch started thinking of anyone as "*just*" anything, that would be the first step on a well-worn path that could lead to, oh, to poisoned apples, spinning wheels, and a too-small stove ... and to pain, and terror, and horror and the darkness [*Shepherd's Crown* 194].

Resisting the compulsion to Other those who are different is a constant challenge for Pratchett's characters, and the fact that Pratchett portrays this philosophy as something difficult speaks to its necessity as well as its importance. The line between good and bad, right and wrong, light and dark, is razor thin. No one knows this better than Tiffany and her fellow witches. "A witch is always on the edge," Pratchett writes, "between the light and the dark, good and bad, making choices every day, judging all the time. It was what made her human" (*Shepherd's Crown* 165). Being a witch, being human, comes down to making the right choice even when the decision is difficult. "But what [is] it," Tiffany ponders, "that [makes] an elf?" (*Shepherd's Crown* 165).

Thus far in the Discworld series, elves have been characterized by their extreme egotism and amorality, aligning them closely with the Anglo-Saxon concept of *ælf*. To be an elf is to be a parasite, a disease, a creature that exists only for the pleasure of itself. Nightshade's expulsion from Fairyland alters this dynamic by presenting the reader with at least one elf who appears capable of changing her nature. Following Tiffany's example, Nightshade begins helping humans without the expectation of reciprocation, first carrying a heavy basket for an old woman on the road and then assisting Tiffany in caring for an old lady on her deathbed. Nightshade subsequently experiences "a little *glow*," which Tiffany explains often happens to those who help others: "she will probably feel what we call *a little glow*, because she has helped someone who needed help. It will mean that she is glad that she is not in his circumstances. You could say that she can see what his world is like, and—what can I say?—she comes away feeling hopeful" (*Shepherd's Crown* 222, 209). Here again, Pratchett emphasizes the human quality of empathy, which involves the ability to think creatively in order to imagine the world from someone else's perspective. When Tiffany asks how Nightshade felt when she offered to help the old woman with her basket, Nightshade "[looks] puzzled," replying, "I'm not sure [...] But I'm not sure I felt like an elf should ... is that a good thing?" (*Shepherd's Crown* 211). By learning to think of those outside of herself as something other than things, Nightshade effectively loses her claim to elfhood. The implication of this phenomenon is not only that empathy can be taught but that *anyone* can learn it. Upon learning to empathize and, more importantly, *act on* said empathy, one achieves humanity at the expense of one's monstrosity. Taken within the context of Stuart's earlier argument that elves cannot "appreciate the rights of [their] fellow beings to life, happiness, and material comfort" (316), it would seem apparent that the queen is well on her way to no longer being an elf. This fact is unequivocally confirmed during the ensuing battle between the witches and the elves when Nightshade is brutally executed by one of her former subjects:

> "Why do you follow this ... perfidious elf?" the Queen demanded of the elves. "*I* am your rightful queen, and I say that you do not have to do this. There are ... other ways." She spun on the spot, her velvet robes spiraling around her slim body. "I have learned this. And this girl"—she pointed at Tiffany—"is my *friend.*"
> Tiffany couldn't stop what happened next.
> "Friend?" Peaseblossom spat. "There are no friends for elves."
> He raised his arm and his saber tore through Nightshade with a terrible swishing sound. The elf Queen fell, crumpling to the ground at Tiffany's feet, where she writhed for a moment that seemed to last a lifetime, myriad faces and shapes appearing and disappearing, flickering in and out of substance, before finally lying still, a forlorn heap [*Shepherd's Crown* 253].

We will never know how Nightshade would have behaved had she succeeded in regaining control of the throne. Based on her characterization in *The Wee*

Free Men, it is entirely possible that Nightshade's altruism was actually self-serving, as she makes it clear from the moment of her exile that she intends to "get [her] kingdom back," while also realizing that she needs Tiffany's help to do so (*Shepherd's Crown* 212). While Nightshade appears to have embraced the value of helping others, she still exhibits a certain amount of vindictiveness and gives "not a particularly pleasant smile" when Tiffany asks her to provide the witches with a demonstration of elven magic (*Shepherd's Crown* 229). Yet despite these apprehensions, Nightshade's declaration of friendship with a human is all that it takes for Peaseblossom to decide that the Queen is too far gone in her humanity to be saved.

That Pratchett ultimately deviates from the Anglo-Saxon model of elves should not be quite so surprising, since Pratchett's usual method involves making use of literary conventions for the purpose of dissecting and analyzing their various parts. In this case, Pratchett makes use of the medieval past in order to convey valuable lessons about community and what it means to be human. In the first book of the Tiffany Aching series, Pratchett repeatedly demonstrates the importance of "[speaking] up for those who don't have voices" (*Wee Free Men* 29), examples of which include caring for the elderly, being mindful of others, and having compassion for the physically and mentally ill. The distinction between elves and humans in this respect is an important one. However dangerous elven amorality can be, it is nothing when compared to the human tendency of failing to act. The capacity for empathy is what sets humans apart and ultimately what enables Tiffany to defeat the Queen and save her brother. This message later evolves in *The Shepherd's Crown* to encompass the notion of service. "Humans need other humans," Tiffany asserts, "it's as simple as that" (*Shepherd's Crown* 209). Like most witches, Tiffany strives not to "think of [herself]" but to "think for all" (*Shepherd's Crown* 46), and this is ultimately what makes her worthy of the shepherd's crown as the voice of her land rises up to proclaim, "*Tiffany Aching is the first among shepherds, for she puts others before herself...*" (*Shepherd's Crown* 238). Essential to this notion of service, however, is the understanding that no one person can act alone, something that elves intrinsically do not understand. Tiffany is *the first* among shepherds, but she is by no means the only one.

The question of literary origins is hardly ever straightforward, but the combination of linguistic and historical evidence does seem to suggest that Pratchett's work may indeed have been influenced by the Anglo-Saxon concept of *ælf*. Though Pratchett's elves may have the potential to inflict even more harm than their Anglo-Saxon predecessors, their major characteristics remain the same. Both Pratchett's universe and the Old English texts present elves in a predominantly negative light, and Pratchett draws specifically on their Old English associations with disease and madness in order to address important concepts about morality. Pratchett's reliance on these Anglo-Saxon origins demonstrates the continuing relevance of the medieval past in today's fantasy. Pratchett's Anglo-Saxon elves serve as a foil to the main character, working to further the primary themes of the Tiffany Aching novels: the importance of speaking for the voiceless and putting others before oneself. Such themes clearly held a special significance for Pratchett, who said in a 2013 interview with Cory Doctorow, "The Tiffany Aching series is what I would most like to be remembered for, and I couldn't have written Tiffany Aching when I was seventeen. I just wouldn't have had the tools" (Pratchett). There is a noticeable urgency, especially in Pratchett's later work, for cooperation, tolerance, and compassion in the face of injustice and cruelty. Tiffany's demonstration of these qualities, in contrast to Pratchett's medieval-inspired elves, stands as a reminder that humanity is not determined by one's species, but by one's actions and that one's capacity to change rests not on one's supposed nature but on one's willingness to learn. For "If you learn things," Tiffany suggests, "you might learn to build a different kind of kingdom" (*Shepherd's Crown* 212).

Notes

1. The term "English" here refers specifically to the cultural and linguistic traditions of the Anglo-Saxons, as opposed to those of the Britons, Picts, and other groups indigenous to the British Isles. Examples of these early Anglo-Saxon texts include such works as *Beowulf, Bald's Leechbook, Leechbook III*, the *Lacnunga*, and the Anglo-Saxon metrical charms. While contemporary fantasy writers can and do draw from broader folkloric traditions, generally thought of as "British" versus "English," this essay focuses on the extent to which Anglo-Saxon themes are present in Pratchett's work.

2. Pratchett's elves make their first appearance in the novel *Lords and Ladies* (1992), and it is here that Pratchett first begins experimenting with the conventions of medieval Anglo-Saxon folklore. Since many of the themes present in *Lord and Ladies* carry over to and are expanded upon in the Tiffany series, I have chosen to narrow my focus to *The Wee Free Men* and *The Shepherd's Crown*, both of which capitalize on the implications of elfin morality initially presented in *Lords and Ladies*.

3. The legends surrounding Arken Hill in the *Wee Free Men* resemble the passage in *Beowulf* (2232–2277) describing how the dragon came to reside in the "beorh eallgearo," which Roy Liuzza translates as "a waiting barrow" (2241). While this is not enough to prove a direct correlation to the text, the evocation of dragons, treasure, and barrows certainly underscores Anglo-Saxon cultural beliefs surrounding these structures. The word beorg can also be translated as "hill" or "mountain" (McGillivray 184). Additionally, one can draw comparisons between the dragon story here and the medieval legend of Saint George, who slew "a plague-bearing dragon" known to "poison everyone who came within reach of his breath" (De Voragine 238).

4. In her article "On the Origin of Fairies: Victorians, Romantics, and Folk Belief," Carole Silver reports that Dadd claimed to have actually *seen* the fairies he painted "when they modeled for his Bedlam masterpiece" (Silver 145).

5. For a similar description of the Queen's very first unmasking by the former witch Magrat Garlick, see *Lords and Ladies* (255–6).

WORKS CITED

Bonser, Wilfrid. "Magical Practices Against Elves." *Folklore*, vol. 37, no. 4, 1926, pp. 350–363. *JSTOR*, url: http://www.jstor.org/stable/1256144.

De Voragine, Jacobus. "Saint George." *The Golden Legend: Readings on the Saints*, translated by William Granger Ryan, Princeton Univ. Press, 1993, pp. 238–242.

Hall, Alaric. *Elves in Anglo-Saxon England: Matters of Belief, Health, Gender, and Identity*, Anglo-Saxon Studies, vol. 8, Boydell, 2007.

Jolly, Karen Louise. "Elves, Demons, and Other Mind Altering Afflictions: Evidences of Popular Practices." *Popular Religion in Late Saxon England: Elf Charms in Context*, U of North Carolina P, 1996, pp. 132–168.

Liuzza, R.M, translator. *Beowulf*. 2d ed., Broadview Press, 2013.

McGillivray, Murray. *Old English Reader*. Claremont: Broadview Press, 2011.

Pratchett, Terry. "A Conversation with Terry Pratchett, Author of *The Carpet People*." *BoingBoing*, 5 November. 2013, https://boingboing.net/2013/11/05/a-conversation-with-terry-prat.html

———. *Lords and Ladies*. Harper Torch, 1992.

———. *The Shepherd's Crown*. HarperCollins Publishers, 2015.

———. *The Wee Free Men*. HarperCollins Publishers, 2003.

Semple, Sarah. "A Fear of the Past: The Place of the Prehistoric Burial Mound in the Ideology of Middle and Later Anglo-Saxon England." *World Archaeology* vol. 30, no. 1, Jun. 1998, pp. 109–26. *JSTOR*. url: http://www.jstor.org/stable/125012.

Silver, Carole. "On the Origin of Fairies: Victorians, Romantics, and Folk Belief." *Browning Institute Studies*, vol. 14, The Victorian Threshold, 1986, pp. 141–156. *JSTOR*, url: http://www.jstor.org/stable/25057792.

Simpson, Jacqueline. "On the Ambiguity of Elves." *Folklore* vol. 122, no. 1, Apr. 2011, pp. 76–83. *JSTOR*, url: http://www.jstor.org.libproxy.csudh.edu/stable/41306567. Web. 5 Mar. 2015.

Stuart, H. "The Anglo-Saxon Elf." *Studia Neophilologica*, vol. 48, 1976, pp. 313–20.

Constructing Identity Through Language in Discworld

Elise A. Bell

When writers give voice to a character, the language they choose conveys (at least) two levels of intent. First is the intent of the author: what should this character's speech say about them to the reader? Second is the intent of the character, whose mind the writer must inhabit to answer the question "What should my speech convey to my listeners?" Skilled authors manage both levels, giving their characters voices within the narrative informed by, but separate from the author's own. Terry Pratchett uses a variety of linguistic manipulations in his Discworld series to work on both these levels. Commonalities in language link members of each group together and also distinguish humans and other non-human groups from each other. Furthermore, the group-level linguistic characteristics serve to evoke stereotypes about real-world language use, and to demonstrate how particular aspects of language use reflect both positively and negatively on speakers. On the level of the character, we see individuals from each group taking advantage of their linguistic creativity to forge their own personal identity, while on the level of the author, Pratchett's colorful descriptions of non-human languages provide a baseline perception of each group. I explore these tactics as they apply to four non-human groups on the Discworld: trolls, Igors, dwarfs, and goblins.

Before beginning to discuss the linguistic features that set these groups apart, the norm from which they differ must first be defined. While English is the language the novels are written in, Morporkian is the language the characters speak, and it is "standard" Morporkian that provides a baseline against which the speech of others on the Discworld is judged. Throughout,

I refer to a standard dialect of Morporkian, much as a standard dialect of English is referred to in the real world. The standard, which may or may not be the most commonly spoken form of the language, is considered to be the variety that is spoken by the privileged class, and generally conforms closely to the written language. In American English, this standard (American Standard English or ASE) is often referred to as "newscaster" speech. In the UK, Received Pronunciation (RP) was once considered to be the target standard dialect, but has in recent decades declined due to the introduction of local dialects into national broadcasting services. When discussing language through the lens of the field of linguistics, a distinction between *prescriptive* and *descriptive* language analysis must be made. *Prescriptive* grammar is the kind that tells you to never split an infinitive or end a sentence with a preposition, based on archaic rules devised by grammarians who wanted English to conform to the rules of Latin. It is often used as a method of determining who belongs to a particular group, based on the way they speak. *Descriptive* grammar, on the other hand, is value neutral; all dialects are equally valuable and equally grammatical. Where prescriptive grammar would claim that the standard language is the best or most proper way of speaking, descriptive linguistics proposes that the standard is no more or less valuable than any other language variety.

Language is value neutral, but linguistic discrimination remains a major issue in the struggle for equality by most, if not all, marginalized groups. Consider the linguistic stereotypes held by American culture. Non-standard speech is often associated with stupidity, and therefore stupidity is associated with non-standard speakers. This association is spurious, but persistent. African American Vernacular English (AAVE) is a prime example of a dialect of English which, while perfectly grammatical according to its own linguistic rules, does not necessarily align with the grammar of Standard American English (Green 2002). Speaking AAVE indicates nothing more about a speaker than that they speak AAVE, and yet the dialect has been at the center of racial discrimination in education, housing equality, politics, and more for decades. An example closer to home for Pratchett is the association of class stereotypes with specific dialects of British English. Speaking RP is associated with wealth, education, and the upper classes, while speaking with a Cockney accent (sometimes called Estuary English) is associated with poverty, ignorance, and a lower social station. If any dialect of English in Britain can be called standard British English, it may be the Popular London accent, which falls somewhere between the broadest Cockney and the most refined RP (Wells 1982). Other linguistic stereotypes abound, interacting with every social, regional, sexual, or racial contrast in the English-speaking world.

As happens all too often in the real world, the so-called standard speaker of Morporkian, for the purposes of this discussion, is a middle-aged white man. In the case of Discworld, the closest the series provides to a speaker of standard Morporkian is His Grace, the Duke of Ankh, Commander Sir Samuel "Blackboard Monitor" Vimes of the Ankh-Morpork City Watch. Vimes is a native speaker of Morporkian, born and raised in Ankh-Morpork. Although he comes from a lower-class background, his speech does not generally diverge from what might be considered an Ankh-Morpork standard (compare Vimes' speech to that of Havelock Vetinari, the Patrician, whose upper class pedigree is not in doubt). Vimes is generally positioned as the everyman protagonist in the novels in which he appears. Vimes' nature as an observer, and his position as commander of the Watch, also contribute to his suitability as a baseline speaker: he has both the means and motivation to observe the speech (and other mannerisms) of all those he encounters, human or non-human.

Vimes' voice provides color, informing the reader of the prejudices humans hold against various non-human groups which he himself shares, despite his willingness to respect (or not) individuals on their own merits: "Just because someone's a member of an ethnic minority doesn't mean they're not a nasty small-minded little jerk" (*Feet of Clay*). Throughout the series, Vimes encounters one non-human species after another, generally when he, as commander of the City Watch, is pressured to hire a member of said species, or when they appear as a villain or scapegoat in the course of his duties.

In the following sections, I explore the linguistic features Pratchett assigns to each non-human group, including his characterization of their native language (if any) and how each group's spoken Morporkian is represented textually. Subsequently, the contributions made by both these linguistic representations are examined in the light of the real-world stereotypes they are intended to evoke, and how these stereotypes contribute to readers' perception of the characters and groups in question.

Trolls: "You might not be as stupid as you look" (Men at Arms)

Trolls are a non-human species of sentient beings made of living rock. The troll homeland is in the mountains of Uberwald, but many trolls have immigrated to Ankh-Morpork to make a better life for themselves and their children. Detritus, the first troll sergeant in the City Watch, explains to Vimes the circumstances in which he relocated to Ankh-Morpork from Uberwald: "I was a just a pebble when we left dere. Dad wanted a better life in der big city" (*The Fifth Elephant*).

While the native Troll language is never described in any great detail, from the few words ("oograh," "goohuloog," "groophar") Pratchett provides throughout the series, it appears both simplistic and foreign. This perception of simplicity is contradicted in the elaborate Morporkian paraphrases that are supposedly necessary to define a single troll word. For example, the troll word "aagragaah" is translated as "lit'rally der time when you see dem little pebbles an' you jus' know there's gonna be a great big landslide on toppa you and it already too late to run" (*Jingo*). Of course, this paraphrase is not actually necessary, the word could just as easily be translated as "foreboding," but doing so would erode the characterization of Troll as opaque and unknowable to human listeners.[1]

Because examples of the native Troll language are scarce, it is more productive to examine differences between Morporkian as spoken by trolls as compared to the standard represented by Sam Vimes. The most prolific example of troll speech in the Discworld is that of Sergeant Detritus. Although he appeared for the first time in *Guards! Guards!*, Detritus subsequently became a staple character in the City Watch subseries of novels, beginning with *Men at Arms*, when he was inducted as the first troll member of the Watch. Detritus and other trolls' speech differs from that of most Discworld humans in two major ways: in the sound system of their dialect, and in the grammatical structures they use in speech.

Because all speech in the novels must be represented in textual form, the only way to indicate differences in accent is through manipulation of spelling. Pratchett uses a small set of spelling alterations fairly consistently throughout the series in the representation of troll speech. First is the regular substitution of "d" for the "th" found at the beginning of words such as "that." The "th" sound found at the beginning of "thing" is also subject to alteration and replacement by "f." Examples of both these substitutions abound in Detritus' speech: "Yeah, dere used to be a lot of dat sort of fing in der old days.... Dey wouldn't be de real diamond teef, o'course" (*The Fifth Elephant*). Other orthographic indications of accent also occur throughout Detritus' speech, including sound deletion ("of course" becomes "o'course"), vowel alternations (spelling "the" as "der" indicates that it should rhyme not with "tree" but with "huh," assuming deletion of syllable final "r" sounds as part of a baseline British English accent), and reduction of verbs ending in -ing to "in."

The majority of pronunciation differences in troll speech are associated in the real world with negative characteristics based in racist and classist prejudice, due to the stigma attached to the real-world dialects which use these features (including African American Vernacular English, Cockney English, and others). Intentionally or not, Pratchett's work evokes these negative characteristics, which include laziness, lack of intelligence, and a lack of education, in his representation of troll speech, simply through the manipulation of orthography.

Also common in written troll speech is the phenomenon of "eye dialect," or the changing of a word's spelling in a way that does not alter its pronunciation. The spelling of "was" as "wuz," "been" as "bin," or "stupid" as "stoopid" does not necessarily convey any real information about a character's speech, but still successfully conveys a lack of intelligence or education. Eye dialect relies on the reader's knowledge and recognition of the misspelling to formulate the desired perception, and succeeds because of the conflation of inaccurate spelling with the non-standard or speech of those stereotyped as ignorant.

Grammatical differences between troll speech and the Morporkian standard are also fairly consistent throughout the series, if not as consistent as the orthographic changes described above. One of the most consistent patterns of grammatical difference is the lack of a "to be" verb (a feature that linguists refer to as "zero copula") in the speech of many trolls. In *Men at Arms*, for example, Sergeant Detritus says, "You in the Watch now," omitting the word "are." Many, but not all, dialects of English require a "to be" verb for this sentence to be grammatical, but others, including African American Vernacular English, can grammatically omit the copula in many sentence types. In a similar vein, Detritus also occasionally uses copulas that are in grammatical disagreement between the subject and object of a sentence: "Der street doors is open" and "Watchmen is watchmen" (*The Fifth Elephant*). Where standard Morporkian requires "are," the plural conjugation of the copula, Detritus and other trolls often use the singular "is." The omission of articles "a" and "the" is common in troll speech: "Dis is your club with nail in it!" (*Men at Arms*). In combination, these grammatical features elicit the perception of troll speech as not only non-fluent, but non-fluent in a way that also conveys stupidity.[2]

The idea conveyed by the written representation of troll speech is that they are essentially stupid. This assumption generally goes unquestioned within the narrative, and is often lampooned by Pratchett to humorous effect. Trolls knock themselves out while saluting, drink battery acid to become intoxicated, and regularly fail to remember that "When Mister Safety Catch Is Not On, Mister Crossbow Is Not Your Friend" (*Night Watch*). In *Men at Arms*, however, we learn that trolls are not naturally as unintelligent as they usually appear. When Detritus and Cuddy (a dwarf officer of the Watch) are trapped in the freezing temperatures of the pork futures warehouse, Detritus' normally slow brain function improves. As troll brains are silicon-based, their minds function more efficiently at lower temperatures, much like a real-world computer: "Detritus's silicon based brain was, as with most trolls, highly sensitive to changes in temperature. When the thermometer was very low he could be dangerously intellectual" (*Men at Arms*). The emergence of Detritus' intelligence due to the drop in temperature appears linguistically in several ways. Detritus' grammar standardizes ("You're alive," "it looks like a mild skin abrasion"), his vocabulary improves ("I can calculate your trajectory with astonishing precision"), and his characteristic troll accents essentially vanishes ("There are small glazed apertures up there"). All these effects are sadly lost when he is removed from the warehouse's freezing temperatures.[3] The general characterization of trolls as stupid, then, is not due to their innate abilities, but rather to their environment. Trolls who have chosen to leave the mountains and live in the warmer climate of Ankh-Morpork pay with their intellect.

The linguistic features of troll speech work together to characterize them as unintelligent to any reader who is generally familiar with the linguistic stereotypes against almost any modern dialects of non-standard English. Pratchett takes advantage of the stereotypes lurking in the minds of his readers, which ascribe negative qualities to particular accents or dialects of English based on the stereotypical and prejudicial negative qualities assigned to speakers of those accents or dialects. While trolls are not an overt racial analogue to any real group of people, in harnessing the power of extant racially coded linguistic stereotypes, Pratchett indirectly conveys the similarity of Discworld humans' attitude toward trolls to similar racial and class prejudices held by many in the real world.

Igors: "We don't athk quethtionth" (Making Money)

Of all the groups of non-humans represented in the Discworld series, Igors are one of the most homogenous. First introduced in *Carpe Jugulum*, the appearance and speech of Igors evokes the stereotype of the hunchbacked, lisping assistant to the mad scientist of classic horror films. Igors generally share a similar physical appearance, and the same speech characteristics. In *The Fifth Elephant*, Vimes is introduced to multiple Igors, who he repeatedly fails to differentiate before learning to take into account the small details, including the number of forehead stitches and potentially also of fingers.

The characteristic lisp of the Igors is one of the most consistently represented linguistic features throughout the series, and serves to immediately bring a host of characteristics to mind whenever a new Igor is introduced. The consistent lisp of the traditional Igor is realized throughout the series by the substitution of "th" for the sounds "s," "z," or "sh": "Jutht Igor, thir. Alwayth ... jutht Igor" (*The Fifth Elephant*). This is consistent with patterns of lisping in the real world, where a lisp is generally considered to be a physical attribute influencing a person's speech. In early introductions to traditional Discworld Igors, their lisps do appear to be physically based, and appear invariable.[4]

In later books, including *The Fifth Elephant* and *Monstrous Regiment*, readers are introduced to Igors who do not belong to this traditional generation. In *The Fifth Elephant*, Vimes meets a young Igor who is being sent by his father to Ankh-Morpork, where "hith thlight thpeech impediment" won't count against him as it does in Uberwald. This "slight speech impediment," of course, is young Igor's failure to lisp consistently. He occasionally pronounces "thir" as "sir," and neglects to lisp in other suitable environments: "I grow them in special vats. I can do eyes and fingers, too!" (*The Fifth Elephant*). What Igor describes as speech impediment appears to actually be an intentional linguistic choice on the part of young Igor. What better way to set yourself apart from your family than to make sure you don't sound like them? The revelation that an Igor's lisp is more of a performative cultural affectation than a physical necessity is confirmed in *Monstrous Regiment* with the introduction of Igorina.

Igorina is the most overt example throughout the Discworld series of a character not only consciously altering their speech in order to be perceived differently, but also admitting that the change in question was made for the sake of "style," and that in general, female Igors "don't lisp as much as the boys. It's a style thing." In Discworld, as in the real world, speech is one of many tools available in the performance of gender identity. As a social construct, gender is by nature performative, and consciously or not, we all take part. Throughout *Monstrous Regiment*, characters deal with the performative nature of gender. Characters who identify as women alter their clothing, movement, interactional style, and speech in order to be perceived as men, in their successful attempts to join the Borogravian army. For Igorina, out of all the recruits, physical changes are the easiest. Her hair is easily removable (and later, reattachable), and the forehead stitches worn by male Igors are simple to adopt. To alter her speech to match that of a male Igor, she simply had to "remember to lisp." In the end, it was only her failure to do so consistently that led to her companions discovering her deception.

Igorina's adoption of the appearance and speech patterns characteristic of male Igors was voluntarily undertaken, and did not represent her personal gender identification. While she performed masculinity, she remained female-identified. For other characters in Discworld, however, changes in performative gender are neither so elective nor easily achievable.

Dwarfs: "Gender is more or less optional" (Guards! Guards!)

Corporal Cheery (pronounced "Cherie") Littlebottom, a dwarf employed by the City Watch, is one of the first, if not the first, dwarfs to adopt human trappings of femininity in her dress and personal style. To other dwarfs, this makes her an anomaly, and potentially a threat to dwarfish society as a whole. It is important to note that this threat is not leveled against her because of her gender/sex identity (after all, statistically speaking, 50 percent of the dwarfs judging her are also female), but rather because of her decision to openly identify as female. Cheery is greeted with open hostility by other dwarfs on more than one occasion: "B'dan? K'raa! D'kraga 'ha'ak'!" Vimes saw the expression that appeared on Cheery's small round face. Above him there was a clunk as Detritus rested the loaded Piecemaker on the edge of the coach. "I know dat word he said to her.... It is not a good word. I do not want to hear dat word again" (*The Fifth Elephant*).

In traditional dwarf culture, the human concept of "gender" is irrelevant, at least performatively. The only gender is "dwarf," and a dwarf's biological sex is considered irrelevant to anyone but the dwarf in question until such a time as they decide it is relevant for any personal relationships they may be engaged in. As Pratchett describes in *The Fifth Elephant*, "It was simply that they also saw no point in distinguishing between the sexes anywhere but in private."

While Igorina altered her speech in an effort to disguise and alter others' perception of her gender, Cheery Littlebottom undertakes these actions in attempting to *reveal* her true gender identity. Leaving the issue of biological sex aside, when Cheery arrives in Ankh-Morpork and realizes upon learning about the existence of human women, and the feminine gender in general, she begins to identify herself as feminine as well. When Cheery alters her appearance and dress to more closely align with those of human women, she also adopts the Morporkian female pronouns "she" and "her." While this change is not described as difficult for Cheery's human friends and coworkers in Ankh-Morpork to adapt to, it is met with scorn, derision, and disgust among other dwarfs, particularly those traditional "deep-down" dwarfs known as grags (and their supporters).

Because "There [is] no such thing as a Dwarfish female pronoun" (*The Fifth Elephant*), or indeed gendered pronoun contrasts at all, unless a preference otherwise has been stated, dwarfs are generally referred to using "he" in Morporkian. Traditional dwarfs openly oppose the idea of female identification, regarding it as "un-dwarfish" and even unnatural. In Discworld, while humans are used to the concept of a gender binary and generally have no trouble referring to Cheery with feminine pronouns once she begins to dress in a traditionally human feminine way, dwarfs often struggle. In *The Fifth Elephant*, the Low King of the Dwarfs begins to use feminine pronouns to refer to Dee, his advisor, immediately after she reveals her long-suppressed identification as female. "Take ... her away," he says, and despite his hesitation, the king's immediate attempt to alter his speech patterns for the comfort of others is clear (and indeed later indicates to Cheery that he himself is interested in assuming traditionally feminine traits as well).

This change is only apparent when speaking Morporkian, because Dwarfish does not make a gender distinction in its pronouns (*The Fifth Elephant*). Where English or Morporkian would use "she" or "he" (or "her/him"), Dwarfish speakers would use a single pronoun which does not contain any information about the person's gender, much like singular "they" is used in English for someone whose gender is unknown.

While Pratchett's intentions are not explicitly stated, there is an obvious analogue to be seen between Cheery's struggles with her gender identity and the struggles faced by transgender, non-binary, and other gender nonconforming people in the real world. However, in discussing the gender politics of dwarfish culture, Pratchett avoids mentioning both sexual orientation and biological sex, the former hopefully due to oversight from his personal perspective, but the latter likely due to a conflation of gender and biological sex. The question of dwarf gender becomes much more interesting when these two notions are divorced, and a dwarf's identification as female does not necessarily imply anything about their biology.

Describing Cheery's decision to begin dressing in female-coded clothing, Pratchett implies that she has a natural affinity for female-coded clothing, etc., and that once she was exposed to it in Ankh-Morpork, she adopted the aspects of it which appealed to her (makeup, jewelry, hair and beard grooming, and of course, a small sparkly decoration on her traditional battle axe). Cheery's enthusiasm in *Feet of Clay* for Ankh-Morpork standards of feminine dress and behavior ("...you can wear *dresses*! With *colors*!") is one of many hints that Cheery's gendered behavior is due to her biological sex. In doing so, the author makes the assumption that feminine coded appearance is intrinsically linked to gender and sex. This is not in truth the case, not in the real world, and one would presume not in Discworld either, whether or not Pratchett chose to demonstrate that to us in the novels.[5]

Gender identity and the linguistic stereotypes associated with it in the real world are not as solid or monolithic as Pratchett makes them out to be in his descriptions of Cheery and dwarfish culture. Identifying with a gender not assigned at birth can involve much more than an adjustment of wardrobe and pronouns; as Cheery experiences, the greater challenge is not to alter herself, but to alter the world around her.

Goblins: "An entire race reduced to vermin" (Vetinari, Snuff)

Although goblins, as a group, were introduced fairly late in the Discworld series, the linguistic situations and conflicts they face are some of the most complex in the series. It was not until the publication of *Snuff* that goblin culture and language were described in any depth. *Snuff* introduces goblins through the eyes of humans. They are described as "vermin" by Lord Vetinari, and as "stinking, cannibalistic, vicious, untrustworthy bastards" by Vimes. However, Vimes' perception of goblins begins to change when he becomes involved in solving the murder of a goblin girl at the bequest of a goblin who pleads with Vimes for "just ice."

The goblin language (or "heathen lingo" as *Snuff*'s Chief Constable Feeney calls it) is described as sounding like "somebody cracking walnuts under their foot," "a man jumping up and down on a very large packet of crisps," and "crunchy chattering" to human ears, harsh and impossible to understand. However, Miss Felicity Beedle, whose human mother was raised by goblins, informs Vimes that beneath the harsh auditory exterior, "They have the most complex language you could possibly imagine.... The meaning of every word is contingent on the words around it, the speaker, the listener, the time of year, the weather, oh, and so many other things" (*Snuff*). The way that Miss Beedle describes the goblin language employs a number of linguistic tropes that are often used in the real world to exoticize foreign languages.

The claim that some languages have "strange," "unusual," or particularly "complex" sounds or structures assumes, falsely, that there is such a thing as a "usual" language. While it is the case that the world's languages have many features in common, this is due to the fact that all human languages are spoken by humans, using the human vocal tract.[6] Some common misconceptions about "exotic" languages are the idea that "Eskimo" (more properly Inuit) has more than one hundred words for snow ("There's Snow Synonym"), that some languages either have no way to communicate a relatively simple concept in English (such as "hello") or that other languages have "untranslatable" words for which English has no possible equivalent.

This last claim is an example of the often-misunderstood Sapir-Whorf hypothesis, which in its strong version proposes that the language a person speaks determines how they see the world. In past linguistic research, this has taken the form of claiming that speakers of a language which does not have a numeric system will never learn how to count in another language (Dan Everett's work on Pirahã). Many linguists reject the strong Sapir-Whorf hypothesis, but accept the weak version, which proposes that a person's native language may influence, but does not determine, their world view (Baghramian and Carter). For example, languages which require speakers to convey the method by which they acquired reported information (a linguistic property known as evidentiality) may have the effect of influencing speakers to prioritize that knowledge in their observation of the world. Speakers of languages which do not require evidentiality markers are still capable of this type of observation ("I *saw* that it was raining," "I *heard* that it was raining"), but are less likely to prioritize it as a communicative necessity. Asserting that the complexity and beauty of the goblin language enable its speakers to see the world in a different way than humans is an assertion by Pratchett of the strong version of the Sapir-Whorf hypothesis.

Miss Beedle's description of Goblin as "the most complex language you could possibly imagine" valorizes the language, and sets it on a pedestal to be admired. Human speakers of Morporkian cannot grasp the complexities of the language, but goblins can, and do. And because they master and use such a remarkable language, they too must be remarkable. While languages do not intrinsically carry value of their own, Goblin is able to lend value to its speakers by sole virtue of its supposed complexity and impenetrability.

Depictions of goblin identity throughout *Snuff* are best illustrated through a comparison between three specific goblins: Stinky, Billy Slick, and Tears of the Mushroom. All three speak Morporkian as a second language, and it is in the different realizations of their non-native accent and grammar that Pratchett characterizes their different backgrounds and relationships to both goblin and human society. Although it is not explicitly stated, the fluency and comfort with which each character speaks Morporkian reveals that they likely acquired the language in different ways, either through necessity (Stinky), bilingually (Billy Slick), or through formal education (Tears of the Mushroom).

Stinky lives on the outskirts of human society rather than with his fellow goblins. He interacts with humanity on a survival basis, taking odd jobs when he needs to, but making little to no effort to blend in with humans or adapt to human culture. Nevertheless, Stinky successfully interacts with Vimes and other human characters, although his distinctive use of Morporkian sets him apart. Stinky's speech in Morporkian is designed to seem non-fluent, apparently picked up from villagers who despise him. He has an extensive vocabulary and an idiosyncratic grammar in Morporkian, which tends to omit determiners ("the," "a"), tense markers ("will"), and copulas ("is," "are"): "Big trouble, fellow po-leess-maan colleague? Big trouble for a man scared of horses. Damn right!? Hate horse, can smell fear. You take me, po-leess-maan. I fix. No worry" (*Snuff*). *Snuff*, unfortunately, does not provide enough evidence to indicate whether Stinky's non-standard speech is simply the result of learning Morporkian as a second language, or if a goblin–Morporkian pidgin has begun to develop. Altogether, Stinky's non-standard grammar could easily have the effect of portraying him as stupid, were it not for other utterances such as, "There is no race so wretched that there is not something out there that cares for them, Mr. Vimes." By contrasting Stinky's usual cobbled together disfluencies in Morporkian with this perfectly standard utterance, Pratchett ensures that Stinky is taken seriously, not only by Vimes, but by the reader as well.

Billy Slick might well be Stinky's polar opposite. Rather than avoiding assimilation to human culture, Billy actively works to adopt it. Billy is introduced in *Snuff* as a goblin living on the outskirts of Ankh-Morpork, working for Harry King's night soil business. His manner of speaking is essentially human, not very different from the speech of any native Ankh-Morpork human from the lower classes. Billy makes an effort to appear and sound as little like a goblin as possible, wishing to distance himself from the perceptions of his species. When asked why he calls himself Billy rather than a more traditional goblin name, he sneers. "Granny calls me Of the Wind Regretfully Blown. What kind of name is that, I ask you? Who's going to take you seriously with a name like that? This is modern times, right.... Why the fruckle should anyone be proud of being a goblin?" (*Snuff*).

Although Billy still speaks and understands the goblin language, and uses it to translate for his grandmother, if he could, he would abandon the language and his native culture entirely. Billy's desire to assimilate to the culture of the majority echoes the struggle faced by children of immigrant parents in many real-world countries. Many descendants of immigrant families feel caught by the differences between their heritage language and culture and that of the local community. For example, consider Syrian refugees in Britain, or Mexican immigrants in the United States, who are under great pressure to learn English and adopt the cultural practices of their new country. This dilemma often leads to the loss of intergenerational transmission of the native language, as well as to a feeling of separation from the heritage culture, whether willing or unwilling.

While Billy Slick adopts the language and culture of Ankh-Morpork in order to distance himself from the stigma of being a goblin, Tears of the Mushroom does so in order to demonstrate the personhood of goblins to the world at large. Educated by the human Miss Felicity Beedle, Tears of the Mushroom speaks Morporkian in a manner affected by the different grammatical structure of her native language, which Vimes describes as "pulling words out of a rack and then tidily putting them back in their places as soon as they had been said." While her voice still resembles "half a dozen coconuts rolling downstairs" or "a living filing cabinet," her spoken Morporkian is essentially fluent, although clearly non-native. It is her mastery of human language, as well as her uncanny musical ability, that begins to break the barrier of prejudice and hatred held by humans against goblins for eons. Ideally, the acceptance of goblins as (non-human) people in their own right would not be predicated on their ability to adopt human culture: in a truly egalitarian version of the Discworld, goblins would be accepted on their own merits. But just as in the real world, in the Discworld, it is sadly only accommodation to the norms and customs of the powerful that is the key to achieving a level of respect which should have been present all along.

Analogies between the goblins of Discworld and the struggles faced by real world immigrant and refugee communities are easily drawn, particularly when it comes to the variation in language background and use. Stinky and Billy Slick represent the past and present of goblin-kind, existing on the outskirts of human society without the opportunity to assimilate, but Tears of the Mushroom represents the future, and everything that goblins can and will be, when given the respect and inclusion they deserve and have been so long denied.

Conclusion

Throughout the Discworld novels, Pratchett maintains a series of fairly consistent orthographic and grammatical choices in the representation of his characters' speech. He draws upon the cultural consciousness of his readers, taking advantage of the conscious and unconscious social biases acquired simply by living in society. Using linguistic variation and contrasting the speech of non-human characters and groups with an unacknowledged but present linguistic "norm," Pratchett invokes stereotypical perceptions on the one hand, and challenges or overturns them on the other. However, although it is tempting to ascribe only the purest of motivations to Pratchett, it is also important to acknowledge that there are more often than not racial, class, and ethnic stereotypes underlying the characterizations evoked, although it is important to acknowledge Pratchett's long history of critiquing these assumptions as well. Is the invocation of real-world stereotypes damaging to readers who are among those groups being lampooned, or who may find their own speech represented more accurately by characters who are presented as less than intelligent, less than capable, or less than human? That question can only be answered by the reader on an individual basis.

Despite the clear cultural and linguistic differences that set them apart, the humanity of Pratchett's non-human characters is never in doubt. Trolls, Igors, dwarfs, and goblins serve as analogies of varying clarity to real world marginalized groups. They may not be *homo sapiens*, they may not fit into the mold of an average citizen of the Disc, but they are *people*. Idiosyncrasies of speech mark differences, and set groups apart from each other, but the ways individuals craft their personal identities through language remind the reader of the shared humanity of the characters in the Discworld. Angua, in *The Fifth Elephant*, sums it up best: "and so one at a time we all become human—human werewolves, human dwarfs, human trolls ... the melting pot melts in one direction only, and so we make progress."

Notes

1. Of course, Pratchett's sense of humor in the construction of this definition should not be ignored; 'aagragaah' being the sound one makes before being killed in an avalanche cannot be taken entirely seriously.

2. Readers may notice that several examples of Detritus' speech contain words that are inconsistent with the general description of Troll grammar. There is no discernable pattern to these inconsistencies, so I do not attempt to analyze them here.

3. Interestingly, the speech of Chrysophrase, Ankh-Morpork's troll equivalent of a mob boss, conducts his business in the same freezing environment of the pork futures warehouse, presumably for the beneficial effect the temperature has on his mental ability (*Thud!*). However, unlike Detritus', Chrysophrase's accent does not standardize in the cold: "Now den, Mr. Vimes, you know dat don't exist.... Dere's no call for name-callin.'" One of the potential explanations for this is that in later novels (*Thud!* as compared to *Men at Arms*), Pratchett concluded that the non-standard aspects of the troll accent were not in fact markers of impeded intelligence, but rather a value neutral aspect of their dialect of Morporkian. It is also possible that Chryoprase's unwavering accent is an affectation used to perform 'trollness' for the benefit of his human audience.

4. Mel Brooks' *Young Frankenstein* (1974) is almost certainly an influence on Pratchett's depiction of Igors and their speech patterns.

5. Also worth considering, but beyond the scope of this paper, is the development of the feminine dwarf fashion industry as depicted in *Unseen Academicals*.

6. Signed languages, of course, do not rely on the human vocal tract, but are still limited by the nature of human physiology and dexterity.

Works Cited

Baghramian, Maria, and Carter, J. Adam, "Relativism," *The Stanford Encyclopedia of Philosophy* (Summer 2017 Edition), Edward N. Zalta (ed.), https://plato.stanford.edu/archives/sum2017/entries/relativism/.
Editorial. "There's Snow Synonym." *New York Times*, February 9, 1984.
Everett, D., Berlin, B., Gonalves, M., Kay, P., Levinson, S., Pawley, A., ... & Everett, D. (2005). Cultural constraints on grammar and cognition in Pirahã: Another look at the design features of human language. *Current Anthropology*, 46(4), 621–646.
Green, L.J. (2002). *African American English: A Linguistic Introduction*. Cambridge UP.
Wells, J.C. (1982). *Accents of English* (Vol. 2). Cambridge UP.

Rhetoricity of Discworld

Magic and the Ethics of Footnotes

AMY LEA CLEMONS

Terry Pratchett's Discworld series is one that is very aware of its own ethics of language; taking postmodernism at its word, Discworld's physics quite literally allow language and stories to constitute reality.[1] In *Wyrd Sisters,* the Fool's thoughts most clearly explain this notion: "Wizards and witches used words as if they were tools to get things done, but the Fool reckoned that words were things in their own right" (185).[2] Through their words, or rather, through the choices the characters make in the style, timing, and content of those words, the Discworld and its characters are changed in real ways that have real consequences for the story. In other words, pun intended, a major driving force in the Discworld series is what we might broadly call "rhetoric" or "rhetoricity"—the transformative ability of speech, writing, and art.

Through the 41 Discworld books, then, we might be able to construct a Pratchettian rhetorical theory: a declaration of how language works *on* audiences to construct reality and how rhetors *should* use such magical tools. But in these books, too, we see Pratchett not just explaining his theory of rhetoric-as-magic through his characters, but performing that rhetoric himself as Wayne Booth's "implied author." The narrator of the Discworld series both points the audience to an interpretation and provides a space of linguistic ambiguity and play that calls for a cooperative meaning-making process instead of an absolute authoritative statement of truth. While some fantasy genre narrators seek to speak a kind of universal myth or truth (the *Lord of the Rings* series or the *Chronicles of Narnia,* for example), through the use of satire, Pratchett's narrator asks their[3] audience to enjoy the construction of the diegesis and their relationship to it.

First, this essay reviews the relationship between magic and rhetoric, noting how both terms carry with them questions of identity and authority with implications for ethics. The essay then reviews Discworld's version of those rhetorics as seen in Granny Weatherwax's "headology," Samuel Vimes' appeals to the Law, and Carrot Ironfoundersson's ease of identification and persuasion through charisma. The essay finally turns to the ways that Pratchett uses that rhetoric to act on his audiences—what "spells" he chooses to put on his readers through his storytelling that is either similar to the practices of his characters or a correction of it. Ultimately, this essay argues that Pratchett's understanding of rhetoric-as-magic leads him to perform a more ethical rhetoric than what his characters manage, taking care of his audience through the literary techniques of the implied author's style and his infamous footnotes.

Word Magic in Rhetorical Theory

Most scholars today avoid a simple conflation of rhetoric with deception or mere persuasion, but the affective and symbolic power of rhetoric remains lodged in our collective consciousness as something to be concerned about. While the term "rhetoric" has been in the process of reclamation for several decades now, the application of rhetorical theories to fiction is still an uncommon method in literary studies. For a series like Discworld, though, rhetoric is both a literary technique and a theme of the text, because of the series' inclusion of symbolic magic as a major force in the storyworld. A book like *Soul Music*, for example, mashes up the histories of multiple iconic rock bands and singers to argue that music is a life force that can even (temporarily) overcome Death; music, like literature, has a magical quality that mixes aesthetics with persuasion, moving an audience from one state of being and feeling to another. This kind of rhetoric is not the kind of argumentative speech we often teach students, but, as Kenneth Burke argues in *Counter-Statement*, it is extremely effective, since it works at the level of the body: the rhythm of music and poetry, the adrenaline-creating suspense of a well-structured story, and the sense of satisfaction we get from the logic of narrative form measurable responses in the human body, just like a curse or a blessing from a witch.[4]

This relationship between magic and rhetoric is an old one, rhetorician William Covino reminds us. Covino's book *Magic, Rhetoric, and Literacy: An Eccentric History of the Composing Imagination* traces the title's three terms through Western history to discover how they have often been synonymous, or at least strongly associated.[5] Given Discworld's generically European setting and connections between Ankh-Morpork to the history of the Roman empire, medieval England, and the British Empire, Covino's project is a particularly useful tool with which to interrogate the series; his first chapter traces both the classical and medieval treatments of the intersections of language and magic, historicizing his definitions of his terms with a lengthy literature review of the topics.[6] The connection between magic and rhetoric is fairly obvious: "Making language has long been regarded as, in some sense, magical; as a *spell*" (5). Because both magic and rhetoric work by using symbols to constitute reality and create change, the two have long been collapsed into a single idea—and a dangerous one at that: "[t]he magical world is one in which language can bewitch the soul, and it is also unstable and dynamic, spirited and licentious" (6). This association is also why, Covino argues, magic users (especially women magic users) have been seen as dangerous: Without any other agency, they alter the world and people with just words, "disrupting and recreating articulate power" while "generating multiple perspectives" (9) to what Covino calls the official "authorized knowledge" (which is, these days, called "science") (8).

Covino explains how and why our sense[7] of rhetoric-as-spell persists despite the intervention of Science as an epistemological authority. Historically, we have defined magic as that which forms reality through the *resemblance* between signs and signifieds (14), calling upon "phantasies" or "phantasms," ideas that enter the "mind-soul" from the ether (32). Phantasies, for pre–Enlightenment philosophers, call upon something similar to the Platonic form to create communication (33–34), and the resulting images, shared by a discourse community, form the basis of human language (32). While this notion has obviously been abandoned in our current era, the sense of language's mystical appeals and the idea of rhetoric as a kind of mass hypnosis has not faded with time. Words, abstractions of these phantasies and phantasms, are seen as creating something from nothing—"mere" rhetoric, as opposed to objective fact.

Rhetoric and narrative's power is most clearly seen in Discworld through the dwarfish myth of Tak and the resulting dwarfish mythos of words that emerges from that myth. While the dwarfs are "not a naturally religious species,"[8] their creation myth uses spoken word as the foundation:

>The first thing Tak did, he wrote himself.
>The second thing Tak did, he wrote the Laws.
>The third thing Tak did, he wrote the world.
>The fourth thing Tak did, he wrote a cave.
>The fifth thing Tak did, he wrote a geode, an egg of stone.[9]

Tak's word magic speaks the universe into being, and as such, the dwarfs regard the written word as having a kind of ritual weight that extends past individual signified meanings. When Sir Samuel Vimes sarcastically brags to a dwarf official about having been a "blackboard monitor" in school, some of the dwarfs react in awe and others are scandalized.[10] As "deep downer" (what we might call a fundamentalist) dwarf Ardent says, erasing words is "the most heinous of crimes" and is "unthinkable for a true dwarf."[11]. The magic of words for dwarfs—and, as *Thud!* shows later, other symbols—is completely "generative," as Covino would say, and this word magic gives the symbols or words *being* in an almost sacred fashion.

For example, early in *Thud!*, a dying dwarf sketches the symbol for the entity known as "the Summoning Dark"; while "mine sign" is usually shorthand notation for dwarfs working in mines, the Summoning Dark symbol is both a signifier that curses the dwarf's murderers and a being that has agency of its own. In the magic-laden Discworld, using this sign summons the "quasidemonic entity"[12] into Ankh-Morpork, both cursing those responsible for the writer's death and, as word of its appearance spreads, letting the dwarf community communicate their concerns. Such symbol use is generative in that it is an "amplification of possibilities for action"[13] and the "process of inducing belief and creating community"[14]; it does not "arrest" response by prescribing a singular reading of the situation,[15] but allows for cooperative action in the community—ideally, in this case, some kind of disruption of the deep downers' questionable actions. The symbol is, as Lord Vetinari says, "not the thing itself," (336) but it is close: the discourse community using the symbol grants the word its power, and that communal agreement has real consequences. Even as dwarfs cooperatively create the meaning for the symbol, that agreement reflexively creates the community; it is no wonder, then, that the curses associated with the symbols actually work, and the dwarf Helmclever dies of a fright-induced heart attack after being left in darkness with the Summoning Dark symbol nearby. For the dwarfs of Discworld, at least, this definition of rhetoric as magic is appropriate, and other word magics run throughout the series, letting Pratchett and his narrator explain in hyperbole how rhetoric is magical in our own world and why we should use it with such care.

Covino draws part of his argument from Kenneth Burke's playful exploration of the intersection of grammar and glamour. As Covino explains, Burke associates word magic (rhetoric) with the act of *naming*; when we provide a name for a situation, we also implicitly prescribe an attitude and reaction to it. For example, we might call the actions at an American airport "national security" or we might call that same action set "invasion of privacy" ; our names (or misnaming) for things "decree" (Burke, qtd. in Covino 21) an attitude and response. As Covino notes, most curses and blessings in magic are done "in the name of" an empowered entity. Getting groped in line "in the name of" national security or safety (or, in the extreme, patriotism) results in a different attitude and even a different bodily response than getting patted down by agents employed by Big Brother to keep our bodies disciplined.

When we invoke such names, we also re-identify ourselves as either in line with that notion, changing our sense of self: sedately going through a TSA line at the airport is not just an act of security, but it identifies us as *patriots* or at least *cooperative citizens*.

This may be why Sam Vimes is able to defeat the symbol-creature the dwarfs call the Summoning Dark. Throughout *Thud!!* Vimes resists giving power to the darkness and while he uses the dwarfs term grudgingly, he also reminds Vetinari that "[w]e don't do mystic in the Watch" and that he is looking for real evidence, not "a big floaty eye with a tail" (336). Vimes' resistance to seeing the symbol as magic results in a renaming of the signifier as a signified by folding it within the realm of Law. Vimes' use of the word "mystic" is important for rhetoricians: As Grace Veach explains, the mystical is the realm just outside of logos that some rhetorician call the *chora*.[16] Vimes' rejection of the Summoning Dark as part of the *chora*—the space that rejects standard chains of logic and evidence, a space which requires human beings to put it into order—is a firm re-naming of the mystic as logos. Vimes' renaming allows him to interact with the entity as a *thing* bound to rules, law, and command. The novel's title refers to a game for a reason: Games are microcosms of the idea of law. Therefore, instead of letting the name "Summoning Dark" summon in him his worst intentions through a mystic relationship among symbol, being, and action, Vimes reinterprets the symbol as a simple sign-signified relationship. By renaming this symbol as part of the Law, he is able to do what the dwarfs could not: Restrict the symbol's word-act power to the realm of Vimesian ethics.

Fantasy texts can use this naming and identity in order to comment on rhetoric in general. In her review of magic and rhetoric in *Buffy the Vampire Slayer*, A. Abby Knoblauch[17] expands on Burke's grammar/glamour pun: Grammar is the agreed upon structure of language that metaphorically reflects the idea of order itself, while glamour is a reordering that forces participants to see the world differently. Knoblauch tracks this down further than Covino does, by following Mary Daly and Jane Caputi's call for feminists to "recast definitions of common terms" by using alternate spellings that "rattle loose"[18] the oppressive, prescriptive, phallogocentric roots of language, to see the interrelations of our sounds instead of our demarcations of difference in semantics. Doing so, Knoblauch agrees with Burke's and Covino's link of grammar and glamour—glamours are spells that use grammar to re-see the world as something else. But she also connects Daly and Caputi's link of grammar and grimoire, a book of spells, another kind of ordering. In this way, rhetoric becomes not just top-down persuasion, but "symbolic action"—a cooperative, communal acting through shared symbol systems to make real world change. As Grag Bashfull Bashfullsson says, the Summoning Dark and its symbol did not kill Helmclever; instead, "He died of fear and guilt.... That mine bore down so heavily on him."[19] The symbol identified Helmclever as *culpable* for the death of several dwarfs, and that symbol cast a glamour on Helmclever, masking him in guilt so strong that it physically killed him. In Discworld, glamour and grammar and the spells of grimoires are inseparable.

For literary scholars, a more familiar version of this would be J L Austin's theory of speech acts. Austin's speech act theory focuses on how speech can perform more than inform; certain utterances, due to the specific social conditions they are situated in, will not describe reality (that is, have "truth" value) but create or command an impactful action within that reality.[20] While Austin himself does not refer to this theory as concerned with rhetoric, others made the connection easily. Walter Beale (in *Philosophy and Rhetoric*) recommended rhetoricians adopt Austin's theory as a way to reimagine the Aristotelian epideictic genre,[21] while in the field-defining *College Composition and Communication*, Reed Dasenbrock suggested that Austin's speech acts were, in fact, the "New Rhetoric"—the ways rhetorical scholars in English have referred to the version of rhetorical theory (cooperative and based in identification and identity instead of raw power)[22] that has reemerged in the 20th century. In other words, in contemporary rhetorical theory as well as literary theory, words are still magic: language is always an invocation, formed and informed by tradition and social relations that creates real world change upon its utterance.

In our world and in Discworld, rhetoric is language that constitutes reality. But it also constructs and through that construction changes its audience's very being. As Burke says, rhetoric is invitation to consubstantiality; when a speaker speaks, she is asking her listeners to share substance with her and share in some related act. Burke echoes the idea of phantasms when he talks about rhetoric as the formation of shared substance: "For substance, in the old philosophies, was an *act*; an a way of life is an *acting-together;* and in acting together, men [sic] have common sensations, concepts, images, ideas, and attitudes that make them *consubstantial*"[23] (21). Rhetoric is not pure force for Burke, but an invoking of shared experience and identities—what we might call arguing by ethos, in a very broad sense. When we ask others to join us in an act, we form a shared identity with them to do so, and the act leaves both parties transformed: our rhetoric changes us. Such a radical alteration of identity and being through symbol use is certainly a kind of magic that persists despite science being the dominant episteme. In Discworld, *ethos*—the character, identity, and authority of a rhetor—is clearly the key strategy by which words and symbols do the magic of rhetoric.

Ethos in Discworld or, the Problem of Carrot

Pratchett's Discworld extends the metaphorical conflation of magic with rhetoric to its logical terminus: What happens when we take seriously that the world is *written*, constructed, and reconstructed by what is said—and more importantly *how* it is said to the Other? Because in Discworld, rhetoric can literally be magic that acts on both people and things, Pratchett's characters' speech illustrates the effects of rhetoric, both good and bad. And through his characters and their speech acts, Pratchett's theory of an ethical rhetoric emerges in Discworld—one based in how characters manage both their ethos and treat their interlocutors with care.

Many of the Discworld books feature commentary on rhetorical strategies,[24] but this essay emphasizes two of the "sub-series" in Discworld: the Witches stories, featuring Granny Weatherwax's rhetoric, and the City Watch thread, emphasizing the intertwined rhetoric of power seen in Sam Vimes and Carrot Ironfoundersson. Through these two quite different points of view, a complex picture of Pratchett's ethics of rhetoric appears—both from the characters themselves and the narrator forming our attitudes toward them. While Granny's early comments in the Witches sub-series establishes the general ideas of this rhetoric of ethos and identity, the Watch stories complicate that theory, showing the potential problems in rhetorical ethics through Carrot, whose powerful charisma is recognized as a double edged sword: simultaneously capable of saving Ankh-Morpork or leading them into a (worse) dictatorship. Taken as a whole, these characters show the power of ethos in argument, but also the necessary responsibility and care each rhetor must have for their audience.

Granny Weatherwax

Granny Weatherwax initially appears in the third book of the Discworld series, *Equal Rites*. Her identity forms many of the plot developments in the novels about the witches of the small kingdom of Lancre: in her first book, Granny finds herself mentoring Esk, a girl who was mistakenly gifted at birth with a wizard's powers instead of a witch's. When Granny first realizes that Esk has wizardly power, she explains to the child's parents the difference between the magic of wizards and the magic witches use: "Witches is a different thing altogether.... It's magic out of the ground, not out of the sky, and men could never get the hang of it."[25] This division between ground and sky is not explained in the novels, but the Witches subseries narratively shows that Granny's magic, at least, is largely "headology"—a kind of word magic that depends on a witch's ethos and the subject's psychology. What Granny calls "headology" might as easily be called knowing your audience and working with them to accomplish a goal—what Kenneth Burke means when he renames rhetoric as a kind of "acting-together."[26]

The term "headology" itself points to Granny's rhetorical skill and ethical stance. In Discworld, where word magic is everywhere, one must choose one's words carefully. Granny's own language shows her attention to this "acting-together"; instead of the complex language of the wizards, or even the careful notebooks other witches keep like Desiderata Hollow's travelogues that Magrat Garlick inherits. Granny's folksy language enables her to speak to those she helps without placing herself above them; her twin sister Lily's much more formal—and over-wrought—phrasing in *Witches Abroad* suggests that Granny's colloquial language is a choice—one meant to create the "identification" between interlocutors that Burke sees as the method of that acting-together. Choosing to speak plainly, mirroring those around us, is a word magic that all of us engage in every day: we connect with each other through the shared culture of our words and word choices. Granny's "headology"—a far less scientific word than "psychology" and far less mystical than "psychic power"—is both a method and a sign of her method of word magic.

While Granny is certainly capable of using her rhetorical magic for self-gain (and she does, sometimes), she resists using her full power for fear of becoming a black witch. But Granny is never really at risk: as Janet Brennan Croft notes, Granny might not be "nice" (inoffensive) or "good" (rule-following), but she is Right: she "mak[es] decisions that are just but not necessarily merciful, morally correct but not necessarily pleasant."[27] She gives her listeners what they need, not what they want, treating them with compassion and recognizing their humanity.

While Granny does have what we may call true magical power—the ability to influence others' actions and change nature itself—most of her headology is rooted in her identity as a witch and the associations her community has with witchcraft. Like the dwarf belief in word magic, the kingdom of Lancre's belief in the identity of witches constitutes much of the witch's power. This power is seen in *Witches Abroad*, when the witch trio Granny, Nanny Ogg, and Magrat Garlick travel outside of Lancre and discover their ethos no longer holds sway: "At home, if a witch wanted a table to herself it … just happened. The sight of a pointy hat was enough. People kept a polite distance, occasionally sending free drinks to her … [but h]ere they were being *jostled*, as if they were *ordinary*."[28] In Lancre, then, the witches' identities and the people's response to it is a kind of ethos-based rhetoric; in *Wyrd Sisters*, when the Duke attempts to ban witches, he does so because the Fool recognizes this rhetorical power, and the Duchess agrees, realizing the degree to which the citizens' faith in the witches *is* the foundation of the majority of their power.[29] The rumors spread about the witches fail to work, due to the deeply-rooted folklore that forms the community's identity, but the storyline highlights how humans invest in ethos-based arguments. The rhetor's own self and the authority of the symbols they carry with them can influence their audiences in ways that are potentially problematic.

Sam Vimes

Sam Vimes is perhaps an odd figure to consider as a worker of magical rhetorics through ethos. He is first introduced to us as Captain of the City Watch in *Guards!, Guards!* as a cynical and hopeless alcoholic—and he wants nothing to do with magic. His initial character description is less than flattering, but Vimes' emergence from his alcohol-fueled depression is a compelling rags-to-riches everyman story that invites audience identification. Like Granny, Sam contemplates his identity and is quite aware of his authoritative power that is constituted by his position in the Watch.

Importantly, it is Sam's *ethos* as watchman—and later, as Commander, Knight, and Duke (His Grace, Sir Samuel Vimes)—that gives him his power. This power is symbolized by his badge, which he sees as an inherent part of his identity so much so that when he is fired in *Men at Arms*, Carrot and Angua find him with his hand bloodied from holding on to his badge tightly in defiance and despair.[30] While the badge's rhetoricity marks Sam as having authority to discipline others, and he identifies with it strongly, he does not wield that power without good cause: Sam chooses his battles, and it is that choice of when to rely on the authority granted by his various symbolic identities that is of interest here.

Vimes' story adds to the Pratchettian ethical rhetoric by considering the power of stories to fight the darkest impulses of humanity. In *Thud!* Vimes is possessed by the Summoning Dark symbol, but he does not let it take over his identity. The Summoning Dark attempts to unleash Vimes' more violent urges—his desire for immediate, complete justice at his own hand—but finds inside Sam's mind a restrictive force: a mirror of Sam's own self, a policeman inside his head that keeps his use of power in control. This second self reports that he has been created "not to keep the darkness out" but is there instead to keep Vimes from misnaming *guarding* as vengeance.[31] As this is Discworld, though, that second self, the self-disciplining super-ego, seems to have power beyond normal psychology: as Vimes struggles against the Summoning Dark deep in a cave, some part of him realizes he is late for his nightly bedtime story with his son. As he battles the demon, Vimes begins to recite his son's favorite book at the appointed time, and the sound of his voice somehow reaches his son several miles away. The recitation of the story and all of the comfortable feelings Vimes associates with reading to his son breaks the spell and lets Vimes temper his response into something more lawful and less emotional. Fiction's rhetoricity—its social and symbolic power—binds the Summoning Dark and reasserts Discworld's theory of language as magic.

Vimes' restrained inner darkness is not just concerned with physical violence. Sam must also leash his tongue, which tends toward snark, particularly when addressing Lord Vetinari. For example, when Vetinari asks Vimes, who is investigating the attempted murder of a Klatchian prince, if there is "any suggestion that he's anti–Klatchian," Vimes sarcastically answers "Apart from him trying to kill one? Enquires are continuing."[32] But while Vimes is unafraid to let loose his sarcasm on Vetinari, he is more careful with suspects and friends (and all people fit into one of those two categories for Vimes—sometimes at the same time). In *Snuff*, for example, Vimes silences himself at a dinner party when he thinks he may be stepping into territory that would disrupt Sybil's polite gathering. Instead of regaling the party with police stories, he ends his part of the discussion with a leading phrase and promptly shuts himself up to watch the fallout: "[It's e]xceedingly dull around here, I would imagine. From my point of view, this place is as quiet as the ... grave" (109). Silence is both an ethical choice for Vimes, whose snarky comments might hurt his relationship with his peers, but also a rhetorical strategy that lets him listen and blend in with the rest of the crowd. Through Vimes, Pratchett builds on his ethos-based rhetoric to include the problem of using irony and satire among those whose literacy is not sophisticated enough to recognize tone. Vimes' self-policing in both physical and symbolic power usage turns him into "a good man speaking well": recognizing his physical and rhetorical prowess, Sam *chooses* to discipline himself, not in a Foucauldian submission to hegemonic power—an idea that Sam who has climbed to the top of the social class ladder rejects—but a personal moral code. Through our identification with Vimes, readers of Discworld are asked to adopt a similar rhetorical ethics: using the powers of our own identities only for the good of the Other.

The Problem of Carrot

While the City Watch books are arguably the story of Sam Vimes' "rise to the top,"[33] Vimes' story only makes sense when read in parallel to that of Carrot Ironfoundersson. In fact, Sam is initially introduced to readers at the same time as Carrot in *Guards!, Guards!,* and the two characters' *ethoi* work together to show different ways an authoritative ethos might be dangerous, acting to warn audiences about rhetors who seem too charming and problems of relying on tradition. While Vimes' lowly starting place, his tendency toward revenge, and his sarcasm and irony create an identifiable everyman, Carrot's ethos is more complicated—even if he is, indeed, a "simple" man. Carrot, an orphan raised by dwarfs, is the rightful king of Ankh-Morpork—even though the city has not had a king for several generations. Carrot, biologically human but culturally dwarfish, is made aware of his heritage in *Men at Arms*, but chooses to remain a simple Watchman. Carrot's true identity, as per the rules of Discworld, does influence his rhetorical prowess: his kingship, even though it is unknown to most of the population, bleeds through into his speech, and he is able to convince nearly anyone to do what he says, even when it does not make sense. In *Jingo*, Pratchett's nuanced anti-war argument, Carrot convinces the two warring sides, paused in a momentary truce, to play a game of football. Angua notes that "[i]t only works around him"—no one else could serve as a mediator and convince two sides to work together like that.[34] And that truce is only obtained because Carrot, in his understanding of what is good, rereads war as a crime—something he and Vimes can legally stop by arresting both sides.

When considering the Nice, Good, and Right, Croft notes that there are few in the witches' subseries that could be seen as purely "Good"—in fact, that singular label seems only to apply to one character, Carrot. Carrot is "good" in that he is rule-driven, what Dungeons and Dragons players might call "lawful good." Carrot, unlike any other member of the Watch, has memorized half of the giant Ankh-Morpork law book before the end of *Guards! Guards!* (enough so that he can arrest the dragon, citing "grievous bodily harm" done when the dragon burned people alive[35]). He lets the Law and the public good guide his decisions; in *Jingo*, when his lover and coworker Angua goes missing, Carrot does not heroically run after her; instead, he goes to Vimes to report the situation, since he "really did believe that personal wasn't the same as important."[36] Carrot knows his ethos is too powerful and that his kingship would, in the magic of Discworld, overcome and control the people of Ankh-Morpork, taking away their humanity (or dwarfhood or trollishness),[37] and so he, like Vimes, treads carefully with his words and deeds. This approach frustrates Angua, who wants Carrot to be more normal: "You're being reasonable again!" snapped Angua. "You're deliberately seeing everyone's point of view! Can't you try to be unfair even once?"[38] Carrot cannot, though; if he lets his guard down, his kingly ethos will overrun Ankh-Morpork's citizens, taking away their right to respond and choose on their own.

In Discworld, ethos and ethics go hand in hand, recognizing the constitutive power of rhetoric. Because rhetoric is literally magic in this world, the characters tread lightly when engaging in speech acts or any creation with rhetoricity. Sometimes, the characters use these to their benefit, but more often than not, as seen with Carrot, magical-rhetorical power is treated like a weapon: it is used only when needed and not without specific purpose, particularly when the situation gets "political" and considerations of radically different Others are in play.

The Rhetoric and Ethics of Fiction

While these characters in Discworld demonstrate a careful treatment of rhetoric as magic, such a portrayal would be pointless if the Discworld novels themselves did not perform the same word magic for their readers. In some ways, a character's speech is easier to parse as rhetorical: the characters have clear motives and roles in a plot in order for the story to make sense, and with an omniscient narrator, the story can show us the characters' intentions as well as the resulting effects of that speech. We can watch the word magic work and learn, through parable, how we should act. Viewed as such, Discworld is a handbook for ethics, and other scholars have approached the stories as such. Farah Mendlesohn's argues, for example, that at least some of Pratchett's work should be considered *"romans à these"*: novels written to convey a message, or what we might call didactic fiction.[39] For Mendlesohn, Pratchett's romans à these depend heavily on the idea of an individual making choices. These choices ask the character to act while remaining "authentic" to themselves and maintaining the integrity of their identities while questioning their position in the world.[40] Mendlesohn's text seeks out these moments where identity, choice, and reflection meet, concluding that "[t]he moral structure of Pratchett's work rests on a conviction that only personal integrity is a useful foundation for free will and true choice; all else is self deception."[41] If this is the central argument of Pratchett's work, then, we can certainly see Granny, Vimes, and Carrot use word magics rooted in their ethoi to serve as evidence for this argument.

But if the novels themselves are also "argumentative" they may also be seen as, in a sense, magical. Burke's "Lexicon Rhetoricae" describes how the *logic* of a narrative works to move (emotionally and then, ideally, literally in the real world) its audience; he identifies several methods of grounding reasoning, including "qualitative progression" and "syllogistic progression" of plot points that move readers through distinct stages of emotion ("qualitative progression") and logic ("syllogistic progression") to reach satisfaction.[42] In this way, fiction remains outside the scientific and still in the magical: the word-magic of reading, as Covino notes in his explanation of literacy, is tempting to cast in terms of sorcery. How narrative works rhetoric into a kind of magic remains, well, the magician's secret.

James Phelan, perhaps the most well-known theorizer of the ethics of fiction, tackles the other kind of fictional magic and rhetoric: the style of writing in novels and the ethical relationship this creates (or fails to create) between reader and writer. If, Phelan proposes, we recognize literature not as some easily identifiable aesthetic, but a communicative event defined by audience and purpose, we should focus both on "the ethics of the telling" as well as the "ethics of the told."[43] While most scholars who have considered the ethics of Discworld have focused on the latter—the ethics of the storyworld, its characters, and its events—the former has largely been neglected. How, we should ask, are those "ethics of the told" reinforced by Pratchett's rhetorical strategies? Phelan argues that instead of simply borrowing from a few "go to thinkers" as the ethical standard against which we measure an author's telling that we acknowledge that there are a variety of ethical rhetorical strategies that an author might choose, including ones not yet turned into perfectly coherent theoretical systems.

Even though Phelan does not give a strict model to work with, his resulting discussion does reveal some basic principles of what a fictional ethics might look like. Like Vimes, Granny, and Carrot carefully controlling their ethoi, *narrators* (and implied authors) must wield their world-generating powers carefully. The authority of the narrator should not, Phelan implies, overwhelm the reader and her ability to respond, to make choices, and to interpret texts.[44] An author cedes some of their authority of monovocal semantic meaning in favor of granting power to other voices, including that of the audience. We can see this negotiation of meaning and ethos in Vimes, Granny Weatherwax, and Carrot—while they are all effective rhetors and are powerful in their own rights when need be, they do recognize the humanity (or dwarfishness, or trollishness) of the Other they are engaging with their speech. This careful treatment of the Other is not limited to the characters in Pratchett's story, though; it is performed by the Discworld books themselves. Pratchett's careful control of his narrator's storytelling further demonstrates just how much this series is shaped by its author's ideas about word magic.

Discworld's Narrator: Ethos and Ethics

If the characters in Discworld have an implicit theory of ethical rhetorics, we only know of it because the events of Discworld are told to us through a narrator in novel form. Narrative, as Daniel Lüthi notes, is not just the way stories are told, but, in the Discworld stories, an actual substance that controls reality called narrativium.[45] Pratchett and cowriters Ian Stewart and Jack Cohen explain narrativium in detail in the companion series *The Science of Discworld,* and Lüthi reminds us that in the Discworld diegesis, the Disc itself would not exist without this element; it is "literally driven by stories, by narrativium" (135). It controls expectations and allows magic to do all the things magic should do—both pure magic and the rhetorical magic outlined earlier in this essay.

This reading of narrative as foundational is not limited to Pratchett's Discworld books. Lüthi reminds us that other philosophers have proposed man as the storytelling animal (137). But this theory often falls short of explaining what humans *do* with their stories and what stories do to us. We can say Pratchett uses narratives in Discworld to form his stories and convey messages, but there is a further step to take: what actions and attitudes do these stories constitute for their readers resulting in real world changes? Walter Fisher proposes the "narrative paradigm" of knowledge: that humanity is so essentially embedded in narrative that our knowledges are wholly constituted through story.[46] If, as the narrator in *Witches Abroad* argues, our stories get repeated so often that they "become ingrained in our minds and shape our desires"[47]—in other words, if our stories stabilize our norms—then we should be paying attention not just to the message of the stories but how they are told and what actions or attitudes those messages suggest in the telling. Further, we should consider, as Pratchett does with his characters, how the rhetor—in this case, the nameless narrator of Discworld—treats their audience as people instead of things to be manipulated.

The narrator draws their power in part from those repetitions of stories that create the genre of fantasy; Discworld, as Lüthi argues, was initially a parody of the high fantasy genre (à la J.R.R. Tolkien), and the purpose of direct genre critique in the early Discworld books helped form the narrator's identity as an echo of the genre.[48] While "quote about myth vs science basis" does differentiate the Discworld narrator from that of Tolkien in particular, our expectations of that narratorial approach grants the Discworld narrator their initial ethical power: We expect an omniscient (or nearly omniscient) narrator whose authority lets us immerse ourselves in the storyworld without fear of uncertainty or confusion. Despite the disparate threads of the Discworld books, the narrator of the series remains fairly stable in their voice, even if the facts of the series are less consistent in the early books. When *Equal Rites* introduces the Disc, its narrator's voice uses a parody of high style of fantasy mixed with an awareness of its audience and our needs, leading us into the story in a faux-screenplay style:

> Here it comes now. Watch closely, the special effects are quite expensive.
>
> A bass note sounds. It is a deep vibrating chord that hints that the brass section may break in at any moment with a fanfare for the cosmos, because the scene is the blackness of deep space with a few stars glittering like the dandruff on the shoulders of God.
>
> Then it comes into view overhead, bigger than the biggest, most unpleasantly

armed starcruiser in the imagination of a three-ring filmmaker: a turtle, ten thousand miles long. It is Great A'Tuin, one of the rare astrochelonians from a universe where things are less as they are and more like people imagine them to be, and it carries on its meteor-pocked shell four giant elephants who bear on their enormous shoulders the great round wheel of the Discworld [1–2].

The tone of this introduction to the structure of Discworld does not waver in the series itself; while different versions appear and the exposition is shortened and finally disappears in later books, the tone—a play on the grand style favored by Tolkien—remains the same.

Ridiculous and ridiculing figures of speech ("dandruff on the shoulders of God") are prominent tools in the narrator's storytelling toolbox, and the language the narrator uses is carefully chosen to avoid a heavy-handed argument that forces the readers into a singular response. In *Men at Arms*, for example, the narrator treats their audience with care, allowing the readers to reach their own conclusions without a bullying kind of pathos that some narratives employ to create the desired effect. These playful constructions often bleed into the speech of characters. Even Death takes on punning as a way to ease the discomfort of his clients: When dwarf Bjorn Stronginthearm is murdered, Death asks him if he might be "Bjorn again" through reincarnation.[49] Because dwarfs are notoriously incapable of recognizing irony (which the narrator and characters further pun by pointing to the mining of iron in several novels), Death must point out his own pun, a distracting moment breaking up the narrative, which ultimately does exactly what Death had hoped to do in the first place: alleviate the panic of death and horror of murder. That the narrator chooses to include this short interlude shows they share Death's concern: the novel *Men at Arms* takes on the problem of guns and their destructive power. The narrator uses this interlude and others with Death to force readers out of a potentially bleak and controversial argument for a moment; instead of pathetically manipulating their readers into believing all guns should be destroyed (as Carrot does at the end), the ambiguity of language and the humor of wordplay allows for a more measured response.

The ethics of rhetoric in fiction is formed in large part by these choices the author and their narrators must make. *How* audiences are magicked into a storyworld and how they feel once there is a question of ethics—just as Granny insists on seeing people as people and not things, so must an author and narrator treat their audiences as people and not minds or emotions to be manipulated. The interplay between author and narrator can, of course, be tricky, and narratologists have spent significant time working to identify kinds of narrators, narratorial tones and styles, and ways that narrators participate in diegetical and extradiegetical events. In Discworld, we might argue that the narrator is, in fact, the implied author, but that that implied author is not clearly the real person named Terry Pratchett who lives in our world, writing the bestselling series called *Discworld*. Instead, we see Pratchett authoring his narrator, who is in turn authoring the books, adding footnotes for his implied readers. This distance allows the narrator to edit his story through the notes and allows us to see Pratchett as simply providing us with that narrator's text—not agreeing or disagreeing with it, but handing it to us, giving us what we need.

Conclusions

If magic is rhetoric and fiction is rhetoric, we might imagine Pratchett as a kind of particularly ethical witch. By using a narrator, Pratchett provides space between himself and the story, giving even more room for the audience to make reading choices; his authority as canon-creator of Discworld is somewhat undermined by his reliance on his narrator's knowledge that exists outside our own world. But the Discworld narrator also makes room between themselves and Pratchett through the major stylistic feature of the series: the narrator's footnotes, which are at times reflexive, self-editing, and like the companion *Science of Discworld* series, a way to break the generic boundaries of fantasy—a genre that is too often hegemonic, particularly in its formulation of gender, as Lian Sinclair argues.[50] Moreso than the narrator's playful language, these footnotes bear the burden of providing readers with room to respond, letting them have agency and be human instead of objects.

The footnotes have been identified by some as a "postmodern" move that may "interrupt" our "literary belief" as we read.[51] Lüthi begins his discussion of those postmodern notes with an assumption that reader immersion is, in fact, a desirable goal of all fiction; he argues that these notes are humorous and risk breaking reader engagement with the "second world" all readers must construct in their imaginations as they read (much like the phantasms that medieval magicians assumed formed our ability to communicate). And certainly, most fictions do approach writing and fictional rhetoric with total immersion as the goal; but Discworld's continual metacommentary on the magic of language points to a different purpose. Immersion, like all rhetorical effects, can be positive or negative—good or evil—depending on how the audience is treated. And Pratchett and his narrator's end goal is not to immerse us uncritically, but to engage us. This positioning of the speaker to his created world allows readers just enough critical distance to accept or reject the terms the stories provide, creating a different kind of magic: cooperation between author and audience to create meaning both for the storyworld and extradiegetically in the readers' own context.

Notes

1. As Pratchett's own *Science of Discworld* companion text explains, while our "Roundworld" works by a series of rules ("physics"), events on Discworld occur due to the element *narrativium* instead of the rules of physics. Storytelling conventions substitute for scientific laws in Discworld.
2. Pratchett, *Wyrd Sisters*, 185
3. The narrator of the early Discworld books seems likely male, due to some sexist jokes and insight into the behavior of men, particularly explained with the introduction of the dwarf Cheery, who "comes out" as a woman in *Feet of Clay*. As cultural norms regarding gender and sexuality shifted during the two decades Pratchett worked on the *Discworld* series, it is not surprising that his narrator became less sexist and less distinctly male. Such a change in the narrator's tone is also an argument for Pratchett's ethical treatment of his readers: Instead of maintaining the same voice for the sake of continuity, Pratchett allowed his narrator to grow to meet the needs of his audience. For the purposes of this chapter, I use the gender neutral they/them pronouns for this narrator.
4. Burke, *Counter-Statement*. This is a summary of Burke's "Lexicon Rhetoricae," or glossary of rhetoric as it appears in art. While this chapter focuses on the ethical or ethosoriented rhetorical work in Discworld, another fruitful project might read the same ideas initially through logos or pathos, using Burke's Lexicon.
5. Covino, *Magic, Rhetoric, and Literacy*, 5.
6. Covino's book ultimately explains how literacy and all of the structures of dominance that are associated with it developed and changed alongside the shift from magic to the more scientific techne we now call rhetoric. Literacy, he argues, and our discourses about literacy, have often depended on a kind of "magical" thinking of how knowledge of the interpretation of symbols is acquired. Covino points specifically to Paulo Freire's *Pedagogy of the Oppressed* as the kind of magical transformation of the subject through literacy. This essay addresses literacy only inasmuch as any rhetorical theory does implicitly.
7. Covino's definitional work that I borrow from here focuses entirely on treatments of rhetoric, literacy, and magic in the Greco-Roman classical era and the medieval through Renaissance periods in Europe. While Discworld has been translated into non–European languages, Pratchett's own situation as a British fantasy writer logically allows for assuming that his primary audience is British and or citizens in countries that were part of the British colonial project. When I say "we" and "ours" here, then, I am referring to the Western cultural and philosophical tradition, knowing full well that the rhetorical strategies and the narrative logic of Discworld may be quite different when the novels are read by those outside that tradition.
8. Pratchett, *Men at Arms*, 85.
9. Pratchet, *Thud!*, epigraph.
10. The nickname "Blackboard Monitor Vimes" first appears in *The Fifth Elephant*, and the meaning of that phrase grew as the series expanded to explore more of the dwarfish myth of Tak.
11. Pratchett, *Thud!*, 86
12. Pratchett, *Thud!*, 336
13. Covino, *Magic, Rhetoric, and Literacy*, 9.
14. Covino, *Magic, Rhetoric, and Literacy*, 11.
15. Covino, *Magic, Rhetoric, and Literacy*, 9
16. Veach, "Divination and Mysticism."
17. Knoblauch, "From Burke to Buffy." Knoblauch does not track down the ethical implications of identification (the symbolic act involved in creating consubstantiality), but her use of Burke to explain the ways fantasy literature "collapses" rhetoric and magic in explicit ways influences this chapter in significant ways.
18. Knoblauch, "From Burke to Buffy."
19. Pratchett, *Thud!*, 397
20. Austin, *How to Do Things*, 5.
21. Beal, "Rhetorical Performative Discourse," 221.

108   Terry Pratchett's Ethical Worlds

22. Dasenbrock, "New Rhetoric," 292.
23. Burke, *Rhetoric*, 19–22. This section in the *Rhetoric* is the core of Burke's rather complex idea of "identification" as rhetoric, and scholars have been untangling this idea since its inception (as did Burke). Burke's writing is at times difficult to quote, as he uses italics frequently and insists on a universal male pronoun; his writing also relies upon readers being familiar with his prior works to make sense of each new idea. This section of Rhetoric emerged from a similar statement on the "paradox of substance" in his previous work, the Grammar of Motives. Interested readers might consier the implications of magic in that section of the Grammar as well, but to dig that deeply into Burkeian philosophy would belabor the simpler point of this chapter: that Pratchett's hyperbolic treatment of word magic is actually not that hyperbolic, is a statement above all about ethics, and itself is enacted in his narrative style. More difficult ontological questions Burke creates for our Roundworld can be left to others (see Debra Hawhee's *Moving Bodies: Kenneth Burke at the Edges of Language,* 2009).
24. In a longer essay, Moist von Lipwig's rhetoric as invention would be explored in greater detail. Moist's ethos and indeed his overall treatment of language as a tool of the scam reflects the "old rhetoric"—rhetoric as decoration and unexamined power over listeners. Moist may be seen as a complicating character who provides a counter-point to this section; Pratchett's inclusion of Moist's kind of rhetorical savvy and success might serve as evidence for Pratchett's own approach to rhetoric: ambiguity and polysemy that allows an audience to see multiple points of view. Here, Moist stands in opposition to the more rigid ethical rhetorics presented by Granny, Vimes, and Carrot, letting audiences determine for themselves which approach is appropriate.
25. Pratchett, *Equal Rites*, 11.
26. Burke, *Rhetoric*, 21.
27. Croft, "Education of a Witch," 155.
28. Pratchett, *Witches Abroad,* 184.
29. Pratchett, *Wyrd Sisters* 180–184. In one scene Granny bewails her lost power when a cart nearly runs her down (instead of swerving out of respect). In the scene immediately following, the Fool tells the Duke that their smear campaign is working.
30. Pratchett, *Men at Arms,* 241.
31. Pratchett, *Thud!,* 391.
32. Pratchett, *Jingo,* 90.
33. Pratchett, *Snuff,* 38. Vimes' sarcastic response that while cream rises to the top, "so does scum" is ignored by Sybil here, but later in the book, Vimes' cutting class commentary is addressed head on.
34. Pratchett, *Jingo,* 389.
35. Pratchett, *Guards! Guards!,* 367.
36. Pratchett, *Jingo,* 231. This particular line is a callback to Carrot's explanation of why he is still working after Angua's "death" in *Men at Arms*—because while he is upset she is dead, he still has a duty to perform. In that same scene, Carrot destroys some of the evidence that would prove him to be the rightful king, again resisting the power-grab.
37. While Carrot may be aligned with the "Good" and moral, he is not without his own flaws and blindspots. Carrot's distrust and dislike of the undead takes several novels to resolve, for example; he separates his relationship with Angua from his distaste for the vampire and werewolf population. Therefore, while Carrot stands for the *lawful,* and works for the good of the humans, dwarfs, and trolls in Ankh-Morpork, that moral system seems to privilege those three races through a logos-based appeal to the "natural" instead of arguing through ethos, which is his strength.
38. Pratchett, *Feet of Clay,* 280.
39. Mendlesohn, "Faith and Ethics," 239.40. Mendlesohn, "Faith and Ethics," 242–43.
41. Mendlesohn, "Faith and Ethics," 259.
42. Burke, *Counter-Statement*, 124.
43. Phelan, "Rhetoric," 56.
44. Phelan, "Rhetoric," 62–63. In that section, Phelan's main purpose is to discuss how other ethics scholars have ignored the importance of character as both a function of story

and discourse—both the telling and the told, to use his earlier language. Likewise, examining the ethics of rhetoric espoused by the Discworld characters can provide us the same insight and help establish Pratchett's implied theory of ethical communication.
    45. Lüthi. "Toying with Fantasy," 204, 135.
    46. Fisher, "Clarifying," 57.
    47. Sinclair, "Magical Genders," 14.
    48. Lüthi, "Toying with Fantasy,"131–132. Lüthi relies on this assumption to discuss Pratchett's disruption of fantastic belief in Discworld, a disruption that lets readers "play" with the genre.
    49. Pratchett, *Men at Arms*, 86.
    50. Sinclair, "Magical Genders," 8.
    51. Lüthi. "Toying with Fantasy," 132.

Works Cited

Austen, J.L. *How to Do Things with Words*. 2nd ed. Eds. J.O. Urmson and Marina Sbisà. Harvard UP, 1975.
Beal, Walter H. "Rhetorical Performative Discourse: A New Theory of *Epideictic*." *Philosophy and Rhetoric* 11: 221–246.
Burke, Kenneth. *Counter-Statement*. 2d ed. U of California P, 1968.
_____. *A Rhetoric of Motives*. U of California P, 1969.
Covino, William. *Magic, Rhetoric, and Literacy: An Eccentric History of the Composing Imagination*. State University of New York Press, 1994.
Croft, Janet Brennan. "The Education of a Witch: Tiffany Aching, Hermione Granger, and Gendered Magic in Discworld and Potterworld." *Mythlore* 27, no 3/4 (2009): 129–142.
Dasenbrock, Reed Way. Reed Way "J.L. Austen and the Articulation of a New Rhetoric." *College Composition and Communication* 38, no. 3 (1987): 291–305.
Fisher, Walter. "Clarifying the Narrative Paradigm." *Communication Monographs* 56 (March 1989): 55–58.
Knoblauch, A. Abby. "From Burke to Buffy and Back Again: Intersections of Rhetoric, Magic, and Identification in Buffy the Vampire Slayer." *Slayage: The Journal of the Whedon Studies Association*. 8.1 Accessed January 28, 2018, http://www.whedonstudies.tv/up loads/2/6/2/8/26288593/knoblauch_slayage_8.1.pdf.
Lüthi, Daniel. "Toying with Fantasy: The Postmodern Playground of Terry Pratchett's Discworld Novels." *Mytholore* 33, no. 1 (2014): 125–142.
Mendlesohn, Farah. "Faith and Ethics" in *Terry Pratchett: Guilty of Literature*, 2d ed, eds Andrew M. Butler, Edward James, and Farah Mendlesohn, 239–260. Old Earth Books, 2004.
Phelan, James. "Rhetoric, Ethics, and Narrative Communication: Or, from Story and Discourse to Authors, Resources, and Audiences." *Soundings: An Interdisciplinary Journal* 94, no. 1/2 (2011): 55–75.
Pratchett, Terry. *Equal Rites*. HarperCollins, 2008. Dates refer to the mass market reprints of each novel through the Harper imprint.
_____. *Feet of Clay*. HarperCollins, 2000.
_____. *Guards! Guards!* HarperCollins, 2001.
_____. *Jingo*. HarperCollins, 1999.
_____. *Men at Arms*. HarperCollins, 1997.
_____. *Snuff*. HarperCollins, 2011.
_____. *Thud!* HarperCollins, 2006.
_____. *Witches Abroad*. HarperCollins, 2008.
_____. *Wyrd Sisters*. HarperCollins, 2001.
Sinclair, Lian. "Magical Genders: The Gender(s) of Witches in the Historical Imagination of Terry Pratchett's Discworld." *Mythlore* 33, no. 2 (2015): 7–20.
Veach, Grace. "Divination and Mysticism as Rhetoric in the Choral Space." *KB Journal*. 8.1 (2012 Special Issue). Accessed 13 July 2018. http://www.kbjournal.org/ veach_divination_mysticism

The Golempunk Manifesto
Ownership of the Means of Production in Pratchett's Discworld[1]

Janet Brennan Croft

Terry Pratchett is not usually thought of as a steampunk author, since his Discworld is clearly a fantasy world filled with wizards and witches, dwarves, vampires, trolls, werewolves, and magic. After all, it is flat and rests on the backs of four elephants standing on a giant tortoise swimming through space. But Discworld is also full of ordinary people living relatively ordinary lives without the help of magic, and inevitably developing technology to do the things that magic does for the gifted. And Pratchett is notable for bringing the rigors of science fiction to bear on fantasy. If he resorts to "handwavium" in one book for the sake of moving the story along, he will frequently go back to the glossed-over bit in a later book and try to figure out how it "really" works. This is especially evident in what is sometimes called his Industrial Revolution series, a sub-series in which the focus is on various technological advances which have social ramifications all over Discworld.

This series includes *The Truth*, which deals with the introduction of the printing press and the newspaper and their effects on government and the social hierarchy; *Going Postal*, which focuses on the competition of the newly developed "clacks," or semaphore-based telegraph system, with the revival of the post office through the invention of stamps; *Making Money*, which examines the effects of going off the gold standard, the introduction of paper money, and the potential effects of a free, practically limitless power source; and *Raising Steam*, in which the locomotive begins stitching together the far-flung countries of Discworld, with vast social and economic implications. Some also include *Monstrous Regiment* in this series, as it deals in part with the effect of a free press, the telegraph, and photographic technology on the conduct of war. Other books also include technological advances that may not be the prime focus of the book, like the computer Hex, first introduced in *Soul Music,* or the Combination Harvester in *Reaper Man*; or they may be deliberately abandoned, like the "gonne" in *Men at Arms,* the motion picture in *Moving Pictures,* or the space-going craft in *The Last Hero.*

The themes of the Industrial Revolution series overlap nicely with those of steampunk. The primary focus is on the social effects of technology, but there is also an emphasis on the value of hackability (as opposed to magic, where there are no user-accessible parts); on technology made beautiful, as in the designs of Leonard of Quirm, Discworld's equivalent of Leonardo da Vinci, or the continual improvements on Iron Girder, the first of the steam locomotive engines; on the dangers of unchecked technology or poorly designed technology, as in the designs of B.S. "Bloody Stupid" Johnson, whose mail sorter was capable of warping the space-time continuum; and on the intersection of class, money, power, and access to technology. At the same time, Pratchett's Discworld novels also exhibit other characteristics frequently found in steampunk literature: racial inclusivity,[2] a concern for sexual and social equality, and the supernatural as a major plot element.

The aesthetic and setting are also reminiscent of steampunk, at least in the more recent books set in Ankh-Morpork. While the series as a whole is fantasy, the great city of Ankh-Morpork is strongly reminiscent of Victorian London, with its vast divide between rich and poor; its small factories and manufacturing districts, guilds and apprenticeship systems; the docks, markets, and slaughter yards, the prostitutes and thieves; the plots and corruptions gleefully reported in many thriving, competing newspapers. We witness the beginnings of forensic science and a professional police force, and the presence of governesses, butlers, etiquette books, balls, and conspicuous consumption as aspirational class markers for the rising bourgeoisie. The influx of racially diverse immigrants and burdens on the rural hinterland supporting the city cause social tensions, only exacerbated by the city's growing international connections and its rapidly evolving technology. Pratchett does not usually describe clothing and interior decoration in great detail, but the two Mob Films/Sky One television productions based on this time period in the city—*Hogfather* and *Going Postal*—definitely have a very Victorian look, and Pratchett was deeply involved in their production.[3] Ankh-Morpork differs from London in one very key respect, though—it is a city-state, not the center of a kingdom, and it firmly rejects empire-building under the current ruling Patrician, Vetinari.

One of the distinguishing characteristics of Ankh-Morpork is the way it absorbs new races. Every type of being, from trolls to vampires to gargoyles to werewolves to evangelical Omnians, finds its niche in time, and inevitably winds up with a representative on the police force. There are now more dwarfs in Ankh-Morpork than in the rest of Discworld put together—a key contribution to rising tensions and an attempted coup in the Dwarf kingdom in *Raising Steam*. I want to focus here on one particular race, if they can be called a race, because of the way they so perfectly represent two essential elements of the Industrial Revolution: both the steam that powered the machines and the lives of the workers who ran the machines.

Where Golems Come From

Golems, like so many of the elements of Pratchett's Discworld, have their roots in our own world's folklore. In medieval Jewish legends, golems are man-shaped automata, formed of clay, and activated by magic words written on their foreheads. They generally did not have magical powers of their own beyond great strength, speed, and endurance. In the best-known versions of the tale, Rabbi Judah Loew, a great scholar who lived in the Prague ghetto in the 1500s, prayed for a way to help deliver his people from persecution, and received instructions on how to create and animate a golem. There are many stories of the deeds the golem performed at the rabbi's command; collections usually include, among other tales, a version of the familiar Sorcerer's Apprentice motif and a story of the foiling of a Blood Libel plot against the Jews at Passover. Generally, over the years the golem serves the rabbi, he becomes both more human (even, in one retelling, asking for a Bar Mitzvah and a bride [Singer 66]), and less easy to control, and in the end the rabbi must erase the word that animates the golem and let it die (see, for example, Wiesel 89; Rogasky 79, Singer 65). Is it murder? In one version, it is explained that a golem has "no soul, only a nefesh—the kind of spirit that is given to higher animals" (Singer 75). Adam was called a golem in Genesis until he was given the power of speech and thereby a soul (Rogasky 91, Wilson 82, Rosenberg 188), and for this reason golems are generally not given the ability to talk.

The concept of the golem has evolved beyond these roots to become a common metaphor for anxiety about the modern world and the pace of technological change. Frankenstein's story is basically that of the golem, as is any story about a computer or robot developing self-awareness or going out of control. The golem can carry other meanings as well, though. In the original folkloric tales, the golem is strongly connected to the community; he is made by a holy man of a religion that values family; he becomes a member of the rabbi's family; he is brought to life in order to serve the community; and as he becomes more self-aware, he longs to be even more closely tied to the community by participating in its sacred rituals. He is not created, like

Frankenstein's monster, out of "curiosity, striving, and individualism" and he is never "denied family and thus humanity." When he must finally be destroyed, it is "with love, sorrow, and gratitude, and according to religious formulas" (Allison 93). "The rabbi sanctifies the monstrous and responds to it with pity and hope" and does not deny that it has a soul of some sort (94). Most importantly, the creation of the golem is a hallowed act of what J.R.R. Tolkien called *sub-creation*—the right and indeed responsibility of man, created in the image of the Creator, to in turn create. In this view, "the universe is magical. [...] Man's practice of God's magic is not a violation of sacred order but a realization of sacred potential" (Wilson 83). In fact, in earlier, pre-medieval golem legends, the creation of a golem was seen as a proof of a rabbi's learning and holiness (Yair and Soyer 15).

In contrast, later interpretations of the golem tend to emphasize its creation as an act of unrestrained ego and attempted Promethean domination over nature—man meddling where he should not, "magic [as] a result of the fall, Adam's violation of God's law" (Wilson 83). In this interpretation, an act of creation by man too easily crosses the line and becomes a hubristic imitation of God, and therefore "a sin that is fated to be punished" (Yair and Soyer 1). In these stories the golem or its equivalent invariably rebels or runs mad, and turns on and destroys its creator (2); think of Frankenstein's monster, Hal 9000 from *2001*, or the androids of *Blade Runner*.[4] So "[c]reativity becomes a double-edged sword. The creative endeavor is replete with dangers" (Sherwin 24). The golem becomes a locus for concerns such as "skepticism [about] technical progress and [criticism of] the hubris of modern man" (22). Karl Marx drew on the concept of the golem to show that "tensions between men and their creations"—by "creations" meaning both the capitalist system and the working class it created—"predict the destruction of the whole system, culminating in the frustration of the vain hopes of men and their most rational plans" (50). The way I propose to look at Pratchett's golems—as symbolizing both the power source that drives capitalism and the workers swept up in robotic slavery to the capitalist system—is one familiar in Marxist thought; yet as we shall see, Pratchett does not buy into the inevitable destruction of the system. If this seems like a heavy burden of meaning for fantastic and steampunk stories to bear, consider this: as Charlie Stross pointed out in his rather harsh critique of steampunk as a fad, if steampunk accepts the trappings of empire and uncontrolled capitalism without examining its dark underside, it loses its "punk" status and energy and risks falling into an unconsidered "romanticization of totalitarianism." Steampunk at its best should be, instead, an ideal way to explore and confront these issues and imagine a better way.[5]

Pratchett's Golems

With this brief theoretical and historical background in mind, let us now take a look at Pratchett's golems—what they are, how they come into being, what they do in the story, and what they mean. The three Discworld novels most concerned with golems are *Feet of Clay* [*FC*], in which they are introduced, and *Going Postal* [*GP*] and its sequel *Making Money* [*MM*], in which the fate of Ankh-Morpork's golems is intertwined with those of reformed con man Moist von Lipwig and Miss Adora Belle Dearheart, who runs the Golem Trust.

Discworld's golems were invented by the ancient Umnians, some 60,000 years before the current period. They rivaled the best statuary, delicate and beautiful, highly decorated, eggshell thin but nearly unbreakable, with sculpted musculature and "calm, sad faces" (*MM* 325), and were bigger and heavier than later golems (*MM* 216–7). As Adora Belle tells the story, "It was [the Umnians'] only invention. They didn't need any more. Golems built their city, golems tilled their fields [...]." Golems even built other golems. "You don't need weapons [...] when you've got golems instead of city walls. You don't even need shovels" (*MM* 229). And so they brought the technological development of ancient Um to a screeching halt. With golems, what need was there to invent any further tools?[6] And thus we have the first cautionary economic tale about golems—their inventors or their descendants, like H.G. Wells's Eloi in *The Time Machine* or the humans in Jack Williamson's "With Folded Hands," cared for and coddled by machines they can no longer understand, repair, or control.

Later golems were not so carefully and beautifully made, but there was one important advance: the *chem*, the animating holy words, were written on a slip of paper placed inside their hinged hollow skulls instead of carved and baked into their clay, thus making golems re-programmable, and all golems had to allow access to their chem if requested (*FC* 78). The chem contained a set of prohibitions very much like Isaac Asimov's Three Rules of Robotics (for example, golems were not allowed to hurt people [*FC* 97]), and made clear the purpose of the golem's existence: "GOLEM MUST WORK. GOLEM MUST HAVE A MASTER" (*FC* 2, 78, 157). Additionally, golems had to be given time off for their holy day every week (*FC* 81); as Moist muses, "It was part of what distinguished golems from hammers" (*GP* 227).

One character explains, "There are more golems around than you might think. [...] They can work underwater, or in total darkness, or knee-deep in poison. For years. They don't need rest or feeding" (*FC* 78). "Some are walled up in treadmills or at the bottom of shafts. Doing messy tasks, you know, in places where it's dangerous to go" (*FC* 102). But it isn't exactly slavery, at least not to the minds of other races; "You might as well enslave a doorknob" (*FC*

78). Still, "Golems had no concept of freedom. They knew they were artifacts; some even still bore, on their clay, the finger marks of the long-dead priests. Golems were made to be owned" (*MM* 227–8).

At this point in the history of Discworld there is a prohibition against making new golems (*FC* 2, 101) since it is considered the prerogative of the gods to create new life—though golems are technically considered "unalive," in contrast to the by-now-familiar "undead" peoples living in Ankh-Morpork (*FC* 76). Which brings up the question of where the soul of a golem comes from, since they are obviously self-aware.[7] Pratchett gives no clue beyond the fact that a holy man had to write out the words (*FC* 165) and, it is implied, oversee the firing of the clay. Given what we know of Discworld, it's possible to speculate that "ensoulment," like belief (cf. *Hogfather*), just needs something around which to crystallize; in this case, the writing of the chem might focus any spare "soul" floating around, just as at the time of *Hogfather* merely naming the Hair-Loss Fairy precipitates enough spare "belief" to call him into existence.

In the book where we first encounter modern golems, *Feet of Clay*, the golems have begun to chafe against their conditions and desire freedom and self-determination. Perhaps it is just something in the air of Ankh-Morpork, with its churning soup of multiculturalism and constant social upheaval. They attempt to gain their freedom by creating a king-golem, with bits of their own clay mixed in (*FC* 213), but they put too many commands in its chem, asking it to create peace and justice for all, to rule them wisely, to teach them freedom, on and on, begging it to meet all their needs (224). Like the golems of modern literature, it goes mad and starts killing people, particularly those who made it—"it knew who to blame" (215).

There is a strong anti-monarchial strain in Discworld books, particularly the City Watch series of which *Feet of Clay* is a part, and the flawed golem plan bears out this theme. Sam Vimes, the commander of the City Watch, is a descendant of the man who executed the last reigning king of Ankh-Morpork, and in spite of the Patrician's highly successful governance of the city, there are continual attempts by the aristocrats to re-install a puppet king. However, a true king exists—Captain Carrot Ironfoundersson, who serves under Vimes in the watch. Carrot is one of the most intriguing characters in the series; perhaps the most efficient way to describe him is "ruthlessly good." He has no desire to be king, quite sincerely believing that the best way he can serve his City is by being a watchman. And yet he fulfills the mythical functions of a sacral king, particularly in this book, as a healer and gift-giver. He promises the golem Dorfl: "If a golem is a *thing* then it can't commit murder, and I'll still try to find out why all this is happening. If a golem *can* commit murder, then you are *people*, and what is being done to you is terrible and must be stopped. Either way, you win, Dorfl" (*FC* 157).

Carrot is the instrument of *the* turning point in the history of golemhood, which occurs when he saves Dorfl from a mob, tries to take him back to his employer, and winds up buying him for $1, insisting upon a receipt. He then simply *gives* Dorfl to himself by adding the receipt to the chem inside his head. It takes Dorfl a while to truly understand the implications of not having a master, of being his OWN master, but eventually he focuses in on the sense of responsibility for his own actions: "Not *Thou Shalt Not.* Say *I Will Not*" (192). With this newfound freedom of action Dorfl sacrifices himself to kill the king golem, which takes the chem out of Dorfl's head to stop him. Yet Dorfl still lives, and writes out "WORDS IN THE HEART CAN NOT BE TAKEN" (224). And when he is re-baked, this time with a voice, Commander Vimes deputizes him—which seems his usual method of trying to deal with new races in Ankh-Morpork. Can you stick a badge on it and swear it in? Good, now it's a copper, not a golem or a werewolf or a zombie—just a copper.

Vimes says "*he* thinks he's alive, and that's good enough for me" (*FC* 240). Dorfl continually makes a point of his self-ownership and its implication that every single action is now a moral choice (*FC* 234), and compares freedom, aptly enough, to having the top of one's head opened up (243). In any case, soon after being sworn in as a Watchman, Dorfl announces his plan to begin saving his wages and buying other golems and setting them free (244). Here the self-aware "technology" hacks itself, resists authoritarianism, and claims its racial equality and free membership in society—it could hardly be more aligned with the underlying politics of steampunk.

Moist and Adora Belle, with Golems

Going Postal picks up long enough after *Feet of Clay* that free golems are well-established as an everyday fact of life for Ankh-Morpkians, though still somewhat exotic to outsiders. They have become accepted for the most part as persons. "[T]hey never wore out and they worked, all the time. You saw them pushing brooms, or doing heavy work in timber yards and foundries. Most of them you never saw at all. They made the hidden wheels go round, down in the dark [...] But now the golems were freeing themselves. It was the quietest, most socially responsible revolution in history. They were property, and so they saved up and *bought* themselves" (*GP* 45–46).

In this novel, while there is some development of golem lore and the introduction of several golems with distinct personalities, they initially serve as a plot device to bring Moist van Lipwig, a con artist saved from the gallows and tasked with bringing the Post Office back to life, together with Miss Adora Belle Dearheart. Adora Belle[8] is a fine embodiment of the steampunk aesthetic, with her severe dark clothes, high heeled boots, absolute assumption of equality, and take-no-prisoners attitude towards life. She runs the Golem Trust, an organization founded on Dorfl's idea of helping golems buy their freedom, which seeks out new golems to free and serves as an employment office for freed golems. Its motto is "By Our Own Hand, or None" (*GP* 64). Once a new golem was located, the Golem Trust would purchase it, and then the golem would earn its own price back and start contributing to the Trust itself. Adora Belle explains the speechlessness of golems from a different perspective than the religious one offered above: "A lot of the cultures that built golems thought tools shouldn't talk." But when the Trust buys a golem, the free ones give it the ability to speak—she does not know exactly how, but it is not just a matter of baking them a tongue (154).[9]

When they first meet, she takes Moist to task for being too politically correct—"do you get a warm, charitable feeling when [you call a golem Mister]?" (61)—then explaining

> Golems don't have any of our baggage about "who am I, why am I here," okay? Because they *know*. They were made to be tools, to be property, to work. Work is what they do. In a way, it's what they *are*. End of existential angst. [...] And then stupid people go around calling them "persons of clay" and "Mr. Spanner" and so on, which they find rather strange. They *understand* about free will. They also understand that they don't have it. Mind you, once a golem *owns* himself, it's a different matter [63].

And so, in a sort of circular reasoning consistent with the golems' own circular view of cosmology, what do golems own when they own themselves? Like any free being, they own a tool, a means of production, which they then have the free will and right to hire out for their own financial benefit. This does frighten some people; the windows of the Golem Trust are the frequent targets of graffiti and thrown bricks.

For all her prickliness, "Moist noticed that [Adora Belle] spoke to golems differently. There was actual *tenderness* in her voice" (*GP* 159). She checks on all the hired golems once a week to be sure they are treated properly and not forgotten (163). Given her personality and history, one of the things that most appeals to her about golems is that "[t]hey're not frightened of 'forever.' They're not frightened of *anything*" (164). Her hardness and bitterness are not surprising. The other point at which the worlds of Moist and Adora Belle intersect is the clacks. The clacks system, first introduced in *The Fifth Elephant*, is the Discworld equivalent of the telegraph and based on an actual abandoned technology in our world, the semaphore tower system or optical telegraph. Adora Belle's father invented them and her brother was a clacks technician who died under mysterious circumstances—in fact murdered as a result of the efforts of a syndicate determined to buy up all the independent clacks companies, develop a monopoly, and milk them dry with no regard for sustainability. The syndicate also wants to eliminate any potential competition from the post office, which is where Moist comes in.

But why, given magic, would you need such a thing as the clacks? Because of how magic works in Discworld: "Oh, you *could* do it all by magic, you certainly could. You could wave a wand and get twinkly stars and a fresh-baked loaf. You could make fish jump out of the sea already cooked. And then, somewhere, somehow, magic would present its bill, which was always more than you could afford" (147). But even more aptly to our steampunk theme, Moist talks about the enchantment of technology and machinery as opposed to mere magic, delivering a sort of maker hymn to the romance of human ingenuity:

> Ordinary men had dreamed it up and put it together, building towers on rafts in swamps and across the frozen spines of mountains. They'd cursed and, worse, used logarithms. They'd waded through rivers and dabbled in trigonometry. They hadn't dreamed it, in the way people usually used the word, but they'd imagined a different world, and bent metal around it. And out of all this sweat and swearing and mathematics had come this … thing, dropping words across the world as softly as starlight [316].

In the sequel to *Going Postal*, *Making Money*, now that Moist has revitalized the post office, Vetinari aims him at the monetary and banking system. Though we first saw some complaints about golems taking jobs from the other races of Ankh-Morpork in *Feet of Clay*, this is where Pratchett seriously begins to explore the economic implications of golems. Moist is busy questioning the reasoning behind the gold standard and inventing paper money and micro-loans, and realizing that it is the city itself, its people and productivity, that backs the currency: "The city is the magician, the alchemist in reverse. It turns worthless gold into … everything. […] The *city* says a dollar is worth a dollar" (115). "What is a coin compared to the hand that holds it? That's worth! That's value!" (384).

But at the same time, the free golems are bringing to the fore concerns about machines putting humans out of work and upsetting the economic balance by doing the same work for far less money than a human. Though wages are falling because of the immigration of all sorts of people to Ankh-Morpork, it is easiest simply to blame the golems, "who uncomplainingly did the dirtiest jobs, worked around the clock, and were so honest they paid their taxes. But they weren't human and they had glowing eyes, and people could get touchy about that sort of thing" (100).

The novel starts with the Golem Trust learning of a cache of buried ancient golems and sending Adora Belle Dearheart to dig them out. Due to her misunderstanding of an ancient inscription, she was expecting four solid gold golems—which would have had a bad enough impact on the economy by dramatically increasing the city's gold reserves in an instant—but what shows up is 4,000 ceramic guard golems, who march up and form a defensive ring just outside the city walls (316). Not too surprisingly, the other cities immediately see this as a threat—"aggressive defense," as Vetinari calls it (317), saying "Miss Dearheart [...] has been kind enough to bring Ankh-Morpork an army capable of conquering the world, although I'm happy to accept her assurance that she didn't really mean to" (317).

Adora Belle warns "They have no chem that I can get at. [...] There's no way of opening their heads! As far as we can tell they have one overriding imperative, which is to defend the city. And that's all. It's actually carved into their clay" (317). She reports that the freed golems "don't like them. They think they will cause trouble. They have no chem that can be changed. They're worse than zombies." Ancient as they are, they may even have no prohibition against killing humans (374). One of the councilors does propose that they use them to conquer their neighbors: "What a weapon [...]. They could collapse a city in a day" (331). But Vetinari insists "We are not going to have another wretched empire while I am Patrician. We've only just got over the last one" (318). "We didn't intend the Empire," he reminds his council. "It just became a bad habit" (338).

He *is* quite willing to treat them as tools to put to work for the city—initially he says "Those people are resurrected from darkness to turn the wheels of commerce, for the general good. [...] [Miss Dearheart] is doing the city a great service" (29)—until the potentially disastrous economic consequences are spelled out for him. Yes, the golems could do the work of 120,000 men. But that would put 120,000 men out of work. And golems don't spend money on food, shelter, clothing, or entertainment—all they really need is the occasional tube of ceramic cement—so demand for goods and services would drop along with the number of people who could still afford to pay for them, and there would be further unemployment among those not directly displaced by the golems (320). Having that many unfree golems enter the work force at once would ruin the city one way or another, through war, economic upset, or the internal rot that comes from being the heart of an empire.

Moist understands that they need to be removed from the scene and rendered inert, and con man that he is at heart, works out how to command them—then orders them to march ten miles from the city and bury themselves again. "They could do wonderful things for the city, couldn't they?" protests a reporter. But he responds,

> Like embroil it in a war or create an army of beggars? My way's better! [...] I want to base the currency on them! [...] Gold that guards itself! [...] How much are they worth? [...] They could build canals and dam floods, level mountains and make roads! If we need them to, they will! And if we don't, then they'll help to make us rich by doing nothing! The dollar will be so sound you could bounce trolls off it! [332].

At the end of *Making Money*, we are left with Ankh-Morpork on the golem standard, the reserve golems backing the currency. Some of the ancient golems and horses are in use to power the clacks towers and pull the mail coaches, but the rest are safe in their own self-made vault, being good as gold, as it were.

Golems have a far less central role in *Raising Steam* [*RS*]; in this novel the non-human race Pratchett is most concerned with developing is the goblins, first encountered in *Snuff*. *Raising Steam* is another example of relatively ordinary people inevitably developing technology to do the things that magic does for the gifted; in this case, the steam engine locomotive, even though, as Lu-Tze of the History Monks reports, the world isn't ready and it isn't yet "steam-engine time" (*RS* 102). Free golems are thoroughly part of the city's landscape now, working in Harry King's rubbish-sorting operation (44), as guards in the locomotive engine Iron Girder's shed, and as metalworkers for the new railway (87): always punctual, never ill, "every one of them his own man, albeit one made of clay" (87). Though now they are also free to make their own choices about employment; King complains that they can be hard to hire because "They're all off doing landscape gardening and suchlike daisy rubbish" (93).

But there is one interesting minor golem development in *Raising Steam*. Moist is permitted the use of one of the ancient Umnian golem horses by Vetinari, and finds himself wondering if the horses desire their own freedom as much as the humanoid golems do. Subtly disturbed by the horse's "all give and no take" relationship to him, by the fact that he need not perform the "fussing little rituals that defined horsemanship" like seeing to its food and water and so on (225), Moist is moved to ask the creature if it can speak. "Yes, if we want to," it answers. Pressed further, it admits that it does not understand the appeal of relaxation but will obediently attempt to "[r]oll around on the flowers and neigh a bit and gallop about and have some fun" if it will please Moist (150–151). Vetinari complains that upon its return to the stables, the horse demanded "Give me livery or give me death" (176; one suspects the entire incident may have been set up for the sake of this punch line), though it still insists that "[b]eing a horse is my passion in life" (189). As their relationship continues, Moist is moved to offer the horse a name, Flash, and Flash muses "It's a very nice feeling to know who you are. I wonder how I did without it for these past nine hundred and three years" (229). Moist does make use of the buried Umnian golems at a key point in the plot, but as he assures Vetinari, no evidence of this will ever be found (331, 361). Golems continue to be key workers in the railyards and laying track—but it is as Free Golems with names and free will and a paycheck, not wordless and nameless slaves.

Conclusion

Pratchett has, in the Industrial Revolution series, addressed a number of questions that the figure of the golem raises: "What is the legal status of a Golem? Is a Golem a person? [...] Is destroying a Golem murder? Can a Golem be intelligent? Is an 'intelligent' Golem different from other Golems?" (Sherwin 26). More specific to our topic, Pratchett has used his golems to present us with a number of scenarios representing modern economic concerns—the problems of unemployment caused by industrial manufacturing methods abruptly replacing human labor, the difficulties of absorbing the immigration of a new labor source willing to take on the bottom rung of available jobs, the dangers of a major change being implemented without thoroughly thinking through its implications, and change occurring whether the times are ready for it or not. Complicating the issue is the fact of the golems' status as "human for a given value of human" (*MM* 40), meaning that their self-ownership echoes socialist and communist ideas that came about in our own world in response to these same stresses. Golems embody the idea that the means of production should be in the possession of those doing the producing. Yet they problematize the issue, at the same time, by having no physical needs and thus not completing the cycle of production and consumption.

Part of the brilliance of Terry Pratchett as a writer is his skill in making these deep issues of how the world operates, how people live together, what makes a city like Ankh-Morpork run, or what issues we might have to think about in a world of self-aware machines, an integral part of a fast-paced and humorous adventure story. A maker aesthetic underlies the steampunk relationship with technology and culture, and under that aesthetic, what makes things tick, what makes humans work, and what we need to think about to make the future itself function humanely, is an adventure itself. Pratchett is very good at making us think about these things—while we think we are just being entertained.

Notes

1. A shorter version of this essay was published in *Proceedings of the Upstate Steampunk Extravaganza and Meetup*, edited by Gypsey Elaine Teague, Cambridge Scholars Press, 2011.
2. For a discussion of race in steampunk literature and role-playing, with a consideration of gender issues as well, see Goh.
3. Pratchett's Introduction to the film *Going Postal* specifically states that the setting is similar to Victorian London. It is also worth noting the afterword to the historical fantasy *Dodger*, in which Pratchett discusses his interest in and sources for the early Victorian London setting of that book.
4. Or there is the assumption that it will, in spite of all evidence to the contrary, as in the movie *The Iron Giant*.
5. See Killjoy for another and more considered discussion of the potential political

aims of the steampunk movement and a call for a return to the more anarchic and anti-authoritarian ethos of first-generation steampunk.

   6. The terra-cotta soldiers of the Red Army in *Interesting Times* are considered golems of a sort by the wizard Rincewind, who finds that, as with the ones in Ankh-Morpork, the difficult part is actually getting them to *stop* working (260).

   7. In the film *Going Postal*, Adora Belle Dearheart specifically states that golems have souls. In the book, the soul of a dead golem meets Death and asks "Then Who Is This Doing The Listening?" (*GP* 256–257)

   8. In the *Going Postal* movie she is referred to as Adora, in the book it is strictly Miss Dearheart, and it is Adora Belle in *Making Money* and subsequent appearances.

   9. Pratchett indicates the peculiar speech habits of the golems typographically by capitalizing every word they speak and avoiding contractions. In some printings, their speech is rendered in a quasi–Hebrew typeface.

WORKS CITED

Allison, Alida. "Guess Who's Coming to Dinner? the Golem as Family Member in Jewish Children's Literature." *The Lion and the Unicorn*, vol. 14, 1990, pp. 92–97.
Blade Runner. Dir. Ridley Scott. Perf. Harrison Ford, Rutger Hauer, Sean Young. 1982. Warner Home Video, 1999.
Goh, Jaymee. "On Race and Steampunk." *SteamPunk Magazine*, vol. 7, 2009, pp. 16–21.
Going Postal. Dir. Jon Jones. Perf. Richard Coyle, David Suchet, Claire Foy. 20th Century-Fox, 2010.
Hogfather. Dir. Vadim Jean. Perf. David Jason, Marc Warren, Michelle Dockery. Genius Entertainment, 2007.
The Iron Giant. Dir. Brad Bird. Perf. Jennifer Anniston, Harry Connick, Jr., Vin Diesel. Warner Brothers, 1999.
Killjoy, Margaret. "You Can't Stay Neutral on a Moving Train (Even if It's Steam-Powered)." *SteamPunk Magazine*, vol. 7, 2009, pp. 4–7.
Pratchett, Terry. *Dodger*. HarperCollins, 2012.
———. *Feet of Clay*. HarperCollins, 1996.
———. *The Fifth Elephant*. Harper, 2000.
———. *Going Postal*. HarperCollins, 2004.
———. *Interesting Times*. Harper, 1994.
———. *The Last Hero*. Gollancz, 2001.
———. *Making Money*. HarperCollins, 2007.
———. *Men at Arms*. Harper, 1993.
———. *Monstrous Regiment*. HarperCollins, 2003.
———. *Moving Pictures*. ROC, 1990.
———. *Raising Steam*. Doubleday, 2013.
———. *Reaper Man*. Gollancz, 1991.
———. *Snuff*. HarperCollins, 2011.
———. *Soul Music*. Harper, 1995.
———. *The Truth*. Harper, 2000.
Rogasky, Barbara. *The Golem*, illustrated by. Trina Schart Hyman, Holiday House, 1996.
Rosenberg, Yudl. *The Golem and the Wondrous Deeds of the Maharal of Prague*, translated by Curt Leviant. Yale UP, 2007.
"Semaphore Line." Wikipedia. http://en.wikipedia.org/wiki/Optical_telegraph Accessed 15 Nov. 2010.
Shelley, Mary. *Frankenstein*. 1831. Oxford UP, 1969.
Sherwin, Byron L. *The Golem Legend: Origins and Implications*. UP of America, 1985.
Singer, Isaac Bashevis. *The Golem*, illustrated by Uri Shulevitz, Farrer Strauss Giroux, 1982.
Stross, Charlie. "The Hard Edge of Empire." www.antipope.com Accessed 27 Oct. 2010.
"The Three Laws of Robotics." Wikipedia. http://en.wikipedia.org/wiki/Three_Laws_of_Robotics Accessed 18 Nov. 2010.
Tolkien, J.R.R. "On Fairy-stories." *The Tolkien Reader*, Ballantine, 1966, pp. 3–84.

2001. Dir. Stanley Kubrick. Perf Kier Dullea, Gary Lockwood. 1968. Warner Home Video, 2001.
Wells, H.G. *The Time Machine*. 1895. Heinemann, 1964.
Wiesel, Elie. *The Golem: The Story of a Legend*, translated by Anne Borchardt, illustrated by Mark Podwal, Summit, 1983.
Williamson, Jack. "With Folded Hands." *Analog: Writer's Choice. Vol. 5*, edited by Stanley Schmidt, Dial Press, 1983, pp. 8–43.
Wilson, Eric G. *The Melancholy Android: On the Psychology of Sacred Machines*. State University of New York Press, 2006.
Yair, Gad, and Micaela Soyer. *The Golem in German Social Theory*. Lexington Books, 2008.

Neomedievalism and the Ethics of Colonization in Pratchett and Baxter's *The Long Earth* and *The Long War*

Sadie E. Hash

In the series *The Long Earth*, Terry Pratchett and Stephen Baxter create a multiverse where millions of Earths, which are naturally uninhabited by humans, exist in millions of different dimensions. The first two novels of the series, *The Long Earth* (2012) and *The Long War* (2013), explore how governments and individuals alike deal with these newly "discovered" worlds into which humanity can suddenly expand. The caveat to the discovery is that humans have been visiting, intentionally or unintentionally, these worlds for centuries. Much like other discovered lands, the new to one group is familiar to another group. After the plans for "stepper" devices are made public (which becomes known as Step Day), any inhabitant of Datum (the only Earth where humans evolved, our Earth) can "step" East or West into new worlds with the assistance of these homemade devices. There are humans, of course, who can step naturally and without the assistance of these devices as well as humans who find it too physically hard to step and are left behind on Datum. These worlds humans can now step into are devoid of human technology, and most technology cannot be transferred between worlds: "No metallic iron can be carried over, sir. Or steel. You can take through whatever you can carry.... I mean, there's iron ore in the other worlds, and you can dig it up and process it and manufacture iron over *there*, but you can't carry that step-wise either" (*Earth* 60–61). These worlds, labeled collectively the Long Earth, are, to the humans of Datum, seemingly completely undeveloped and untamed. The Long Earth features not only untarnished nature but also strange humanoid species named after the trolls and elves of a wide variety of medievalist and medievalism texts from myth to medieval romance to popular culture, and Pratchett and Baxter draw from Anglo-Saxon tradition onwards to develop the medievalism in these novels. Most importantly, the trolls and elves of the Long Earth have evolved to "step" through the Long Earth and have been "stepping" through Datum since otherworldly creatures have appeared in folklore and literature. In the world created by Pratchett and Baxter, these species are the impetus for all of the tales and mythology involving fairies, elves, and trolls. Not only do these figures invoke medievalism and complicate the relationship between magic and science retroactively in the science fiction narrative, but they are at conflict with and enslaved by humans as the Long Earth is colonized. By analyzing *The Long Earth* and *The Long War* by examining the use of neomedievalism, I argue that Pratchett and Baxter interrogate the ethics of colonizing the Long Earth by intimately connecting the Long Earth with medievalist texts which the narrative characterizes as early British folklore and intertwines with British and American history. This connection complicates the expected genre conventions of science fiction and the usual tropes of colonialism in that genre.

By incorporating elements of medievalist texts into this science fiction narrative, these authors are participating in Leslie J. Workman's "notion of medievalism as the ongoing process of recreating, reinventing, and reenacting medieval culture in postmedieval times" (Emery and Utz 2). Pratchett and Baxter's medievalism, although participating in reinventing medieval culture, is more clearly "the medievalism of popular culture" which can be distinguished through the use of the term neomedievalism which:

> is not simply a new kind of medievalism, as its name might suggest, but, in fact, a completely different (and often irreverent) ahistorical approach to the medieval.... Neomedieval creations appropriate and transform elements thought to be "medieval," often flaunting their historicity or verisimilitude to achieve a particular aesthetic. It is perhaps more akin to the technique of "sampling" in modern context.... its fantastical leaps and juxtapositions [require understanding of] the history, beliefs, and cultural productions of the period from 476 to 1453 [Emery and Utz 6–7].

Neomedievalism allows our authors to take figures and tropes from various pre-modern sources and invoke the popular culture idea of what is medieval. Pratchett and Baxter forge a connection between the structure of the multiverse they have created and the medievalist texts they are referencing by using terms associated with the medieval period, such as Valhalla, Grendel, wanderer, seafarers, trolls, elves, and kobolds. Lobsang, protagonist Joshua's companion and guide through the Long Earth and the representative of a massive corporation with equal access to finances and historical records, summarizes his theory about the trolls and elves: "I've told you of fragmentary reports from old traditions—glimpses of transitory beings, tales from myth. I believe that trolls and other species have been visiting Earth for millennia—perhaps simply to pass through, perhaps for other purposes. The frequency of such reports drops in recent centuries, because of the growth of scientific literacy perhaps.... But in recent decades, and even since Step Day, such sightings have been on the increase again" (207). Although this series is classified as science fiction, Pratchett brings his distinct flavor of fantasy which samples medieval elements. These authors change the rules of their science in their science fiction series to accommodate medievalism. Pratchett and Baxter's use of neomedievalism results in "calling attention to the created nature of any representation of the past" through the "repurposing" of "fragments" of "medievalist texts (history, popular culture representations, conventions, tropes, and the like)" (Mayer 224). Trolls and elves—employed as antagonists of chivalric knights in medieval romances—continuously invite associations with medieval literature, especially since reality in *The Long Earth* "had suddenly become porous" (210). By changing the very fabric of reality, Pratchett and Baxter are experimenting with the idea that these stories have an origin based in the scientific reality of their narrative and invite their characters, and vicariously their readers, to revisit their preconceived notions about these texts and reality.

Pratchett and Baxter use elements of the Middle Ages well known in popular culture to craft a certain ambience in the narrative. In turn, the use of medieval elements in the narrative colors a modern reader's perception of medievalist texts, and Pratchett and Baxter are informing a modern audience's understanding of these elements. This dynamic is not dissimilar to the use of medieval romance elsewhere in literature such as in the 17th century where "to write a romance can be, not a natural act within a living tradition, but an act of conscious medievalism, a revival of the past" (Cooper 14). Helen Cooper argues

> "new readers make news texts"; every generation brings different cultural expectations to works of the past and so finds new meaning and new things to respond to. Even successive recopyings of a single text record a process of shifting interpretations and significations, and those shifts become more marked as traditional elements are re-used in new stories and motifs move across authors, periods, readerships grow, and changing political and linguistic conditions [4].

When the characters of the series come into contact with the trolls and elves, they are being asked to reconsider their experience with myth and folklore. When readers witness a modern society, fully aware of the damage done by and consequences of colonization in their own history, venturing into and colonizing pre-modern worlds, they are being asked to reconsider their notion of progress.

This series also seeks to understand how all the intricacies of society translates to a vast expanse that anyone can attempt to explore and settle. Medievalism is often "a way to challenge class structures rather than to justify them" (Simmons 6) and the Long Earth challenges every societal structure ever put in place. In this text, neomedievalism is operating in two ways in order to question the operation of society in both Datum and the Long Earth. First, medievalism is often used to critique from a distance the author's contemporary society, and the multi-dimensional universe of identical and pre-modern (technology-free, human-free)[1] worlds accomplishes the same goal of allowing the authors the space to critique. The first form of neomedievalism is the building of a multiverse which acts as a text itself and functions in the same manner as a medievalism which transports the reader to a pre–1600 landscape. Second, this influence becomes a part of the plot of the series as the figures of medievalist texts, particularly trolls and elves, become real figures in the text. The nature of the Long Earth and the ability to step from world to world change the origin of fairy tales, folklore, and medieval romance.[2] This second form of neomedievalism is the interpretation and incorporation of these figures into essential aspects of the plot and positioning these figures within the narrative eventually as colonized, antagonistic, and dangerous beings. These two forms of neomedievalism take the salient characteristics of medievalism and incorporate these elements directly into the structure of the multiverse narrative. Pratchett's familiarity with medieval romance (Leverett) is positioned within a science fiction narrative. However, the two genres are not so far apart, particularly when the series participates in the neomedievalism, the fragmenting of medievalist texts and elements, discussed above.

These elements encourage the reader to approach this text as a medieval fantasy as well as a science fiction adventure. Clare A. Simmons's description of medievalism echoes those characteristics which are found in this science fiction series:

> Perhaps a person who is interested in the Middle Ages is enacting some kind of wish-fulfillment, looking for a world where adventure is still possible; or where social order prevails; or where artistry serves to glorify the divine; or where good triumphs over evil. Humor may serve as a means of confronting their expectations, making the subconscious conscious and causing readers to question their preconceptions [110].

The creation of the step-wise Earths caters to many of the wishes of the population of Datum (space unpopulated, nature unpolluted, an abundance of resources), makes adventure possible, necessarily changes the social order, provides an opportunity for invention (the divine here might be represented by Lobsang as the text humorously draws those innocuous connections), and hosts conflicts between good and evil, all the while incorporating Pratchett's signature humor and wit.[3] These technologically barren worlds combined with the medieval elements of the trolls and elves encourage a reading of this text as a work of science fiction neomedievalism. While the genre of fantasy is "one of the major focal points" for medievalism, the "affinity between fantasy and the Middle Ages is built on a pervasive and widespread view of the medieval period as a long age of faith and magic" (Kears and Paz 18). Pratchett and Baxter's creation of the step-wise worlds, trolls and elves who can appear in Datum Earth, and individuals who can without the aid of technology travel the Long Earth changes, within the narrative, that view of the Middle Ages as a time of purely "faith and magic" and gives scientific explanations to magical existence of elves and trolls. The effect interrogates "such seemingly clear-cut distinctions between 'science' and 'fantasy,' between 'the non-magical' and 'the magical'" (19) which Carl Kears and James Paz find problematic.

Pratchett and Baxter use a mixture of futuristic advancement and medieval elements, like colors on a palette, to create a new Middle Ages as the human race works through a transitional period after the discovery of the Long Earth which forces the re-evaluation of their society. The futuristic component of this mixture is the configuration of the Long Earth which both strips steppers of technology and allows the authors to have infinite premodern canvases on which to paint. This futuristic component, the design of the multiverse, then becomes the first form of neomedievalism where the structure of the Long Earth works as a text and mimics the way in which medievalism uses the medieval period to comment on the present. The role of government, class structures, and the ethics of expansion are all concerns of Pratchett and Baxter's 21st-century society and are reflected in the struggles of their fictional society:

> It is virtually impossible, then, to think about medievalism without recourse to the capacious concept of presentism. Applied across the expansive history of medievalism, it discloses a story of twofold temporal mobility; for the idea of the medieval past constantly changes because the present itself is ever moving, receding into the past—perhaps becoming the Middle Ages of some future that will also call itself "the present." [D'Arcens 187].

Pratchett and Baxter, with their medieval present in the Long Earth, effectively change the medieval past for their narrative. This opportunity at a reboot[4] for society extends to almost all people in the novel.[5] Not only do people leave the Datum due to debt or dissatisfying careers, but they also take on the opportunity to right the wrongs of past colonization. For example, from the point of view of an Australian the Long Earth represents a landscape "they would shape ... and no white colonist could ever appropriate" (*War* 86). This viewpoint is juxtaposed with the colonialization of the Long Earth, use and abuse of the trolls, and conflict with the elves.

The authors manipulate these ideas through an endless multiverse and thus transform a literary technique into a form of medievalism which manifests as physical worlds. Pratchett and Baxter are challenging the hierarchy of Earth's society through their creation of the Long Earth and their manipulation of the dynamics of the colonization of Long Earth. Like the use of medievalism in a text, their creation of the Long Earth allows the authors to comment on Datum, or more importantly, contemporary society. Medievalism often creates pre-modern worlds with generalized medieval elements to comment on contemporary society by affording the authors distance so they can safely criticize the society without fear of severe repercussions. Pratchett and Baxter treat all of the Long Earth as a text. Each new, identical, untouched Earth is a new template for the authors to express their critique and their inquiries. They create the same pre-modern worlds over and over so they can have infinite possibilities to critique contemporary society and our society's reaction to the ideas of colonialism. While the worlds of the Long Earth are arguably pre-modern due to the inability of humans to step with any technology containing metal, it is critical to note that each world is exactly the same age: "Every Earth comes with its own universe.... And the stars are the same. The date is the same, in all the worlds. Even the time of day. The astronomers have established that with star charts; they could tell if there were a slippage of a century, or whatever" (*Earth* 63). These worlds may differ in technology but are our world which repeats endlessly in the most basic elements without the influence of humanity. For Pratchett and Baxter, each world is a new variation where they can critique the progress of humanity and demonstrate the dangers of not examining the ethics of settling "unclaimed" worlds. They illustrate these dangers even as this expansion is happening in a futuristic era. It is assumed that if humanity had to spread across a large space again, that expansion and settlement would happen humanely. The creation of these thousands of worlds allows Pratchett and Baxter to show that expansion of the human race would still be problematic in terms of colonialism and respecting the rights of the indigenous inhabitants, flora, and fauna.

Their use of medievalism complicates the typical use of colonialism in a science fiction narrative. While Pratchett and Baxter seem to incorporate the classic conventions of colonialism into their creation of the Long Earth, they also shift the usual dynamics of colonialism to encourage evaluation of the ethical issues. According to Edward W. Said, colonialism "is the implanting of settlements on distant territory" which "are supported and perhaps even impelled by impressive ideological formations that include notions that certain territories and people require and *beseech* domination" (9). These ideological formations are more than just the promises of politicians and the strictures of government. From the beginning of the series, the governments of Datum do struggle with the logistical nightmare of governing settlements which are worlds away and expanding out into the Long Earth by maintaining each Datum country's footprint in the Long Earth worlds. These government issues reinforce the dynamics of colonialism as discussed by Said. However, these governments also grapple with a different ideology which is driving the sudden expansion. The Datum governments seek to maintain control of their citizens and the borders of individual countries even between worlds. Poor or debt-ridden inhabitants of Datum suddenly realize that their freedom is only a few steps away; stepping into a new world free of burden and with a fresh start is now an option and complicates the role of government. While these circumstances are not unusual when it comes to colonies, the ease of an individual's ability to travel with relative ease with a homemade device to the new worlds is quite unusual. The governments of Datum seek to control this freedom as economies begin to collapse. In Pratchett's usual witty manner, he encourages his reader to examine the place of government in the Long Earth: "'Oh, don't be absurd, man.' The Prime Minister sat back in his chair. 'Come on. We can't just ban a thing because we can't control it.' The minister responsible for health and safety looked startled. 'I don't see why not. It's never stopped us before'" (*Earth* 68). Pratchett and Baxter remind their readers that this struggle between the control of the government and the will of the citizen is a familiar problem. The government seeks to expand to give their overpopulated areas relief and, more importantly, to control their citizens their wayward citizens. The citizens seek new opportunities and freedoms from old burdens. The colonizers are actively fleeing from structure and the oppression of an overcrowded world. The ideology driving the humans of Datum out into the Long Earth is that of freedom and space. Not unexpectedly, however, it is that same freedom and space which most humans deny to the current inhabitants of the Long Earth. The inhabitants of Datum assume that there are no intelligent beings equivalent to humans in the Long Earth. This assumption leads the reader to the next point in Said's commentary on colonization: the colonized people are necessarily viewed as rightfully subjugated.

Once the colonizers, settlers, and explorers of the Long Earth begin to encounter the inhabitants of the Long Earth, the human's treatment of the trolls and the elves exemplifies Said's explanation of the Other and colonialism. In the second book of the series, *The Long War*, the elves are feared and the trolls are enslaved, sometimes abused and used for experiments, and held up as a rallying point by the colonies striving for independence from Datum. The premodern nature of the Long Earth makes the help of trolls seemingly essential and, at first, cooperative:

> The reason for the rapid expansion had been possible, he learned, was the trolls. Trolls were useful, trolls were friendly, companionable—and, crucially, ever ready to lift a heavy load, an exercise they took much delight in. This donation of muscle

power had helped the colonists here overpower their lack of manpower, draft animals and machinery [*Earth* 309].

However, by the beginning of the second novel *The Long War*, the reader (and audience within the narrative viewing newsfeeds across the Long Earth) are confronted with the scene of a cowering troll, "if a beast built like a brick wall covered in black fur could be said to cower at all—and she held her cub to her powerful chest" (*War* 1). Here a troll mother protects and defends her child from being ripped away from her for an experiment meant to further the exploration of the Long Earth. Later in the novel, the characters are confronted by the fact that the overseers of trolls carry whips and weapons (*War* 115 and 120), a distinct change from the communal living situation between humans and trolls in the early settlements of the first novel. The treatment of the trolls and elves embodies Said's representation of the Other in the dynamic of colonialism; the right to colonize the Other is fueled by "words like 'inferior' or 'subject races,' 'subordinate people,' 'dependency,' 'expansion,' and 'authority'" (Said 9). Typically, colonization features a dynamic which clearly develops the Other as a category to be subjugated. In these two novels, the Other are the inhabitants of the Long Earth such as the trolls and elves. They are seemingly vastly different from humans, even though they are repeatedly characterized as humanoids. The consensus of the general public as it spreads out across the Long Earth is as follows:

> Whatever the reason, the alternate universes into which Earth's pioneers poured out were mostly dark, quiet worlds. Worlds of trees, a spark of civilization, one circle of firelight beyond which the shadows spread to infinity. There were humanoids out there, descendants of lost cousins of humanity, but people knew they would never encounter a humanoid that was anything like as smart as they were. Never a humanoid that could speak English, for example [*War* 329].

This quote encapsulates the expected colonialist attitude towards the inhabitants of the colonized area. The homeland of the colonialist is the height of civilization. Not only is Datum the center of civilization, but it is the source of the most important life and the only intelligent life. To this point of view, there is nothing unethical about the treatment of the trolls and the elves. The Others who are outside of that civilization are inferior and, therefore, do not have the rights afforded to the colonizers. Both of Said's explanations of colonialism, where colonizers are ideologically driven and the Other is made to be subjugated, focus on the ethics of the class structures surrounding those who are perceived as inferior by society. The authors prompt interrogation of these dynamics through the way they dismantle the structures of society by scattering humanity across so many worlds.

These colonialist assumptions are constantly undermined by the text. Political movements are fueled by either the opposition to or support of the rights of these strange creatures. The troll sign language used by the mother troll to declare "I will not" is repeated in defense of the rights of colonists. Politicians make campaign speeches based on governing the Long Earth and the situation regarding the trolls, and revolutions are centered around bringing rights to trolls. Clear ideological stances are taken by various factions of society based on the view that inhabitants of the Long Earth are classified as the Other. Even this othering of the trolls and elves invokes a sense of the medieval romance:

> Above all, they are other in a fuller sense than almost any of the ways in which the term is now used. Most "others" are alien because of unfamiliarity, or sexual or cultural difference, or social or geographical distance: unfamiliarity and difference and distance that ultimately offer the possibility of closer knowledge and understanding. Fairies come from the Otherworld, and are unassimilable. It is never going to be possible to bridge the gulf between the two worlds, even though a being from one side may occasionally take up habitation on the other [Cooper 173–174].

Pratchett and Baxter want their audience to the trolls and the elves as the fairies, and they have begun to close the distance between the fairy world and the real world. Even though the trolls are being othered by those seeking to use them, the text with its frequent refenced to humanoid, bipedal, and, most importantly, mythological stance, repaint these strange creatures as recognizable. Through this constant summoning of a familiar, though fragmented, medieval past, the authors reverse the expectation that those who are colonized are completely identified as the Other in the multiverse of Long Earth. The authors subtly weave in the idea that the presence of the multiverse, while new to the vast majority of humanity, has been in existence since the beginning of time and has interacted with humanity since the trolls and elves have learned to step from world to world. The trolls and elves, therefore, although being encroached upon by humanity now, are the superior and more developed beings in the environment of the Long Earth. Instead of humans being superior in every way, or at least perceived as superior to the inhabitants of the Long Earth, humans are at a disadvantage to the trolls and especially the elves when it comes to navigating the Long Earth. For example, protagonist Joshua's first encounter with the elves ends poorly as the elves have advanced and intricate hunting techniques which rely on quickly stepping from world to world in order to better surround their prey (*Earth* 238). While some humans are the "arrogant colonialists invading" and believe the inhabitants of the Long Earth to be "technologically inferior civilization[s]" (Rieder 4), humans are attempting to colonialize places inhabited by species which are more adept at navigating the Long Earth than they are. This advanced ability and the metal-stripping nature of the Long Earth counteracts any technological advances human may have on Datum. The narrative of the second novel blatantly states that the assumption of Datum superiority and human superiority is incorrect (*War* 329).

The neomedievalism of the novels entwines the inhabitants of Datum and those of the Long Earth and makes these species are more familiar than those typical classified as the Other by lengthening the period of contact the trolls and elves have had with humans. Trolls and elves are more a part of the Datum folkloric identity and history than most humans of Datum realize. Pratchett and Baxter proceed to recount a fictional interview from their bestselling yet controversial Professor Woltan Ulm of Oxford University who argues that "'[i]f [nomadic species such as trolls] *have* had contact with mankind, you might think we would know about it. Well, in a sense, we do. It's remarkable how much human folklore can be explained away if you postulate humanoid races that can move stepwise at will" (*War* 331). This idea is picked from the most prominent explorers of the Long Earth Lobsang and Joshua. Lobsang, Joshua's guide, explains earlier on in the novel: "I would like to suggest we label these creatures elves. I'm drawing on more mythology, partial records of more tentative, misunderstood encounters, with mysterious, slender, human-like creatures who passed through our world ghost-like. The existence of a variety of stepping humanoids could justify a large body of mythology" (223). These creatures are not completely foreign and new as the Long Earth dimensions may, at first, make them seem or as the colonizers and Datum governments may choose to assume. These creatures are part of the folktales and literature which are so familiar to any reader of the fantasy genre and even to popular culture in general.

The trolls and elves and such creatures of the Long Earth become the second form of neomedievalism in these two novels. The creation of the trolls and the elves is more than an anachronistic feature or an allusion to medievalist texts. As shown above, the existence of these figures within the series create a reciprocity between medievalist texts and the narrative world of their series. Because Pratchett and Baxter are breathing life into these figures, these Long Earth inhabitants become figures of medievalism by connecting to a greater narrative and adapting aspects of medievalist texts. Pratchett and Baxter are taking the usual form of medievalism, medieval romances, medieval tropes, folklore, characteristics, or features, and crafting them into actual beings with a scientific explanation in the multiverse. The trolls and elves are no longer the figures of medievalist texts and lore creatively conjured from the past but are real beings, extant, surviving pieces of real (in this multiverse) medieval life.

Trolls and elves are physical embodiment of the folklore of Britain. Here the authors are explicitly acknowledging their reshaping of our view of folklore. The introduction of these medieval elements into a futuristic world prompts re-evaluation of those medieval texts and the folklore through which contemporary society knows those medieval elements. Pratchett participates in this reincorporation consciously, and he acknowledges his use of folklore in his works: "I am not a folklorist, but I am a vast consumer of folklore—an end user, if you like. I think about folklore in the same way that a carpenter thinks about trees, although a good carpenter works with the grain of the wood and should endeavor to make a table that will leave the tree glad that it became timber" (159). The original folklore of early Britain is to the authors' adaptation of folklore in the series as a tree is to a decorated table. Scholars might question the ethics of the authors' consuming and repurposing of British folklore in order to adapt it into a literary product that some might find unrecognizable. However, as Sandra Ponzanesi argues, "Adaptation is understood as remediation, a translation of one text into a new format: adaptation as reformatting and transcoding" (124–125). *The Long Earth* series illustrates Pratchett's views about folklore as he takes the familiar folklore of trolls and elves and adapts those figures into a mechanism for commentary on his contemporary society. The authors utilize folklore in their creation of the two forms of neomedievalism inherent to the narrative of the series. Ultimately, by incorporating early British folklore securely into the rationale of the Long Earth universe, Pratchett and Baxter use two forms of neomedievalism (the multiverse structure and folklore rationale) to interrogate the ethical issue of colonization that, starting with Britain's foundation myth of Brutus's colonization of Albion, is an inescapable part of British history and national identity. With the trolls eventually conscripted to help build towns and harvest crops, the colonization of the Long Earth mimics the usual colonialist enterprise. Humanity literally uses avatars of their early mythology and folklore to build their future. However, the humans' employment of trolls inevitably leads to exploitation, abuse, and the usual ill-effects of colonization.

It is important to note that colonialism is a trope of science fiction, and Pratchett and Baxter are complicating the genre of science fiction through their use of the colonial tropes critiqued by neomedievalism. John Rieder posits that "colonialism is a significant historical context for early science fiction.... Most historians of science fiction agree that utopian and satirical representations of encounters between European travelers and non–Europeans ... form a major part of the genre's prehistory" (2), so it is not surprising that colonialism is a major aspect of this series as it is a standard trope of the early science fiction narrative. The trope of colonialism allows these authors to produce a narrative which is familiar to their readers on the surface but also complex enough to complicate the usual trope and to promote a reevaluation of the development of humanity as whole. Rieder also notes that "colonialism made space into time [which] gave the globe a geography not just of climates and cultures but of stages of human development that could confront and evaluate one another" (5). The geography of the multiverse of the Long Earth with its identical, pre-modern worlds allows for an extended and more developed version of this element of science fiction. Space becomes time as humans are forced technologically backwards. The Long Earth allows for unlimited and uncharted space for the human race to explore and colonize. These new dimensions also provide different stages of development as the dimension closer to Datum are more developed and are built with more similarity to the original structures of Datum because of ease of access for materials and government agencies.

The invasion of one species or another into one space or place inhabited by another species and the repercussions of these colonializations are clearly evident in the narrative of many works of science fiction. In this series, Pratchett and Baxter have developed a narrative which embodies Rieder's argument regarding science fiction and colonialism. Rieder argues that science fiction uses colonialism of new worlds and new unexplored spaces for a very specific purpose:

> For colonialism is not merely an opening up of new possibilities, a "new world" becoming available to the "old" one, but also provides the impetus behind cognitive revolutions in the biological and human sciences that reshaped European notions of its own history and society. The exotic, once it had been scrutinized, analyzed, theorized, catalogued, and displayed, showed a tendency to turn back upon and re-evaluate those who had thus appropriated and appraised it [3].

Expansion into new spaces eventually requires expansion of the mind in some form and Pratchett and Baxter are already reshaping European notions of history and society with their approach to folklore and medievalist text. They intensify the effect described by Rieder. These worlds act as a new painting which illustrates the authors' critiques of the structure of contemporary society and yet still distance themselves from these critiques; these critiques are a signature mark of medievalism. They create endless new worlds which are the "impetus behind cognitive revolutions" which slowly take place as scientists eventually learn how to communicate with trolls and military expeditions become less about intimidation and more about communication and service. However, these authors foreground that these cognitive revolutions are slow in coming. They track a number of characters' reactions to the developments of Long Earth throughout the series. One such character is Professor Ulm who gives his opinion on the assured emptiness of the worlds of the Long Earth excepting swamps (*Earth* 8) and the instincts of the settlers: "People are expanding into all that room! Of course they are! This is a primal instinct. We plains apes still fear the leopard in the dark" (*Earth* 9). This is the same Professor Ulm who is featured in *The Long War* and was discussed earlier in this essay as reacting against Datum superiority and discusses the misperceptions of the trolls and elves. This character's development between the first two novels embodies how the possibilities of the Long Earth require interrogation of preconceived notions. Pratchett and Baxter have created a situation in which they have endless possibilities to explore various problems and issues facing contemporary society. They have also created the ideal environment to visibly demonstrate a massive the restructuring of history and society.

While these colonialist tropes are expected in a type of science fiction such as the *Long Earth* series where a new dimension is suddenly available to the whole of humanity, the use of medievalism allows the authors to complicate an expected genre convention of addressing the issues inherit to colonialism. Almost conversely to the typical science fiction narrative, as humanity spreads out across the new frontier, those individuals in initial excursions into the Long Earth are stripped of any technology containing ferrous metals. The farther humans push into these new science fiction dimensions, the more deeply ensconced into the pre-modern world they are. The mechanism of the science fiction produces the medievalism. For this narrative, the creation of the Long Earth works as an inventive type of neomedievalism incorporated into a science fiction setting. As the settlers expand into the Long Earth, through a futuristic advancement by exploring new dimensions, they return to pre-modern technologies the farther they travel into those dimensional worlds. The identical dimensions of Long Earth itself become a medievalism text through which Pratchett and Baxter can safely investigate their contemporary society. This complication is important as it allows a fresh approach and genuine evaluation of the issue of colonization and expansion. Pratchett and Baxter exhibit genuine interest in the complexity of human beings being faced with such an enormous shift in their worldview. These authors provide depth in their characters by not boxing them into binaries such as right/wrong or good/evil and present ethical issues in a realistic manner. Ronald J. Horvath argues, "The changing morality of colonialism contributes to our lack of understanding. People feel strongly about colonialism—it has either been a dirty business engaged in by evil people or a praiseworthy endeavor undertaken by fine gentlemen for the noble purpose of saving the wretched, the savage, the unfortunate" (45). Pratchett and Baxter present characters who are idealists and hope for a better future for their children as well as characters who are opportunistic and interested in only a profit. These authors strike a tone with their portrayal of the colonialization of the Long Earth which acknowledges the advantages to the expansion of humanity in to new and wide-open spaces and allowing societies to run on favors[6] rather than money as well as the malfeasance of irresponsible actions of settlers and governments. Often the characteristics of the different tourists of the Low Earths, those looking for salvation "in these paradisiacal worlds," explorers, settlers, colonizers, and entrepreneurs are blurred together in the eyes of the protagonist Joshua; they "trample all over *his* secret places" and get "in the way of the Silence" (*Earth* 52). This narrative explores the gamut of conflicting approaches to the Long Earth where settlers are indentured and entangled with Datum governments or refuse to deal with the government agencies so far away. Even the British Prime Minister of the British Datum government admits, "What a farce it is, this business of government. To imagine we were ever to control our destinies" (*Earth* 70). By developing a narrative with endless dimensions, these authors recreate the era of humanity which struggled so much with the rights and wrongs of exploration, colonization, and governing those enterprises.

Pratchett and Baxter not only subvert the expectations of the usual tropes of science fiction, but they also accentuate the interconnectivity of the two genres. The genre of fantasy and the genre of science fiction are intimately connected, and so much so that often only a slash separates the genres on the bookshelf. Richard C. West argues that "science fiction is really fantasy that puts a supposedly scientific veneer on the marvels it depicts" (13). This is true perhaps for some medieval texts as marvels were once depicted as "early scientific exploration, consistently attempting to measure, map and count the alien, the weird, the inhospitable" (Kears and Paz 9). Kears and Paz suggest that, at least for medieval science fiction/fantasy, it is our change in perception of the meaning of science which causes the some of the interconnectivity between the genres (7). This permeability between the genres in connection with medieval literature is why the use of neomedievalism is so effective in this series. The magic of a medievalist text becomes the science of the Long Earth. Cooper posits that in medieval romances:

> Magic may be at its most compelling in a romance when it does not behave magically, but a being from another world—from the other world, the world of fairy—who showed no supernatural qualities would be a sad disappointment. It is the fairies' difference from ordinary humanity, or even heroic humanity-their freedom from the pains and limitations of morality; their ability to break the rules of nature and time and physical space; their capacity to bestow unstinted wealth; their independence of moral conventions; their sheer unpredictability—that gives them their narrative interest [173].

Pratchett and Baxter allude to this type of fairy realm by having the worlds of the Long Earth being "the thickness of a thought away" (*Earth* 143), by having Irish granddads being able to "step lively" through "fairy ways" (*Earth* 305) and by having Lobsang point directly to what he refers to as myths but have the recognizable, albeit fragmented, traits of medieval romance (*Earth* 207 and 223). Pratchett and Baxter neither adhere to one medieval source nor to scientific explanation. The science fiction found in the first two novels of *The Long Earth* series take on many elements inherent to medievalist texts and sometimes offers little to no scientific explanation. Carl D. Malmgen argues, "The *worlds* of [pure fantasy] are under no obligation to be faithful to a scientific epistemology; in such *worlds*, various forms of magic can govern the relations between human and natural realms, and all sorts of fantastic or impossible actants might flourish, without any scientific motivation or rationale" (260). Pratchett and Baxter are blurring the line between the two genres by providing unexplained science, even to the narrative's scientists, and drawing clear connections to the medievalist texts which are ruled by fairies and magic. According to the narrative of series, the trolls and elves an influential force on humanity and its culture. This interconnectivity with the what should be the Other of Long Earth complicates humanity's progress through the Long Earth and puts the colonizers direct conflict with its own culture. By colonizing the Long Earth, enslaving the trolls, and warring with the elves, humanity is struggling with its own identity and its literary history.

With the authors' utilization of neomedievalism in several forms, the trope of colonialism is complicated by the idea that the soon-to-be colonized Long Earth has inhabitants which are familiar to the reader through medievalist text and folklore and are an essential and no longer fictional aspect of the development of the British and subsequently American identity. By using neomedievalism and scattering fragments of adapted medievalist texts throughout their own text, Pratchett and Baxter demonstrate that the colonizers, settlers, and explorers of the Long Earth are more intimately connected to the inhabitants of the Long Earth and have been influenced by the Long Earth through the development of Datum's folklore. Pratchett and Baxter encourage their readers to evaluate their current journey through the lens of their roots. *The Long Earth* provides an explanation for British folklore and medievalist texts. The authors rely on the readers' familiarity with folktales about people falling into fairy places to make their own connections regarding the various intentional and unintentional natural steppers. As humanity colonizes the Long Earth, the reader, along with the protagonist Joshua, learns the reality behind the folktales, as it is revealed that trolls and elves are humanoid species that evolved in the Long Earth and step to Datum—a revelation important to understanding the identity of these creatures. By connecting them to British folklore, which entangles their identity with the identity and history of humans, Pratchett and Baxter question the ethics of colonizing the Long Earth, and their use of two distinctive forms of neomedievalism complicates and critiques our perception of colonialism and reflect an ongoing concern with humanity's ethical progress.

Notes

1. As the series progresses, advancements in technology and travel are made. Large vessels, known as twains (a reference to Mark Twain, whose works, coincidentally, also

engaged in medievalism), are developed to move people and materials more easily through the worlds. However, this technology is slow in developing and expensive. This argument focuses on the slow process of exploration, expansion, and development which takes place over many years in the first two novels of the series.

    2. The lines between these categories are blurry due to Pratchett and Baxter's use of neomedievalism and the "fragmentation" of the source material. Pratchett and Baxter do not point to any one category but rather allow the reader to make their own connections to their literary and popular culture experiences concerning elves and trolls. This blurriness allows for instances in the text such as an English soldier comically mistaking trolls for Russians when he unwittingly steps out of France into the Long Earth during World War I.

    3. Pratchett and Baxter purposely set up these dynamics in order to continuously undermine them and remind the reader how complicated these issues are. One such undermined dynamic is that between the wayward citizen and the government. Although citizens may be fleeing in the Long Earth in order to start fresh and various governments' responses has been, at times, antagonistic, there are government agents, as the Long Earth develops, whose duty it is "to give a ride to a place of safety to the wounded, or even just the severely embarrassed, who had given up after their first winter without electricity, or a visit by an unexpected bear or pack of wolves—or maybe the odd dinosaur-descendant if you went far enough" (*War* 154–155).

    4. One early settlement is even named Reboot.

    5. There are those who cannot leave Datum for health reasons or find stepping too physically jarring. Some of these people are left home by their families and become antagonistic to the Long Earth and those who can step, especially naturally, as a whole.

    6. Favours are "small trades" which happen in communities in place of the use of money. Rather than bartering being limited to hard goods available at the time, favors take the idea a step further. Some good that isn't useful to you now, "but it certainly is to Franklin the smith, [can be handed] over to him in exchange for favour, to be repaid at some future time. So you are now owed a favour, which might be something solid, or even an offer to bring back store-bought goods next time he has to go to Hundred K or the Datum. Or whatever. It's no system to run a civilization on, but a pretty good one for a colony of a hundred people every single one of whom you know personally, and they know you. No point in cheating" (*Earth* 199).

Works Cited

Cooper, Helen. *The English Romance in Time: Transforming Motifs from Geoffrey of Monmouth to the Death of Shakespeare*. Oxford UP, 2004.
D'Arcens, Louise. "Presentism." Emery and Utz, pp. 181–188.
Emery, Elizabeth, and Richard Utz. "Making Medievalism: A Critical Overview." Emery and Utz, pp. 1–10.
Emery, Elizabeth, and Richard Utz, editors. *Medievalism: Key Critical Terms*, D.S. Brewer, 2014, pp. 1–10. *Medievalism*, vol. 5.
Horvath, Ronald J. "A Definition of Colonialism." *Current Anthropology*, vol. 13, no. 1, 1972, pp. 45–57. *JSTOR*, https://www.jstor.org/stable/2741072.
Kears, Carl and James Paz. "Medieval Science Fiction: An Impossible Fantasy?" *Medieval Science Fiction*, edited by Carl Kears and James Paz, King's College London, 2016, pp. 3–27.
Leverett, Emily. "Medieval English Romance and Gendered Spaces in Terry Pratchett's *Guards! Guards!*" 2016 Southeastern Medieval Association Conference, 7 October 2016, Knoxville, Tennessee.
Malmgren, Carl D. "Towards a Definition of Science Fantasy." *Science Fiction Studies*, vol. 15, no. 3 [46], Nov. 1988, pp. 259–281. *JSTOR*, https://www.jstor.org/stable/4239897.
Matthews, David. *Medievalism: A Critical History*. D.S. Brewer, 2015.
Mayer, Lauryn S. "Simulacrum." Emery and Utz, pp. 223–230.
Mendlesohn, Farah. "Faith and Ethics." *Terry Pratchett: Guilty of Literature*, 2d ed. Edited by Andrew M. Butler, Edward James, and Farah Mendlesohn, 239–260. Old Earth Books.

Ponzanesi, Sandra. *The Postcolonial Cultural Industry: Icons, Markets, Mythologies.* Palgrave Macmillan, 2014.
Pratchett, Terry. "Imaginary Worlds, Real Stories." *Folklore,* vol. 111, no. 2, Oct. 2000, pp. 159–168. *JSTOR,* https://www.jstor.org/stable/1260601.
Pratchett, Terry, and Stephen Baxter. *The Long Earth.* Harper, 2012.
_____ and _____. *The Long War.* Harper, 2013.
Rieder, John. *Colonialism and the Emergence of Science Fiction,* Wesleyan UP, 2012. *Project MUSE,* https://muse.jhu.edu/book/22738.
Said, Edward W. *Culture and Imperialism.* Vintage Books, 1993.
Simmons, Clare A. "Humor." Emery and Utz, pp. 109–115.
_____. *Popular Medievalism in Romantic-Era Britain.* Palgrave Macmillan, 2011.
Utz, Richard. *Medievalism: A Manifesto.* Arc Humanities Press, 2017.
West, Richard C. "Where Fantasy Fits: The Importance of Being Tolkien." *Mythlore: A Journal of J.R.R. Tolkien, C.S. Lewis, Charles Williams, and Mythopoeic Literature,* vol. 33, no. 1, 2014, pp. 5–36. *Mythopoeic Society,* http://www.mythsoc.org/mythlore/mythlore-125.htm.14

Appendix
Works and Adaptations

Discworld Novels

The Colour of Magic (1983)
The Light Fantastic (1986)
Equal Rites (1987)
Mort (1987)
Sourcery (1988)
Wyrd Sisters (1988)
Pyramids (1989)
Guards! Guards! (1989)
Eric (1990)
Moving Pictures (1990)
Reaper Man (1991)
Witches Abroad (1991)
Small Gods (1992)
Lords and Ladies (1992)
Men at Arms (1993)
Soul Music (1994)
Interesting Times (1994)
Maskerade (1995)
Feet of Clay (1996)
Hogfather (1996)
Jingo (1997)
The Last Continent (1998)
Carpe Jugulum (1998)
The Fifth Elephant (1999)
The Truth (2000)
Thief of Time (2001)
The Last Hero (2001)
The Amazing Maurice and His Educated Rodents (2001)
Night Watch (2002)
The Wee Free Men (2003)
Monstrous Regiment (2003)
A Hat Full of Sky (2004)
Going Postal (2004)
Thud! (2005)
Wintersmith (2006)
Making Money (2007)
Unseen Academicals (2009)
I Shall Wear Midnight (2010)
Snuff (2011)
Raising Steam (2013)
The Shepherd's Crown (2015)

Discworld Short Stories

"Turntables of the Night" (1989) (features Death as a character, with a non–Discworld setting)
"Troll Bridge" (1992)
"Theatre of Cruelty" (1993)
"The Sea and Little Fishes" (1998)
"Death and What Comes Next" (2002)
"A Collegiate Casting-Out of Devilish Devices" (2005)

Appendix

In-World Supplemental Texts

Nanny Ogg's Cookbook (2002) (with Tina Hannan)
The Discworld Almanak (2004) (with Bernard Pearson)
Where's My Cow? (2005)
The World of Poo (2012)

Discworld—Other

Maps, Guides, Quiz Books

The Streets of Ankh-Morpork (1993) (all maps co-authored with Stephen Briggs)
The Discworld Companion (1994) (2003 updated re-release as *The New Discworld Companion*; 2012 updated re-release as *Turtle Recall: The Discworld Companion ... So Far*)
The Discworld Mapp (1995)
The Unseen University Challenge (1996)
A Tourist Guide to Lancre (1998)
Death's Domain (1999)
The Wyrdest Link (2002)
The Wit and Wisdom of Discworld (2007)
The Compleat Ankh-Morpork City Guide (2012)
Mrs. Bradshaw's Handbook (2014)
The Compleat Discworld Atlas (2015)
Discworld Diaries and Discworld Calendars (ongoing)

Science and Folklore

The Science of Discworld (1999) (all science books co-authored with Ian Stewart and Jack Cohen)
The Science of Discworld II: The Globe (2002)
The Science of Discworld III: Darwin's Watch (2005)
The Folklore of Discworld (2008) (co-authored with Jacqueline Simpson)
The Science of Discworld IV: Judgement Day (2013)

Art

The Josh Kirby Discworld Portfolio (1993)
The Discworld Portfolio (1996)
The Art of Discworld (2004)
The Unseen University Cut Out Book (2006)

The Long Earth *(with Stephen Baxter)*

The Long Earth (2012)
The Long War (2013)
The Long Mars (2014)
The Long Utopia (2015)
The Long Cosmos (2016)

Other Works

The Carpet People (1971; revised edition 1992)
The Dark Side of the Sun (1976)
Strata (1981)
The Unadulterated Cat (1989)
Diggers (1990)
Wings (1990)
Good Omens (1990) (with Neil Gaiman)
Only You Can Save Mankind (1992)
Johnny and the Dead (1993)
Johnny and the Bomb (1996)
Truckers (1998)
Rainbow Mars (1999) (authored by Larry Niven; jointly conceived by Niven and Pratchett)
Nation (2008)
Dodger (2012)
Jack Dodger's Guide to London (2013)
Dragons at Crumbling Castle (2014)
The Witch's Vacuum Cleaner (2016)
Father Christmas's Fake Beard (2017)

Collected Short Works

Once More* With Footnotes (2004)
A Blink of the Screen (2012)
A Slip of the Keyboard (2014)

Film and Television

Truckers (1992)
Johnny and the Dead (1995)
Wyrd Sisters (1996)
Soul Music (1996)
Johnny and the Bomb (2006)
Hogfather (2006)
The Colour of Magic (2008)
The Light Fantastic (2008)
Going Postal (2010)
The Wee Free Men (announced in 2016, not yet released)
Terry Pratchett: Back in Black (2017) (docudrama)
Troll Bridge (2018) (short film)
Good Omens (2019)
The Watch (in production, 2019)
The Amazing Maurice and His Educated Rodents (announced, 2019)

Graphic Novels

The Colour of Magic/The Light Fantastic (1992–1993; reissued 2008)
Mort (1994)
Guards! Guards! (2000)
Small Gods (2016)

Theater

Discworld stage/screenplay adaptations by Stephen Briggs (ongoing)

Other Theater Adaptations

Lords and Ladies (1995, 2016)
Eric (2003, 2004)
Small Gods (2011)
Terry Pratchett's Night Watch (2012)

Thief of Time (2013)
Lords and Ladies (2014)
Monstrous Regiment (2014, 2015)

Soul Music (2016)
Witches Abroad (2016)

Radio

Guards! Guards! (2008)
Mort (2008)
Night Watch (2008)

Small Gods (2008)
Wyrd Sisters (2008)
Eric (2013)

Games

The Colour of Magic (1986) (video game)
Discworld MUD (founded 1991, ongoing) (online role-playing game)
Discworld (1995) (video game)
Discworld II: Missing Presumed...?! (1996) (video game)
GURPS Discworld (1998; re-release 2002) (role-playing game)
Discworld Noir (1999) (video game)

GURPS Discworld Also (2001) (role-playing game)
Thud (2002) (board game)
Cripple Mr. Onion (2003) (card game)
Discworld: The Colour of Magic (2006) (mobile phone game)
Guards Guards (2011) (board game)
Ankh-Morpork (2011) (board game)
The Witches (2013) (board game)
Clacks (2014) (board game)

Music

Dave Greenslade: *Terry Pratchett's From the Discworld* (1994)
Keith Hopwood: *Soul Music—Terry Pratchett's Discworld* (1998)
Steeleye Span: *Wintersmith* (2013)

About the Contributors

Elise A. **Bell** obtained a Ph.D. in linguistics from the University of Arizona. Her research investigates the challenges people face in learning the sound system of a second language, with a focus on bilingualism in a community of Welsh and Spanish speakers in Argentina.

Livia **Bongiovanni** received a MA in literature from California State University Dominguez Hills. She is a recipient of the university's Presidential Outstanding Student Award and a two-time Student Research Day award winner. Her other research interests include medieval literature, folklore, 19th century British literature, and contemporary science fiction and fantasy.

Kathleen **Burt** is an assistant professor of English at Middle Georgia State University. She studied Classics and English at St. Olaf College and earned a Ph.D. in English at Marquette University, focusing on Middle English debate poetry. She is working on a study of science fiction and rhetoric in Chaucer, and mythological and folkloric approaches to contemporary fantasy authors.

Amy Lea **Clemons** is an assistant professor of English at Francis Marion University in South Carolina. Her work explores the intersections of rhetoric and literature, with particular attention to the rhetorical strategies involved in the writing and reading of dystopian, fantasy, and science fiction texts.

Janet Brennan **Croft** is a librarian at Rutgers, the State University of New Jersey. She is the author of the award-winning *War in the Works of J.R.R. Tolkien* (2004) and several book chapters on the Peter Jackson films. She is editor or coeditor of many collections of literary essays. She edits the journal *Mythlore* and serves on the board of the Mythopoeic Society.

Sadie E. **Hash** is a Ph.D. candidate in English and American literature at the University of Houston. Her research focuses on medieval literature and medievalism, and she has been awarded two travel grants to present her work at conferences. She is also an editorial assistant of the UH English Department Newsletter Forum.

Emily Lavin **Leverett** is an associate professor of English at Methodist University. Her interests include medieval romance, medievalism, and the ways that the romances of medieval Britain have made their way into contemporary arts, specifically English author Terry Pratchett's Discworld novels. When not teaching or researching, she is an editor and writer of science fiction and fantasy.

Kristin **Noone** is an English instructor and Writing Center faculty at Irvine Valley College. Her research explores medievalism, adaptation, heterotemporalities, fantasy, and romance. She has published on subjects ranging from Neil Gaiman's many Beowulfs to depictions of witchcraft in Terry Pratchett's Discworld to Arthurian references in *World of Warcraft*. Under a pen name, she also publishes fantasy fiction and romance fiction.

Mike **Perschon** is an assistant professor of English at MacEwan University in Edmonton, Alberta. He has written articles focusing on steampunk, notably for the anthology *Steaming into a Victorian Future* and *Like Clockwork*, and magazines and journals, as well as his research blog, steampunkscholar.com. He is the author of *Steampunk FAQ* (2018).

Index

Aching, Tiffany 47, 52–58, 59n10, 59n13, 62–75, 75n2
adolescence 48, 59n16
African American Vernacular English (AAVE) 78, 80
Angua 43n8, 89, 101, 108n36
Ankh-Morpork 6, 36–37, 39, 41, 43, 47, 62, 79, 82–85, 88, 90n3, 92, 94, 97, 101, 108n37, 111–121, 122n6
Arad, Kin 13–16
Asimov, Isaac 114
Auditors (characters) 46, 49–51, 58n5

Baxter, Stephen 2, 4, 124–138, 139n2, 139n3
Beowulf 63, 64, 69, 70, 75n1, 75n3
The Builders (characters) 5, 14–16
Bulgozdi, Imola 22–32
Burke, Kenneth 92, 94–96, 98, 102, 107n4, 108n23, 108n26, 108n42

Carter, Lin 25, 28–29, 33n3
choice and ethics 2–4, 5–7, 10, 12, 14–17, 34, 39–41, 56, 64, 72, 83, 89, 91, 98–100, 102–106, 116, 120
Cicsery-Ronary, Istvan, Jr. 8, 9–10
City Watch 34, 40, 43, 43n7, 79–81, 84, 95, 97, 99–100, 102, 115
clacks system 8, 110, 117–118, 120
Clute, John 2, 6, 13, 15–16
Cockney English 78, 80
Cohen the Barbarian 3, 19–32
colonialism 4, 9, 125, 129–130
The Colour of Magic 21
community 1, 3, 4, 7, 56, 59n11, 72, 74, 88, 93–94, 98–99, 112–113
compassion and ethics 1–2, 4, 5–6, 11–13, 16–17, 74–75, 98
The Computers (characters) 5, 14–16
Conan the Barbarian 3, 4, 19–32, 32n1, 33n2, 33n3, 36
Cooper, Helen 34–35, 37–39, 41–42, 126, 132, 137

Covino, William 92–95, 102, 107n5, 107n6, 107n7, 107n15
creation: as ethical act 1–4, 5–17, 40, 101, 113, 125, 129; myths in Discword 93

Dadd, Richard 66, 75n4
D'Arcens, Louise 35, 128
Datum (Long Earth) 124–138, 139n5, 139n6
Dearheart, Adora Belle 114, 116–119, 122n7, 122n8
Death (character) 16, 46, 50, 58n5, 92, 105, 122n7
De Camp, L. Sprague 22, 25, 28–29
Detritus (character) 78–82, 84, 90n2, 90n3
Dever, Michael 11–12, 16–17
Dever, Suzannah 11–12, 16–17
dialects 77–90, 90n3
Dios 46, 48
Dorfl 115–117
dragons 7, 37–38, 40–42, 43n6, 63, 75n3, 101
dwarfs 3, 37, 66, 77, 84–90, 90n5, 93–96, 98, 101, 103, 105, 107n3, 107n10, 108n37, 112

economics 118
elves 3, 4, 53–55, 61–75, 75n2, 125–128, 130–134, 136, 138, 139n2
ethos 96–97, 107n4, 108n24, 108n37; and Carrot Ironfoundersson 100–103; and Granny Weatherwax 97–99; heroic 3, 21; and narratorial voice 103; and Sam Vimes 99–100; and steampunk 121n5

Feet of Clay 79, 85, 107n3, 108n38, 114–116, 118
The Fifth Elephant 79–85, 90, 107n10, 117
folklore 1–2, 4, 61–63, 67, 75n2, 99, 112, 125–127, 133–135, 138
footnotes as rhetoric 3–4, 91–92, 106
Frankenstein 112–113; *Young Frankenstein* 90n4

Gaiman, Neil 2, 57–58
Garlick, Magrat 55, 75n5, 98

147

148 Index

gender identity 83–85, 106, 107n3, 121n2
goblins 3, 63, 66, 77, 86–90, 120
Going Postal 110–111, 114, 116–118, 121n3, 122n7, 122n8
golems 4, 110–121, 122n7, 122n9
Good Omens 4, 56–58
Guards! Guards! 3, 35–43, 43n2, 80, 84, 99–101

Havelok the Dane 35–39, 41, 42, 43n1
Herenna the Henna-Haired Harridan 21
heroism 3, 5, 7, 12, 16, 19–32, 35–36, 40–43, 57–58, 137; heroic fantasy 20–22, 29, 32, 33n2
Hills, Matthew 7, 9, 12
history and identity 4, 11–12, 15, 30, 39, 41, 48, 50, 52, 61, 120, 125–126, 128, 134–138
Hogfather 7, 111, 115
Homer (poet) 27–30
Howard, Robert E. 19–32, 32n1, 33n2
Hrun the Barbarian 21
humor 2, 6, 11, 81, 90n1, 105, 106, 121, 127
Hyborian Age 3, 19, 28, 32

identity construction 1–4, 5–7, 13, 15, 17, 34, 36, 41–42, 45–58, 59n6, 59n9, 77, 83, 92, 95–104, 133–134, 138
"'#ifdefdEBug + 'world/enough' + 'time'" 2, 9–13, 15, 17
Igors 3, 49, 77, 82–83, 84, 89, 90n4; Igorina 83
Industrial Revolution 35, 110–112, 121
Interesting Times 20, 23, 24–27, 31, 122n6
Ironfoundersson, Carrot 3, 34–43, 43n1, 43n5, 43n7, 43n9, 43n10, 92, 97, 99, 100–103, 105, 108n24, 108n36, 108n37, 115–116

James, Edward 2, 26, 42, 43n10
Jingo 80, 101

Kochhar-Lindgren, Gray 1, 7–9, 11, 13, 15

Lancre 6, 62, 66, 97, 98
language and ethics 1, 3, 4, 8, 38, 55, 77–89, 91, 93, 95–100, 105, 106, 107n7, 108n24, 132
The Last Hero 20–21, 23, 27, 29–32, 111
LeJean, Myria (Unity) 46, 47, 49–50, 54–55
The Light Fantastic 21–24, 26
Lipwig, Moist von 108n24, 114, 116–120
Littlebottom, Cheery 84–85, 107n3
Lobsang (Discworld) 49–52, 55–56, 58
Lobsang (Long Earth) 125, 127, 133, 137
Locke, John 45–56, 58
London 57–58, 78, 111, 121n3
Long Earth series 4, 17n2, 124–139
Lords and Ladies 47, 75n2, 75n5

magic 3, 8, 21, 39, 41, 61, 65, 67, 74, ; and rhetoric 91–106, 107n7, 108n23, 110–113, 118, 120, 125, 128, 137–138

maker aesthetic 118, 121
Making Money 82, 110, 114, 118, 120, 122n8
maps 6–7, 28, 34, 137
Marvel comics 19, 21, 22, 25
Marx, Karl 113
medieval romance 3, 34–43, 43n2, 125–127, 132–133, 137
medievalism 3, 8, 16, 35, 41, 43, 125–138, 138n1
Men at Arms 79–82, 90n3, 99, 101, 105, 108n36, 111
Mendlesohn, Farah 2, 5–6, 16, 25–26, 41, 102
Mob Films/Sky One television productions 111
Monstrous Regiment 83, 110
Moorcock, Michael 21, 29
Moving Pictures 111

Nac Mac Feegle 54, 62–64, 71
narrative causality 1, 3, 5, 34, 39, 41, 43
neomedievalism 2, 4, 124–138, 139n2
Neverwhere 57
Night Watch 6, 34, 81
Nightshade (character) 54–55, 71–74

Ogg, Nanny 47, 66, 98
orcs 69, 70

parody 4, 20–24, 26–27, 30–31, 61, 104
prescriptive versus descriptive grammar 78
Pyramids 46–49, 52, 59n6

Raising Steam 17n2, 110, 112, 120
Reaper Man 111
Received Pronunciation (RP) 78
Red Sonja 20, 21, 22
rhetoric 2, 3–4, 91–106, 107n4, 107n6, 107n17, 108n23, 108n24
Rieder, John 9, 132, 134–135
rightful heir trope 34–37, 39, 41–42
robots 112–114

Said, Edward W. 129–131
Sapir-Whorf hypothesis 86–87
Schwarzenegger, Arnold 21–25, 30, 33n2
science fiction 1–4, 5–17, 17n2, 110, 125–129, 134–138
The Science of Discworld 103, 106, 107n1
semaphore technology 8, 110, 117
The Shepherd's Crown 3, 47, 52, 54–55, 59n13, 61–62, 64, 66, 69, 71–75, 75n2
Silver Horde 23, 30
Simpson, Jacqueline 61–64, 71
Slick, Billy 87–89
Snuff 86–88, 100, 108n33, 120
Soak, Ronnie (Kaos/Chaos) 51
Soul Music 92, 111
Stardust 57–58
steampunk 2, 4, 17n2, 110–113, 116, 118, 121, 121n2, 121n5

inky (character) 87–89
o Helit, Susan 49–52
rata 2, 4, 5–7, 9, 13–17
ıb-creation 113
he Summoning Dark 94–96, 99–100
Suvin, Darko 9

Tears of the Mushroom (character) 87–89
Tennyson, Alfred Lord 27–32
Teppic (Pteppic) 46–49, 52, 56, 58
Thief of Time 46, 49–53
Thompson, Darren 10–13, 17
Thud! 90n3, 94–95, 99
Tolkien, J.R.R. 32, 35, 61, 104, 105, 113
trolls 3, 4, 69, 119; in Discworld 77, 79–82, 89, 90, 90n2, 90n3, 101, 103, 108n37, 110, 111; in Long Earth 119, 125–128, 130–138, 139n2
The Truth 110
Twain, Mark 138n1
Twoflower (character) 21, 26

Uberwald 43n8, 79, 83
Ulysses 27–32
Unseen Academicals 90n5

vampires 68–69, 108n37, 110, 111
Vetinari, Havelock 43n1, 79, 86, 94, 95, 100, 111, 118–120
Vimes, Samuel 37, 40, 43n2, 79–80, 82–84, 86–88, 90n3, 92, 93, 95, 97, 99–103, 107n10, 108n24, 108n33, 115–116

Weatherwax, Granny 53, 54, 56, 59n13, 92, 97–99, 102, 103, 105, 108n24, 108n29
The Wee Free Men 3, 52–54, 61–71, 74, 75n2, 75n3
werewolves 43n7, 90, 108n37, 110, 111, 116
witches 17, 47, 53–55, 66, 72–74, 91, 92, 97–99, 101, 104, 106, 110
Witches Abroad 98, 104
Wyrd Sisters 91, 98, 108n29

Young, Adam 56–58, 59n16

www.ingramcontent.com/pod-product-compliance
Ingram Content Group UK Ltd.
Pitfield, Milton Keynes, MK11 3LW, UK
UKHW042017140426
5217IPUK00015B/1221